what is this th called philosopny of language?

What is This Thing Called Philosophy of Language? explores some of the most fundamental yet most technical problems in philosophy, such as meaning and reference, pragmatics and propositional attitudes. Some of its greatest exponents, such as Gottlob Frege, Ludwig Wittgenstein and Bertrand Russell, are among the major figures in the history of philosophy.

In this clear and carefully structured introduction to the subject, Gary Kemp explains the following key topics:

- the basic nature of philosophy of language and its historical development
- early arguments concerning the role of meaning, including cognitive versus expressive meaning, context and compositionality
- Frege's arguments concerning sense and reference; non-existent objects
- Russell and the theory of definite descriptions
- modern theories including Kripke and Putnam; arguments concerning necessity, analyticity and natural kind terms
- indexicality, context and modality
- Davidson's theory of language and the 'principle of charity'
- propositional attitudes
- Quine's naturalism and its consequences for the philosophy of language
- the challenges presented by the later Wittgenstein.

Chapter summaries, annotated further reading and a glossary make this an indispensable introduction to those teaching philosophy of language and will be particularly useful for students coming to the subject for the first time.

Gary Kemp is Senior Lecturer in Philosophy at the University of Glasgow, UK.

GARY KEMP

what is this thing called philosophy of language?

 Routledge
Taylor & Francis Group

LONDON AND NEW YORK

First published 2013
by Routledge
2 Park Square, Milton Park, Abingdon, Oxon, OX14 4RN

Simultaneously published in the USA and Canada
by Routledge
711 Third Avenue, New York, NY 10017

Routledge is an imprint of the Taylor & Francis Group, an informa business

British Library Cataloguing in Publication Data
A catalogue record for this book is available from the British Library

Library of Congress Cataloging in Publication Data
Kemp, Gary, 1960 Oct. 15–
What is this thing called philosophy of language? / by Gary Kemp.
p. cm.
Includes bibliographical references and index.
1. Semantics (Philosophy) 2. Meaning (Philosophy) 3. Linguistics–
Philosophy. I. Title.
P325.K46 2013
121'.68–dc23
2012034831

ISBN: 978-0-415-51783-6 (hbk)
ISBN: 978-0-415-51784-3 (pbk)
ISBN: 978-0-203-06894-6 (ebk)

Typeset in Berling and Arial Rounded by
Saxon Graphics Ltd, Derby

Printed and bound in Great Britain by
TJ International Ltd, Padstow, Cornwall

CONTENTS

FIGURES AND TABLES

• FIGURES

• TABLES

• WHAT IS THIS THING CALLED PHILOSOPHY OF LANGUAGE?

Most beginning students are baffled by the philosophy of language – in a way that they are not by moral philosophy, political philosophy or epistemology. Like learning to surf or to ski, they find it excruciatingly difficult to find their feet with the subject, because the hardest steps come right at the beginning. But like surfing or skiing, the rewards promised by studying the subject are superb: when the subject snaps into place, a mighty architectonic structure takes shape that is uniquely satisfying, perhaps one that provides a peek out of Plato's cave.

To get the student to that point, however, that's the rub. The second-order character of the philosophy of language is at least partly responsible for this – its being language about language, rather than being, in the familiar way, language about the world. That can't be helped. But it's also partly because a lot of the primary materials are written at a very high level, with many technical terms assumed to be already understood, and with many asides that will be Greek to the neophyte.

Indeed, when I first encountered the philosophy of language – in the mid-1980s – there was scarcely anything like a textbook on the subject. There have since appeared some excellent ones, but few for the genuine beginner. A couple of the best are geared towards postgraduate (graduate) students and final-year undergraduates who have had a course in logic; for the students I'm aiming at, they're just too difficult. There are others, but I'll name one text that is pitched at roughly the same level as this: William Lycan's *Philosophy of Language: A Contemporary Introduction* (Routledge, second edition 2008). The book is outstanding, and I only wish I could write with as much humour, learning and intelligence as its author. But there are large differences between his book and this one. His book is arranged topically, it is full of names and isms, and the problems, replies and counter-replies come thick and fast. Unquestionably the approach works for very smart students, who will come away well-equipped to take part in more recent debates. By contrast, this book is for the most part theory-based, and more concerned to keep one's eyes fixed on the larger issues, with far fewer names mentioned, a much smaller range of problems considered, and – crucially – a slower pace. There is no getting round the difficulty of the first steps, but this book tries to help the reader without simplifying misleadingly.

It attempts to immerse the student into a few paramount theories and their authors – Frege, Russell etc. – in order to get them used to thinking within the author's point of view, to get them perhaps to see why one would think as the author does, and even to get them to take sides.

In addition, and perhaps most importantly, I hope the student will come away with a coherent picture of the history of the subject. The history will not be thorough; the sketch is only of the main lines, and only of those lines – if such there be – which are for the newcomer relatively easy to learn. It is designed to fit comfortably into one semester or one trimester of teaching. There is nothing or precious little of Carnap, Ayer, Church, Dummett, Geach, D. Lewis, Montague, Stalnaker, Sellars, Tarski, Schiffer; only bits of Grice, Searle and Kaplan. Nothing or precious little of teleose-mantics, conceptual role semantics, game-theoretic semantics, dynamic semantics, intention-based semantics, expressivist semantics, logical positivism, verificationism, inferentialism, realism versus anti-realism, relevance theory or the theory of truth. I hope that students will be able to pursue those topics once they've got their feet wet in the philosophy of language by studying this book and the authors it discusses.

A likely criticism of the book is that it is old-fashioned. This boils down to a philo-sophical difference about how to teach the philosophy of language. I may be wrong, but my view is that the subject is, sad to say, not like mathematical logic or geometry, which normally are taught in complete detachment from their histories. The subject is too contentious, as evinced by the range of isms and types of semantics just mentioned. And I think that one is better placed to review more recent material and controversies if one first has a solid understanding of the basics of Frege, Russell and so on; one otherwise would run the risk of being lost in the detail. A related criticism is that philosophy of language has in recent years shifted towards empirical linguistics – informed by a more detailed conception of syntax and pragmatics – when in this book those subjects are relatively minor. My response is simply that the subject of this book is not linguistics or the philosophy of linguistics, but the philosophy of language as understood in the past one hundred years; one has one's eyes on the pursuance of philosophical questions through reflection of language, on the funda-mentals of thought and meaning, rather than a detailed theory of actual language. Another likely criticism is that outside the study questions, it is not very critical. I admit but do not repent. I do feel that a big mistake that is often made in teaching the philosophy of language is to criticise a position almost the moment it's on the table. In my experience, it takes a long time for a position to sink in, especially to see why one might hold it. If the teacher criticises the view from the get-go, the student is likely to think it not worth spending time on it – aside from exam-taking purposes – and may wonder why the position is being taught if it is so obviously full of holes. At the risk of betraying my Californian roots, I want to put a more positive spin on the material.

Thus from Frege, this book considers Russell, then Kripke and Putnam, then elementary possible worlds semantics and the theory of indexicals through the lens of

Kaplan, then the basics of pragmatics – Austin and Grice – then the main episodes of propositional attitudes centring on the problems raised by Frege and Quine; then Davidson, and finally the rather different directions of later Quine and later Wittgenstein.

I needn't say that the chapters are supposed to be read in sequence. But the chapters are written so as to be relatively self-contained; it is not impossible to depart from the order in which the chapters are presented. Two chapters – Chapter 5 on possible worlds and indexicals and Chapter 7 on the propositional attitudes – are slightly more difficult than the others. You won't hurt my feelings if you skip them.

At the end of each chapter are four items:

1 Some historical notes; including a few remarks tracing connections among the philosophers discussed, some connections with other philosophers, and some gossipy material.
2 A chapter summary.
3 Study questions, which are not just questions for which the answers are present in the chapter, but are designed to get one to think more reflectively and critically about and with the material.
4 Suggested further reading; I take it every reader knows how to obtain the relevant entries in the *Stanford Encyclopaedia of Philosophy* and the *Internet Encyclopaedia of Philosophy*, so I save a little space by not listing them except when I think what they offer is especially valuable; but generally they are both excellent resources whose investigation I encourage. I list the crucial references from, for instance Frege, as 'Primary reading'; and in some chapters I've also listed some items under 'Secondary reading'. At the end, you'll find a glossary of terms introduced in the book.

I stress that the primary reading is essential to any serious course using this book. I don't think any textbook can *replace* the original works; as mentioned above, the subject is too contentious to be like chemistry or calculus, with only historians interested in the original texts. This book, I hope, will serve as an initial exposure to the writers, issues and arguments in the philosophy of language, and as a concise map, serving to orient the reader through the primary reading.

Dr. Gary Kemp
12 April 2012

INTRODUCTION

Western philosophy has been explicitly concerned with language since the early twentieth century, and at least implicitly for much longer. Indeed, for much of the twentieth century, some people thought that the philosophy of language just *was* philosophy. Why? What exactly has language got to do with philosophy, or philosophy with language?

Here are some preliminary ideas, ones that have tended to motivate the philosophy of language:

- As philosophers we can ask 'What is Justice?' or 'What is the nature of Justice?'; but we can also ask 'What is the meaning of the word "Justice"?'. Questions about the essence of a thing, or even about the nature of reality, can seemingly be transformed into questions about semantics or the meaning of words. Some see such shifts as philosophical progress (others reckon it trivialises philosophy).
- Language *expresses thought*. The study of language is one way to study thought – its character, its structure and its relation to the world. Furthermore, unlike thought itself, language is out in the open, open to objective scrutiny in ways that thought is not.
- Language *represents the world*. The study of the more general or abstract features of language might be thought to reveal the more general or abstract features of the world.
- The study of language is itself partly a philosophical enterprise: language exists in the real world, and is thus open to scientific scrutiny, but it is not obvious what a scientific theory of language would be like, or what exactly the relevant data would be. So we have to reflect in an *a priori* way before we know what sorts of questions to ask, what would count as a scientific understanding or explanation of language, whether such things are possible, and so on.
- The analysis of language – especially the theory of *meaning* as informed by *logic* – enables us to understand what *clarity* is. Since one of the defining features of philosophy is its struggle to clarify difficult, contentious or otherwise problematic ideas, the enterprise assists philosophy in its task.

Each of these might be denied or quibbled with in various ways. However, they are collectively and individually plausible enough to motivate the philosophical investigation of language.

We can get more of a handle on the philosopher's interest by considering a simple case of linguistic behaviour, a typical **speech-act**, to employ the term made famous by

John L. Austin. A twelve-year-old girl is returning home from a semi-final doubles match she just got through playing in the local junior tennis tournament. She bursts triumphantly into the kitchen. 'We won!' she cries. What did she do, in speaking thus? She:

1 breathed out, vibrating her larynx;
2 moved her tongue, her mouth, her lips;
3 made certain sounds;
4 caused a certain disturbance in the atmosphere;
5 caused a certain mirror, hanging on the opposite wall, to vibrate imperceptibly;
6 made a certain cat perk up;
7 uttered certain phonemes;
8 uttered them in a certain order;
9 said the words 'we' and 'won' in that order;
10 joined subject to predicate in matter sanctioned by the grammatical rules of English;
11 said something that is true, if and only if she and her partner did win the match;
12 referred to herself and to her partner;
13 said, of herself and her partner, that together they won the match;
14 expressed a certain meaning;
15 represented a certain state of affairs;
16 ascribed the property, or the idea, or the attribute, of having won a certain match, jointly to herself and her partner;
17 communicated what had happened at the match;
18 conveyed her knowledge of what happened at the match;
19 asserted a certain proposition;
20 expressed her excitement at winning the match;
21 drew attention to herself, and away, it so happens, from her younger sister seated at the kitchen table, who was, at the time of the utterance, in the middle of describing the picture she had just drawn to her mother;
22 said something that entails that she and her partner won more sets than their opponents did;
23 implicitly communicated that she and her partner are now to play in the final;
24 took advantage of the situation, of her knowledge that her listeners would realise that by saying 'We' she would be taken as referring to herself and her partner, and not, for example, to herself and the cat.

… and many more. Some of these might be denied on theoretical grounds, some might be thought more fundamental than others, and some might be thought redundant, as saying the same thing as another elsewhere on the list. Nevertheless, except for the first six actions in the list, these are roughly the sorts of things that interest philosophers about such behaviour. We want not just to systematise such facts, as if we were engaged in bookkeeping, but ideally to understand such facts in a compendious and unified way by means of certain fundamental concepts and principles.

From its beginnings in the latter half of the nineteenth century, it has become normal to divide the discipline now known as *theoretical linguistics* into three main areas – **syntax, semantics** and **pragmatics** – corresponding to numbers 7–10, 11–17 and 18–24 of the above list. *Syntax* deals with relations between symbols and symbols, or signs to signs. It is most fundamentally concerned with grammaticality: it aims to discover those basic principles that determine whether a given string of signs is a sentence. *Semantics* deals with relations between symbols and what they mean, express or are about. It is more contested how to characterise its fundamental concern, but for example some semanticists conceive it as formulating a system of rules which determine the **truth-condition** of an arbitrary declarative sentence. *Pragmatics* is yet more various in its aims, but broadly speaking it is concerned with the **use** of sentences – given that a certain sentence has certain basic semantic properties, what sorts of acts can or ought to be accomplished in actual communicative situations by uttering it?

These divisions should by no means be regarded as absolute; considerations from one sub-discipline may have repercussions for another, disputes break out over which of two sub-disciplines is the more fundamental, and sometimes the rationale is called into question for maintaining the tripartite division in the first place.

But this is not a book about the science of linguistics – it is about the philosophy of language; its domain is narrower on the one hand, but deeper on the other, than that of linguistics. At the core of the philosopher's interest in language is the attempt to devise a theory of meaning, represented by 11 through 16. These include facts of **reference** – of *aboutness*, or *of-ness* – of truth, and **cognitive content**. It is broadly speaking the same as semantics, but in practice when one speaks of the theory of meaning, one is usually concerned with the fundamentals or foundational issues – trying to explain, get at the nature of, or explicate, the roles of truth, reference and meaning itself – whereas when one speaks of semantics, one is usually concerned with comparatively fine-grained matters of detail. We will not worry about that distinction very much. And we will say comparatively little about syntax, covering only the rudiments needed to convey the various approaches to the theory of meaning we shall discuss. We will have more to say about pragmatics, not only for its intrinsic philosophical interest and importance, but also because pragmatic considerations tend to relieve some of the lingering worries one might have about the main ideas of semantics or the theory of meaning.

An outline of what's ahead

This book begins by exploring certain classical theories of meaning or semantics – classical in the sense that they continue to serve as the reference points for more recent theories of meaning, and as the kernel of philosophy of language with which most philosophers in other fields are familiar. Although it has its precursors in such figures as Plato and John Locke, the philosophy of language reached its first maturity relatively recently, with the work of Gottlob Frege (1848–1924), and Bertrand Russell (1872–1970); these are the subjects of Chapters 2 and 3.

In Chapter 1 we discuss a relatively simple theory that appeals to common sense; we call it 'naive semantics'. In some sense it formed the basis of both Frege's and Russell's theories, but it has problems, responses to which formed the basis of their more sophisticated and polished theories. In describing the theory we take the opportunity to introduce some elementary logical notions – singular term, predicate, truth-functional connective and so on (those who have already studied logic can easily skip over some of the chapter). Chapter 4 deals with a modern alternative that arose in the 1960s and 70s, largely in response to Frege and Russell, namely the direct reference theory popularly associated with Saul Kripke; the theory has various ramifications for other branches of philosophy, especially for metaphysics. Chapter 5 deals mostly with a topic that grew in stature from the late 1960s on, namely the context-variability of what are known as 'indexicals', such as 'I' and 'here'; we'll consider the topic through the lens provided by David Kaplan.

Pragmatics is the subject of Chapter 6. We can think provisionally of it as subservient or less fundamental than the theory of meaning, but as will become evident, it is difficult to keep matters of meaning strictly so-called separate from pragmatic matters (some theorists argue that pragmatics is *more* fundamental than semantics or the theory of meaning as conceived by Frege and Russell).

Chapter 7 delves more thoroughly into a very puzzling area that inspired many of the main moves in both Frege's and Russell's philosophies of language, and which continues both to puzzle and inspire students at all levels. This is the subject of the semantics of **propositional attitudes**, by which we mean the meanings of sentences that ascribe, for example, beliefs to people, such as 'Darwin believed that human beings and gorillas have a common ancestor', or 'Bob believes that he has measles'. Theories here often have direct consequences for epistemology and the philosophy of mind.

The theories discussed in Chapters 1 to 5 do not attempt to *define*, in any sense, the concepts of meaning and reference. They *use* those concepts, albeit in ways that are much more disciplined than the ways they are used ordinarily, in our 'folk theory', our standard ways of talking about meaning. The finished concepts are sharper and more lucid than the corresponding folk-concepts, but are in some sense implicit in them. Similarly, Newton's theory of gravity doesn't define the concept of gravity, but contents itself with using a sharper version of it, relating the concept to others such as mass and distance. But as familiar as they are, the concepts or phenomena of reference and meaning can seem, at least to some, a little spooky. What sorts of phenomena are they? Are they like digestion or electrical charge? Or are they like something mathematical, or some other kind of non-physical properties? When I refer in conversation to, say, the highest placed pebble on Mt. Kilimanjaro, by using those words, are there some sort of meaning-rays, or referential-rays, that connect my mind or the words to the object?

Chapter 8 discusses a celebrated theory due to Donald Davidson (1917–2003) that attempts to describe the facts underlying meaning and reference *without* simply helping itself to those concepts. Strictly speaking, the theory does not define those concepts either, but attempts to provide explicit instructions enabling one to apply them to arbitrary language users without simply assuming that one already understands their language. The process, as Davidson describes it, is one of *radical interpretation*.

Other figures have been more doubtful of the prospects for a theory of meaning. W. V. Quine (1908–2000) – the subject of Chapter 9 – thinks that no rigorous or scientifically acceptable account of meaning is possible. Although serviceable for ordinary purposes, nothing more precise can be made out of the common-sense concept of meaning, and thus, considered from a fully objective, rigorous, scientific point of view, there is no such phenomenon as the meaning of words or sentences. The subject of our final chapter, Ludwig Wittgenstein (1889–1951), in a sense agrees with Quine that such attempts as Frege's, Russell's or Davidson's at devising a rigorous theory of meaning are deeply mistaken, but proposes instead a way of looking at the phenomena according to which, he believes, the main problems disappear. Unlike the scientifically minded Quine, Wittgenstein thinks that as a matter of fact we do mean things and refer to things; but these are not deep facts, and no systematic theory of such features is anything other than misleading.

Each chapter contains a summary, historical notes, suggestions for further reading – primary and in some cases secondary – and study questions which are designed to make you think a bit harder; there is also a glossary after the last chapter (which is not merely perfunctory). By the end of the book, you should know the most celebrated names and theories in the philosophy of language, and be conversant in its paradigmatic arguments, theories and kinds of criticism. But if you really want to know your stuff, it is essential that you study the works listed as initial primary reading. And there is *much* more to the field, especially with recent developments; look at the historical notes and initial secondary reading for guidance.

We begin with a few foundational points. Some of what follows is debatable, but it will help to have certain structures before us that, in one sense or another, are more or less accepted by all of the main figures that we discuss up to Chapter 8.

• 1 SIX PREPARATORY NOTES

1 You have may have noticed already that key technical or theoretical terms, when first used, are printed in **boldface**; these terms are in the glossary. *You should also pay close attention to anything written in italics.*
2 A few later sections are marked 'Further Discussion'; they are philosophically interesting but are harder than our main concerns, or just less essential to them.
3 We need to be clear about the use of *quotation* marks to talk *about* language. For example, the following are true:
    (a) Boston is a city on the East coast of the USA.
    (b) 'Boston' contains six letters.

That is, (a) says something about a city, whereas (b) says something about a *word*, the name of a city. As we say, (a) **uses** the word 'Boston', whereas (b) only **mentions** it. Strictly speaking, (b) does not say anything about Boston. 'Boston' is a *name* of Boston, what we call a quotation-mark name. The following sentence both uses and mentions 'Boston':

(c)   'Boston' names Boston.

We can go further, nesting quotation marks within quotation marks. For example:

(d)   '"Boston"' is used to mention the name of Boston.
(e)   '"Boston"' names 'Boston'.

Compare (e) with (c). Whereas (c) says that a name of Boston names Boston, (e) says that a name of a name of Boston names a name of Boston.

This might seem to be nit-picking, but in some contexts it can make all the difference. If we are going to talk about language, then we had better make sure we know which bit of language we are talking about, and we had better make sure we are not talking about the world when we mean to talk about language, or language when we mean to talk about the world. Serious philosophical errors have been made precisely by being sloppy over this (the logician-philosophers Quine and Kurt Gödel famously took Russell to task over it).

A word to the wise: When writing philosophy essays, *never* use quotation marks for any other purpose. That is, never use 'scare quotes', as I just have, in speaking of scare quotes. For really I meant to say something about scare quotes, not about 'scare quotes'. The use of scare quotes is an evasive way of using a bit of language while at the same time distancing yourself from it, leaving your reader wondering whether you quite stand by what you say.

4 Ask yourself: how many words does the following sentence contain:

Your dog bit my dog.

Trick question; it depends on what we mean by a 'word'. The sentence has two **tokens** of the **type** 'dog'. So the sentence has five words counted as tokens, four counted as types. We may also say that the word-type 'dog' *occurs* twice in the sentence.

5 A word about what 'is' is. An argument-parody concerning the great blues musician Ray Charles runs: 'God is love; and love is blind; but Ray Charles is blind; therefore Ray Charles is God'. Maybe indeed Ray Charles is God, but the reasoning doesn't support that conclusion. The fallacy is to interpret 'is', at every occurrence, as indicating *identity*, as in '=' or 'is the very same thing as', or 'is identical with' – rather than as indicating **predication**, as in 'The cat is hungry'. Charles is blind; but he is not *identical* with blindness. Stevie Wonder is also blind, but he is not identical with blindness either. Indeed, if we thought otherwise, then according to the

symmetry of identity – that if a=b then b=a – and its transitivity, that if a=b and b=c then a=c – Stevie Wonder and Ray Charles would be the same man! But they are two men, not one. So we must distinguish the two senses. In this book, we will use the equals sign, the identity sign '=', for the 'is' of identity, reserving 'is' for predication.

6 Consider again the relation between 'Boston' and Boston. We can say that the former *refers to* the latter; we can also say that word *designates, denotes, indicates, picks out, mentions, names, is the name of, stands for, has the content of, signifies* the city. At least in this case, these terms all mean more or less the same thing. We shall stick throughout to saying that the word *refers* to the city. **Meaning**, meanwhile, is the cognitive significance of a term, what we understand by it. To give a term's meaning might in some cases be the same as giving the term's reference, but it might not.

The idea of the relation reference in the case of words like 'Boston' seems relatively clear. Less clear is the idea of the relation between *general* terms like 'wisdom', or of parts of speech like 'is wise', and what they mean or refer to. It is also unclear and indeed contentious what sorts of entities are the things meant or referred to; are they concepts, universals, properties, sets, ideas-in-the-mind? It seems that these are real questions, not to be settled by stipulating a way of speaking as when we say that names refer to their bearers. We'll say more about this in Chapters 1 and 2.

● 2 COGNITIVE MEANING AND EXPRESSIVE MEANING

Consider the following pair of sentences:

> Her cat died.
> Her pussycat passed away.

Do these sentences mean the same, or not? In one sense, they do, in another sense, they don't. What they have in common is what is generally called **cognitive meaning**. We cannot define this precisely at this point. But it's common sense to say that the two sentences can be used to *convey the same objective fact* or the *same information*, namely the death of a certain feline. They have the same **truth-condition**: in any conceivable circumstance, they are either both true or neither (assuming that 'her' refers to the same girl or woman on each occasion, and that the relevant cat did not die between the two utterances). Cognitive meaning is generally regarded as that aspect of meaning that potentially affects the truth and falsity of sentences.

The manner in which they differ is what Frege called 'tone' or 'colouring'. This is the domain of rhetoric and spin: the same information, it seems, can be conveyed in different ways, conveying different subjective attitudes or feelings about it. Our official term for this, following David Kaplan, will be **expressive meaning**. Not all language is equally possessed of expressive meaning; in our example the first sentence is relatively flat or colourless in comparison with the second. And the expressive meaning of scientific language, especially when mathematical, seems to be minimal and even absent.

A sometimes vexing question is whether the distinction between cognitive meaning and expressive meaning can always be drawn. Sometimes, it seems justified to complain about the way in which a claim is put, even though we are not prepared to say that the claim is *false*. But are we always happy to say, 'I admit that what you say is *true*, but I don't like the way you say it'? The question obtrudes conspicuously in the case of racial epithets. Do such terms have the *same* cognitive meaning as inoffensive terms, and differ *only* in tone or rhetorical connotation? Tricky. Another way in which the distinction emerges is in connection with Ethics and Value: according to the most extreme variety of ethical *expressivism*, 'x is morally good' has *no* cognitive meaning, but only expressive meaning. There are no *facts* of goodness, according to this view.

In what follows, we are concerned almost entirely with cognitive meaning, as this is what links up most directly with enduring philosophical issues of epistemology and metaphysics. Except where ambiguity threatens, we will speak simply of meaning, as short for 'cognitive meaning'.

• 3 MEANING AND FORCE

(A) The most conspicuous purpose of language, if not its only purpose, is *communication*. Communication is achieved by means of *linguistic acts*, or **speech acts**.

With some exceptions, one can perform a speech act, say something, only by uttering a *complete sentence*, or by uttering something that is intended in such a way as to be equivalent, for the purposes at hand, to a complete sentence. For example, if questioned 'Are you a student?' you might answer 'Yes'. What you say is not a complete sentence, but it is equivalent for the purposes at hand to 'I am a student'. (The obvious exceptions are greetings such as 'Hello!', and exclamations and the like such as 'Crikey!').

Consider now the following sentences (pretend they are being addressed to yourself):

    (1)   You are going to eat raw fish.
    (2)   Are you going to eat raw fish?
    (3)   Eat raw fish!

The first is a sentence in the **declarative** (also called indicative) **mood**, the second in the *interrogative mood*, the third in the *imperative mood*. They have a certain something in common, namely the idea *that you are going to eat raw fish*. The first would normally be used to *assert*, or *say that*, you are going to eat raw fish; the second would normally be used to *ask whether* you are going to eat raw fish; the third would normally be used to *command* or *enjoin* you to eat raw fish.

What is this thing that these have in common, which we can express by means of the clause *that you are going to eat raw fish*? We will say that this common element is a **proposition** – the proposition that you are going to eat raw fish. (a) to (c) all express this proposition, but in forms normally used to (1) assert that it is true; (2) ask whether it is true; (3) command or enjoin that it be made true. We sum this up by saying: (a) to (c) all *express the same proposition*, but each, when used to carry out its normal function, attaches a different **force** to the proposition. (a) is normally used to attach **assertoric** force to it, (b) *interrogative* force to it, and (c) *imperative* force to it. One can *utter* 'You are going to eat raw fish' without actually asserting anything, as a stage actor might do. By varying one's intonation, one could ask a question using that form of words – 'You are going to eat raw fish?', one might ask incredulously. And so on. Whether one actually attaches a given type of force to a proposition is determined, at least in part, by the intention with which one speaks and the context in which one speaks, not just by the form of words uttered. Still, each of the three *grammatical moods* exemplified by (a) to (c) is *normally* used to express a *characteristic* force: it is by using the *appropriate* mood that we typically make it known *which* force we attach to the proposition expressed. Mood is a feature of grammar, or more technically of syntax; force is a feature of pragmatics.

(B) From now on, we are mostly going to *ignore* non-declarative sentences. Thus when speaking of 'sentences' we are speaking of declarative sentences. We need to say more about the nature of what we have just called the proposition, and its relation to the sentence. Consider:

> Snow is white.
> Schnie ist weiss.
> La neige est blanche.

These declarative sentences, we should naturally say, are *synonymous*, in the sense that they are correct translations of each other. They mean the same thing, namely that snow is white. Again, the common element is the proposition, *not* any particular form of words – not a sentence, and not a clause of English such as 'that snow is white'. We can put this by saying that they all *express* the proposition that snow is white: the meaning of a sentence is the proposition it expresses. Another way to put the same point is that these sentences all have the same *content*; another is that they *express the same thought*.

Now in this case we are speaking of a *meaning* as if it were a special kind of *entity*: we have said that propositions are sentence-meanings, different from sentences or clauses. They are what is common to synonymous sentences, just as the number 4 is what is common to the Beatles, the Evangelists, and the John Coltrane Quartet, along with every other four-membered set or collection. As we will see, it is very natural and useful to speak as if there really are these entities, namely propositions, just as there are numbers.

● 4 CONTEXT-DEPENDENCE

Now that we have declared that a proposition is the meaning of a sentence, we have to take it back, slightly. Consider the sentence:

I am the father of Julius Caesar.

What is the meaning of this sentence? If propositions, as we are assuming, are the meanings of sentences, then *it does not have a complete meaning.* For the same sentence expresses different propositions depending on *who utters it* (and when). The word 'I' picks out or refers to different persons depending on who utters it: 'I' refers, whenever uttered, to the utterer. The sentence expresses a certain proposition if uttered by Julius Caesar's dad, another one if uttered by Groucho Marx. There are many words like this, words that refer to different things depending on time, place, identity of speaker or hearer, and other facts concerning what we call the **context of utterance**. Further examples:

here	refers to place of utterance
now	refers to time of utterance
you	refers to person addressed by speaker
this, that	refers to object indicated by speaker

These are simple examples of context-dependent expressions; there are more complex ones. Sentences that contain context-dependent expressions (called **indexicals**, or deictic expressions), which are themselves context-dependent: the things they refer to vary with the context of utterance. Consider:

Octavian is Emperor of the Roman Empire.

The indexicality resides in the present tense of the verb 'is'. This sentence would have expressed a false proposition before Octavian (Augustus Caesar) became Emperor in 27 BC, but a different, true one, for a while after that (until his death in 14 BC). We can think of the copula 'is' (along with 'am' and 'are') as implicitly accompanied by 'now'.

Terms such as 'this' and 'that' constitute a special class of indexicals called **demonstratives**: they often require an accompanying pointing gesture or suchlike in order to pick out an object. It is standard to call the accompanying gesture or other device a **demonstration**.

For this reason it is really more correct to say that propositions are the meanings of *utterances* of sentences (actual or possible); better, more exactly, a proposition is what a sentence means *with respect to*, or *at*, a context. A context, we will say, is a set containing at least the time of utterance, place of utterance, identity of speaker and audience, objects indicated by demonstrations, if any. Strictly speaking, then, the meaning of a *sentence* is a rule, or function, that determines what proposition, if any, the sentence would express at a given context (equally: the **statement** that would made my uttering it at a given context). So the picture is like this:

Sentence + Context ⟶ Proposition

Context sensitivity or relativity makes itself known in further ways. 'Benjamin Higgins is rich' might be thought false in the context where one is taking the relevant *comparison class* to be the members of the House of Lords, but true in a context where one takes it to be the world population. But this phenomenon will not figure in this book. In fact, for the time being, we are going to *ignore* all forms of context dependence. We will consider sentences that do, like 'Snow is frozen water', always express the same proposition, or we will ignore context-dependent features. We will return to this issue much later, in Chapters 5 and 6.

● 5 THE ROLES OF PROPOSITIONS

(A) A proposition, we are assuming, is neither animal, mineral or vegetable: it is not something that might be inspected with a microscope or a telescope. Like the number 2, it is not a material object at all; it is an *abstract entity*. But we can characterise propositions in terms of certain roles they play and relations in which they stand (similarly, we might not be able to say what the number 2 is 'in itself', but we can say that it follows 1, precedes 3, is the number of ears belonging to Prince Charles, and so on). We have just said that the proposition that snow is white is the meaning of the three sentences above. That is one role of propositions: to be the meaning of a sentence (at a context of utterance). There are two more.

(B) The second role of propositions concerns what Russell called the **propositional attitudes**. Consider John, Pierre and Hans. They speak, respectively, only English, only French, only German. But they all believe that snow is white. There is that phrase again, a that-clause:

> *that snow is white*

We have:

(1)   John believes that snow is white.
(2)   Pierre believes that snow is white.
(3)   Hans believes that snow is white.

Intuitively, John, Pierre and Hans *believe the same thing*. That is, there is one thing that John, Pierre and Hans all believe. That thing, as you will have guessed, is the proposition, the proposition that snow is white.

Consider the inference from (1) to (3) above to:

(4)   There is something that is believed by John, Pierre and Hans.

The argument from (1)–(3) to (4) certainly seems valid. If so, *then our normal way of reasoning about beliefs commits us the existence of propositions* – or so it seems.

Propositions, then, are the objects of belief. To believe is to stand in a certain relation to a proposition. Belief is a propositional attitude: an attitude towards a proposition. There are other propositional attitudes: one may *believe* that the fish is fresh, but one may also *doubt* that the fish is fresh, *wonder whether* the fish is fresh, *hope* that the fish is fresh, and so on.[1]

(**C**) The third role that propositions play is that of truth-vehicles. Here it is useful to delve back into context-relativity for a moment. Consider the following exchange:

> Phocas: *I* am the rightful Emperor of the Roman Empire.
> Maurius: *I* am the rightful Emperor of the Roman Empire.

Phocas and Maurius, of course, disagree. They take it for granted that there is only one rightful Emperor of the Roman Empire. But they utter the very same sentence. The difference is that Phocas says that Phocas is Emperor, and Maurius says that Maurius is. Phocas implicitly denies what Maurius asserts, and Marius implicitly denies what Phocas asserts. In fact, Maurius speaks truly, Phocas falsely (Phocas was a barbarian usurper). They use the *same* sentence, but express *different* propositions. One and the same thing cannot be both true and not true (similarly, the same light cannot be both on and not on). Thus, this thing cannot be the sentence. The thing that is true is the proposition that Maurius is the rightful Emperor of Rome. This is the content asserted by Maurius, and implicitly denied by Phocas.

Propositions, then, are:

the meanings or contents of sentences (together with contexts of utterance);

the objects of propositional attitudes;

the vehicles of truth and falsity (the things that can directly be true or false).

• 6 COMPOSITIONALITY AND STRUCTURE

Back to context *independence*. It is plausible that to understand a sentence is to *know what it means*. In view of the foregoing discussion, we can take this quite literally: since what a sentence means is the proposition it expresses, to understand a sentence is to *know which proposition it expresses*. But if you think about it, merely knowing what a sentence means is not quite sufficient for *understanding* it. If someone reliably tells me that a certain sentence of Urdu means that snow is white, I might thereby come to know that that sentence means that snow is white; but it seems wrong to say that I thereby come to understand the sentence. In order to understand a sentence, I must *know the meanings of the individual words*, and must grasp its meaning *on the basis of how it is put together*. Consider 'Snow is white'. What makes it right to say that I understand this sentence is that I know the meaning of 'snow', 'is' and 'white', and I understand the significance of putting those words together in that way.

So we can formulate and set off for emphasis:

> **The principle of compositionality:** the meaning of a sentence is determined by:
>
> the *meanings of the words* it comprises; and
>
> the *semantic significance* of the *grammatical structure* of the sentence.

The first requirement is relatively transparent, but it is also important to stress the importance of the second requirement. It implies, for example, that merely having an English-Burmese dictionary would not enable a Burmese speaker to understand sentences of English. To take an obvious illustration, the same words constitute 'The dog bit the baby' and 'The baby bit the dog', but the *order* of the words makes all the difference to the meaning.

We can dig a bit deeper. There are countlessly many possible sentences of your language, such that you have never heard, spoken or read, but which you would readily understand if you did hear or read them. Likewise, one is endlessly creative; one's ability to produce novel sentences is amazing but seldom remarked because it is so commonplace. How is that possible? Answer: because you know the meanings of the words they comprise, and you know the semantic significance of the syntactic structure of sentences.

In fact, even though each of us has a finite brain, and knows only finitely many words and grammatical principles, there are *infinitely* many sentences that this finite knowledge enables us potentially to understand. A trivial illustration: competent speakers of English can understand 'He is her father', 'He is her father's father', 'He is her father's father's father', and so on, without upper bound. Of course, if it gets too long, then we might get confused or fall asleep before understanding it; the point is that the understanding one has of 'father' is sufficient, *in principle*, to determine the meaning of any of these sentences. This behaviour of 'father' is known as its being **recursive**, or its being **iterative**; it is a basic example of the sort of thing that underlies the capacity for genuine creativity, of the capacity to comprehend novel sentences. It makes a potentially infinite capacity out of finite means. Insofar as we are like digital computers, the finitude of our actual capacity is due merely to the hardware, not to intrinsic limitations of the programme or software.

This capacity is often thought to mark the difference between human language and language-like behaviour of parrots, chimpanzees, gorillas, dogs etc. – they may use or respond appropriately to an impressive array of individual words or signs, and may even use them in combination to approximate sentences, but it's controversial whether they show any evidence of genuine iterativity. (On the other hand, there are movements afoot that seek to deny that compositionality is a feature of *all* human languages; one case is claimed by Daniel Everett (2008) to exist, the language of the

Pirahã of the Amazon basin, which is evidence that compositional structure is not hardwired as part of the human genetic endowment, in the way that Noam Chomsky has famously argued.) But we have no need to take a stand on this; recursion is integral to the sorts of languages we'll be concerned with, and the exploits and potentials of other animals does not bear on the concerns of this book.

The principle of compositionality is probably the single most important principle of semantics. It's kind of like the principle of natural selection in biology (which also admits counterexamples). Languages, it seems, have to conform to this principle; one might well think that if they did not, then it would be an utter mystery how we could understand sentences that are new to us.

• NOTE

1 This is not to say that propositions are *mental entities*. In fact it seems we can prove that they aren't mental entities. The argument is valid from 'Galileo believed that the Earth moves' and 'Richelieu doubts that the Earth moves' to 'There is something believed by Galileo that is doubted by Richelieu'. But that self-same thing cannot be both in Galileo's mind and in Richelieu's mind, any more than Galileo's spleen can be in Galileo's body and also in Richelieu's; Galileo has his spleen, and the Cardinal his. Each mental entity can only be in one mind.

1

naïve semantics and the language of logic

Language is an enormously complex phenomenon. As with many complex phenomena, it would be pedagogically extremely hard, in one fell swoop, to begin with a complicated theory that accounted for all its many aspects. Compare physics, in which one studies a model of a ball rolling down a frictionless plane – ignoring friction, air pressure and resistance, imperfections in the ball and in the surface of the plane, and so on. We can learn a lot from the model, and think profitably about its most important features, without forgetting that the actual phenomenon has many other features.

We will thus begin by considering a simple theory of language, one grounded in common-sense ideas of how language functions: **naïve semantics**. Later, one can make larger adjustments to the theory, or start over from a more informed perspective. Indeed, many philosophers hold that naïve semantics is almost *completely wrong*. But if it's wrong, it is wrong in something like the way that Newton's classical physics was wrong: it is a good start, and is intuitively satisfying in many respects. Further, in order to see why a different theory is needed, it's useful to see where it breaks down. This then will provide an excellent basis from which to consider the more elaborate Frege-Russell outlook, which is often nowadays called *classical semantics* or the *classical theory of meaning*, which are the subjects of Chapters 2 and 3.

A warning: this is unquestionably the driest and most boring part of the book! Impatient students who have had a course in logic may skim Section 1 Parts (A) and (B), and omit Section 3.

• 1 NAÏVE THEORY: SINGULAR TERMS AND REFERENCE

A sentence is made out of words. Words fall into different grammatical types or classes, *syntactical categories*. To these categories correspond different *semantical categories* – categories of meaning. According to the classifications of traditional grammar, these include proper names, nouns, pronouns, verbs, adjectives, definite and indefinite articles, adverbs, prepositions, quantifiers and more. Those classifications have been partly superseded in modern linguistics, largely because that discipline has a firmer grasp of what such classifications are *for*. For our purposes, the purposes of the philosophy of language, many of these distinctions don't matter; we'll carve up language in slightly different and in some respects cruder ways – ways, primarily, that in the first instance directly affect the *truth-conditions* of statements. Also, the individual words are sometimes best treated not as semantically significant parts in themselves, but only as parts of parts that do have meaning. What all this means will be much easier to see once we get going.

We first introduce and explain the notion of an **atomic sentence**, such as 'Jane smokes' or 'The cat is on the mat'.

(A) Singular terms

Consider:

    (1) Mars is red.
    (2) Mars orbits the sun.

Both (1) and (2) contain the name 'Mars'. 'Mars' is a name of Mars. It *stands for* it, *names* it, *picks it out*, *denotes* it, *designates* it. According to a decision announced in the Introduction, it *refers* to it; Mars, the actual planet Mars with all its red dust, is its *referent*, i.e. the thing it refers to. It is customary to call 'Mars' a **singular term**. We will also formulate naïve principle 2 (naïve principle 1 will be introduced shortly):

    (NP2) The meaning of a singular term is its referent.

We are not going to try to give a precise definition of 'singular term'. It is too hard. But our intuitive classification is sufficiently reliable: we are thinking simply of words whose *role*, whose *function*, is to stand for an object, a certain individual – a person, a city, a planet (so all these things are *objects*, in an extended but philosophically standard sense of 'object').

Thus 'the sun', as it occurs in (2), is also a singular term. It refers to the sun. Here are more singular terms:

    (3) Jupiter
    (4) Prince Charles' mother
    (5) the river that runs through Prague
    (6) the fastest mammal

(3) is a proper name, but (4) and (5) are not (though (4) and (5) *contain* proper names or titles as parts). As you can see, singular terms may be *simple* (containing no expressions as parts), as in the case of (3), or *complex*, as in the case of (5).

(B) Predicates I: Syntax.

If we remove the name 'Mars' from (1) and (2), we get:

(7) _____ is red.
(8) _____ orbits the sun.

These, in the logical sense of the word, are **predicates**. In general: *The result of removing a singular term from a sentence is a predicate.* In writing down (7) and (8) we used underlining to indicate blanks or gaps – the places vacated by the singular terms we removed. It is convenient to refine this practice, using Greek letters to indicate the gaps:

(9) α is red
(10) β orbits the sun

The Greek letters do not *mean* anything. They are not *variables*, either (as we use in logic to express quantification, or in algebra to speak of numbers in general, as in '$2(x + y) = 2y + 2x$'). They are just there to mark the gaps, the places in predicates where names can be inserted (if this were a hard-core course in logic we would take care to distinguish these from 'open sentences', which become *closed sentences* when the blanks are filled with suitable expressions). We call this procedure *predicate extraction*. Obviously, predicates are often complex, built up out of words; but for our purposes – of philosophy of language as opposed to linguistics – we will often ignore this.

Clearly we can attach any singular term to a predicate such as (9) or (10), and the result is a sentence. In particular, we make a sentence this way by replacing the Greek letter with the singular term. Thus we can attach (4) to (10), yielding the sentence:

(11) Prince Charles' mother orbits the sun.

It's not likely that anyone would ever say this, but nevertheless there is nothing grammatically wrong with it as a sentence. This operation – 'completing' a predicate by filling its gaps with singular terms – is the operation of predication.

The predicate (10), you may observe, contains a singular term. The sentence (2), from which we derived (10) by deleting a singular term, contains two singular terms, not just one. If we now delete the remaining singular term from (10), inserting another Greek letter in the vacated space, we derive:

(12) α orbits β.

This, too, is a predicate (in the logical sense of the word). But unlike (9) and (10), which are **one-place predicates**, or monadic predicates, (12) is a **two-place** or binary predicate.

To construct another sentence from (12), we can replace both Greek letters with singular terms (either different ones, or the same one used twice). There are also three-place predicates, such as:

(13) α gave β to χ

There is in principle a predicate of n places for *any* finite n, no matter how large.

Unlike (10), no further predicates can be derived from (12) or (13) by removing singular terms. (12) and (13) are what we shall call **pure predicates**, by which we mean that not only are they without singular terms as parts, they also do not contain sentential connectives such as 'and' and 'or', or quantifier-words such as 'something' or 'everything'. We shall consider sentential connectives and quantifiers later in the chapter. We will also set aside adverbs such as 'quickly' (although the presence of an adverb does not disqualify a predicate from being a pure predicate).

We adopt a rule governing our use of Greek letters: when replacing Greek letters with names (or later, with variables) to form a sentence, always replace *every* occurrence of each Greek letter with the same name (or variable). For example, we regard the following as *different* predicates:

α killed β
α killed α

Thus 'Jones killed Jones' is correctly obtained from either of these predicates, but 'Jones killed Smith' cannot be obtained correctly from the second one. This reflects the fact that the concept of *suicide* could be defined in terms of the concept of *killing* (one commits suicide just in case one kills oneself), but that of killing could not be defined in terms of suicide.

Such sentences as (1), (2) and (11) are the simplest sentences: Each is constructed from a pure predicate and the requisite number of singular terms, and contain nothing else, no other kind of expression. Indeed, any such sentence contains exactly one (pure) predicate. Sentences of this kind are called **atomic sentences**.

> An **atomic sentence** is a sentence comprising nothing besides one n-place pure predicate and n singular terms.

What about verbs?

In traditional grammar, it is customary to say that every sentence must contain a *verb*. But the notion of a verb is really of no use to us. For what, indeed, is a verb? In grammar we say that 'is', as it occurs in (1) for example, is a verb. But what does that mean? What is a verb? 'Is', unlike 'orbits', is not literally an 'action word'. There is no *action* indicated in 'Snow is white'. So what does it mean to call it a verb? From our point of view, that question is pointless. What *is* clear is that a sentence cannot be formed simply from two singular terms, as in:

(14) Mars Charles' mother

Nor from predicates alone, as in:

> (15) is red orbits is red

The words in (14) and (15), so to speak, don't stick together. Rather than the grammarian's claim about verbs, we repeat that atomic sentences are all and only those expressions that can be formed by correctly replacing all the Greek letters in a pure predicate with singular terms (it is straightforward but tedious to extend the point to cover all sentences). A string of words containing only singular terms and pure predicates that is *not* constructed in this way is simply not a sentence.

(C) Predicates II: Semantics

The meaning of a singular term is an object. What is the meaning of a predicate? Let us begin with one-place predicates.

The intuitive idea of a singular term is that of an expression that stands for something: its being meaningful consists in the fact that it refers to an object. Our intuitive ideas about predicates are less clear, and much more varied. It used to be said that whereas proper names **denote** their objects, so-called **general terms** or general names **connote** something that can be *ascribed to* objects; for example what 'dog' connotes can be meaningfully applied to an object by means of the predicate '__ is a dog'. For the most part we will ignore the distinction between general terms and predicates; to go into it would be unremuneratively tedious. But something of the same idea can be expressed as follows: whereas the meaning of a singular term – an object – is *what we say things about*, the meaning of a predicate is *what we say about* an object. This fits with what we said about syntax: syntactically speaking, a (one-place) predicate is what is left over from deleting a singular term from a sentence; semantically speaking, the meaning of a (one-place) predicate can be significantly ascribed to any object.

Consider, for example, (1) above, 'Mars is red'. Whereas 'Mars' refers to Mars, 'α is red' *applies* to Mars, since Mars is red. Another way to put the same idea is that the predicate is *true of* the object Mars. Yet another way is that the object *satisfies* the predicate.

Although 'Mars is red' is true, the meaning of 'α is red' is not the planet Mars. If it were, then 'Mars' and 'α is red' would be synonymous, which they are not, and there would be no semantical difference between 'Mars is red' and 'is red is red', which obviously there is. Whereas Mars is the only thing named by 'Mars', 'α is red' denotes or applies to lots of other things besides Mars. And some pairs of predicates have their *separate* meanings despite applying to just the *same* things; 'α is a continent bigger than Africa' and 'α is a continent that contains China' both apply to exactly one thing, Asia. So applying to a thing must be different from naming a thing: singular terms and predicates have different sorts of meanings.

One candidate for the meaning of a predicate such as 'α is red' is an *idea* in the minds of users of the term; John Locke held something like this view in the seventeenth century. But, for various reasons, in the modern era the idea has not proven popular. For one thing, such 'ideas' cannot be mental pictures or images, because many predicates, even simple ones, stand for things for which it is implausible to say we have mental images, such as 'α is a theory'. And in cases where it is not so implausible, your mental image and mine can be rather different – your idea of a dog may be of a French Bulldog, mine of an Irish Wolfhound – yet the predicate means the same in your mouth and mine, in the sense that the criterion for object's falling under the predicate 'α is a dog' doesn't vary depending on which dog-image we employ, French Bulldog or Irish Wolfhound. This is connected with the observation that whereas ideas are necessarily private and subjective, what we communicate, the meanings of our words, is in some sense objective and public. *Singular terms* are connected in our minds with subjective and private ideas – for example, I have particular ideas of Paris – but they are also connected with public objects as their referents – like the city of Paris itself. Likewise with predicates; this way, sentences can express meanings with public parts corresponding to singular terms and predicates, so the fact of communication is no mystery.

A slightly better candidate, one that does not fall foul of what we will call the *requirement of publicity*, is the *set of red things*. More generally, the idea is that the meaning of a one-place predicate is the set of things that satisfy the predicate. In logic or the theory of meaning this is called the **extension** of a one-place predicate. Thus we might suppose that:

> *(NP3*)* The meaning of a predicate is its extension.

The asterisk is there because we are not going to use this idea in constructing the naïve theory. More powerful reasons for rejecting (NP3*) will emerge later, but two simple reasons that are sufficient for now are as follows: (1) as already mentioned, many predicates that are satisfied by exactly the same set of objects have different meanings; in addition to the example given above, there are pairs of predicates such as 'is a round square' and 'is a human being taller than the Eiffel Tower' that have the same extension, namely the empty or null set, but their meanings differ; (2) the extension of the average predicate is always changing (every moment, some things become red, others cease to be red); yet it seems wrong to say that the *meaning* of the predicate thereby changes.

Much better is this:

> *(NP3)* The meaning of a (one-place) predicate is the property for which it stands. The meaning of a (two-place) predicate is the relation for which it stands; similarly for three-place predicates etc.

The property that 'is red' stands for is *redness*. Is it plausible to say that if 'is red' came to stand for a different property, then its meaning will have changed? Yes. Is it plausible to say that one understands 'is red' just in case one knows that it stands for redness? Yes. Is it plausible to say that properties are in the relevant sense public, rather than private? Yes.

Note that our use of the word 'property' is much more liberal than the ordinary one. Ordinarily we use it to mean such scientifically interesting features as *hardness, flexibility*, and the like. Whereas we intend the meaning of any one-place predicate whatever, such as 'α used to go to bed early'.

Moving now to two-place predicates, such as 'α orbits β'. Such predicates stand for *relations* (two-place, or *binary* relations, in this case). Relations, like properties, are *universals*.[1] So we could say: the meaning of a predicate is a universal; for example, both whiteness and love are universals, but the latter is a relation, the meaning of 'a loves b'. But, since in practice it is easier to treat one- and two-place predicates separately, we will speak of properties and relations, rather than lump them together as universals (we could also speak of properties and relations as *attributes*).

Thus according to the naïve theory, properties and relations are simply the referents of predicates. So the meaning of a singular term *or* a predicate is its referent – it is either an object, property or a relation. Now we have not yet considered all types of expressions, but we have said enough perhaps to motivate:

> **NP1 (the fundamental principle of naïve semantics)** The meaning of every expression is its referent.

The idea is that the meaning of an expression is what it stands for: m*eaning = reference*.

• 2 TRUTH AND MEANING FOR ATOMIC SENTENCES

(A) Naïve atomic propositions

Remember from the Introduction that the meaning of a sentence is the proposition it expresses (in a context). So that idea, along with NP1, entails that propositions are the referents of sentences. This is a little weird. But we do speak (naïvely!) of *facts* as the referents of *true* sentences; and if facts are just true propositions, then maybe NP1 is not so weird after all.

We cannot take any set of referring expressions and expect them to cohere meaningfully, as expressing a proposition. 'Socrates' and 'Groucho Marx' do not together make up a meaningful sentence; at most they constitute a *list* – perhaps a list of great raconteurs – not a sentence. This problem will crop up again later; it is known as the 'list problem'.

Since atomic sentences are sentences, their meanings are propositions. We call these **atomic propositions**. According to the principle of compositionality, the meaning of a sentence is determined by the meanings of its parts, together with its structure. And what, according to naïve semantics, do the meanings of the parts of an atomic sentence have to do with the meaning of the sentence? Simple: the proposition expressed by an atomic sentence – its meaning – is actually *composed* of the meanings of the parts of the sentence. The proposition is a *composite object* whose parts are the meanings of the sentence. Thus the proposition expressed by an atomic sentence is composed of, made up of, the referents of the expressions occurring in the sentence:

> **(NP4) Naïve semantics for atomic sentences:** the proposition expressed by an atomic sentence containing *n* singular terms is composed of the referent of its predicate and the *n* referents of those singular terms.

We can think of an atomic sentence as being like a picture or diagram of its meaning. The proposition expressed by 'Mars orbits the sun' can be shown in diagram form as:

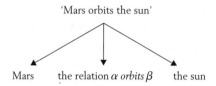

Figure 1.1 The proposition expressed by 'Mars orbits the sun'

The structure is an abstract sort of structure – the mode of composition is not physical – but otherwise it is very like a physical structure. The proposition is some-thing like a pod, and the referents of the expressions are the peas. Or better: the *relation* (the meaning of the predicate) is like the pod, and the referents are like the peas, slotted in.

Further discussion

There is one problem with this conception of propositions. We have said that the proposition expressed by 'Mars orbits the sun' contains, or is made up of, Mars, α *orbits* β, and the sun, but we have not said how this differs from the proposition expressed by 'the sun orbits Mars', which it surely does. Those two propositions assemble the three constituents in different ways; the *direction* of the relation is different in the two cases. Although it is clear that the difference in meaning is indicated by the differing linear order of the constituents of the *sentences*, we have not explained what, in propositions, reflects this difference.

Compare this situation with the notion of a *set* or *class* in mathematics. Like prop-ositions, sets are abstract objects that contain entities as parts or elements. But unlike the case of propositions, a set is said to be defined by its members: that is, it is necessary and sufficient for A and B to be the very same set in that they contain the same members. So {Pluto, Venus} is the same set as {Venus, Pluto}. Whereas, as we just saw in the case of the propositions expressed by 'Mars orbits the sun' and 'The sun orbits Mars', two distinct propositions may have the same parts or constituents.

This difference must be a difference of *structure*; unlike sets, propositions have an inner structure of some kind. But we will not try to explain what this might be. For the moment, we are simply going to assume that something in the propositions does reflect the semantically significant syntactical difference between 'Mars orbits the sun' and 'The sun orbits Mars'.

(B) Naïve truth for atomic propositions

Remember from the Introduction that propositions are the *vehicles of truth*. The things to which the predicates 'is true' and 'is false' immediately attach are not sentences, but the propositions they express.

We can now define what it is for an atomic proposition to be true. For simplicity, we continue to confine our attention to atomic propositions containing only properties or binary relations. We will call these *one-place* atomic propositions and *two-place* atomic propositions.

Common sense seems to approve the idea that truth is in *correspondence with reality*. The simplest way to explain this is as follows.

(a)   The proposition that Mars is red is true if and only if the object Mars *possesses* the property redness. That is, it is true if and only if the object *actually has* that property – *exemplifies*, *instantiates* it. These are all ways of saying the same thing: this abstract notion of an object's *possessing* a property is the key.

(b)   The proposition that Mars orbits the sun is true if and only if those two things stand in the relation denoted by 'a orbits b': That is, it is true if and only if Mars bears that relation to the sun, stands in that relation to it. Here the crucial notion is that of one object *bearing* a relation to another.

Thus in general:

> **(NP5) Naïve definition of truth for atomic propositions.** An atomic proposition is *true* if and only if: (i) it is a one-place proposition comprising an object o and property P, and o possesses P; or (ii) it is a two-place proposition comprising an object o_1, a relation R and an object o_2, and o_1 bears R to o_2.[2]

It is worth noticing the following consequence of this theory. Consider again the proposition that Mars is red. According to NP5, we have:

> The proposition expressed by 'Mars is red' is true if and only if Mars possesses the property redness.

But it is clear that:

> Mars is red if and only if Mars possesses the property Redness.

Putting these two together, it follows that:

> The proposition expressed by 'Mars is red' is true if and only if Mars is red.

That is undeniably correct; that the naïve definition should entail it corroborates the definition. Alfred Tarski, the Isaac Newton of the theory of truth, said (roughly) that the real test of a theory of truth is that it should entail sentences of the above, trivial form, which he called **T-sentences**.[3]

Note finally that none of this actually prevents us from speaking of *sentences*, or *utterances* or *statements*, as being true or false. A sentence, utterance or statement is rightly called 'true' if and only if the proposition it expresses is true. According to this way of thinking, to speak of a sentence as being true is simply elliptical for speaking of a proposition as true. Similarly with beliefs: a belief is true just in cases the proposition believed is true.

Further discussion

It is natural to suppose if truth is *correspondence* then it must be correspondence with *fact*, or *the way the world is*. But what is a way the world is? According to one of these ideas, there is only one way that things are, which is THE way that things are. The way things are is the way the world is – the whole world. So the way things are is what in metaphysics we call the Actual World. Similarly, there are ways that things aren't – these are what in metaphysics we call Possible (but non-actual) Worlds (some philosophers think that there are also *Impossible* Worlds, ways that things not only aren't, but couldn't be!).

According to the other idea, there are many ways that things are. A way that things are, according to this idea, is a *fact* or *state of affairs*. There is, for example, the fact that snow is white, that Arsenal won the English Premiership title in 2002, that $2 + 2 = 4$. Facts are configurations of entities: for example, the fact that snow is white is composed of snow and the property whiteness. Singular terms that stand for this fact include: 'Snow's having whiteness', or 'Snow's being white', or 'the fact that snow is white'.

It is simple, and probably more intuitive, to use this latter notion of a way things are in characterising truth for atomic sentences. Of course, all the ways that things are according to the second idea make up the way that things are according to the first idea. The world, as Wittgenstein once put it, is *all that is the case*, that is, all the facts.

Thus we might try the following characterisation of truth for atomic propositions:

> *(NP5*) Naïve definition of truth for atomic propositions**: An atomic proposition is *true* if and only if: (i) it is a one-place atomic proposition containing an object o and property P, and the fact that o has P exists; or (ii) it is a two-place atomic proposition containing objects o_1 and o_2 relation R, and the fact that $R(o_1, o_2)$ exists.

But Russell pointed out that there is a serious problem with this idea (hence the asterisk). Consider the *fact* that Mars orbits the sun. Compare this with the *proposition* that Mars orbits the sun. They are *both* composed entirely of Mars, α orbits β, and the sun. So what is the difference between them? They have to be different in some way, else they would be identical, in which case *every atomic proposition would be true* – no meaningful sentence could be false – since there would be a fact to which it corresponds, namely itself. But on the other hand, it is very hard to see what the difference would be between the true proposition and the fact. If so, then to explain 'true' in terms of 'fact' would get us nowhere: we would have no characterisation at all of the difference between those propositions that are facts and those that are not.[4]

• 3 LOGICAL SYNTAX AND LOGICAL OPERATORS

So far, we have been speaking only of atomic sentences. Also, we have been speaking vaguely of 'language', and using English to illustrate the points we wish to make. But the idea we have in mind is that *all* languages have atomic sentences, hence singular terms and predicates. Indeed, the naïve idea is that all languages *must* have such devices, because the *world* is made up of objects having properties, and objects standing in relations. A language without singular terms and predicates could not really talk about the world, could not represent it, because it could not reflect its structure. As Tarski once put it, the idea of the semantical categories cuts so deeply into our intuitions that it is difficult to imagine the possibility of an alternative. Thus we have been using English merely to *illustrate* points whose import *is fully general*.[5] So although we will stick to English, you should bear in mind that we are trying to theorise about language in general. English is not our actual subject matter.

The trouble is that once we move beyond atomic sentences English is complicated and confusing in ways that, for our purposes, are best avoided as much as possible. For now, we will restrict our attention to just a few devices in English, ones corresponding to the **sentence-connectives** and **quantifiers** that you may have learned in a logic course. But we won't assume that you have had such a course; our use of them will be quite simple.

A. Sentence connectives

We will make regular use of the expressions 'not', 'or' and 'and'. We will assume that these are **truth-functional**, by which we mean that for any two sentences P and Q:

> **Conjunction:** 'P & Q' is true if both P and Q are true, false otherwise.
> **Disjunction:** 'P or Q' is false if both P and Q are false, true otherwise.
> **Negation:** 'Not P' is true if and only if P is false.

Negation in English is expressed in a variety of ways. For simplicity, we pretend that it is always expressed in the form 'It is not the case that'. Since that is a pain to write out, we just write 'Not: _____.'. For example, for 'It is not case that Jupiter orbits the sun' we write:

> Not: Jupiter orbits the sun.

But it is much more controversial whether the conditional 'if-then' of English is truth-functional. For now we will ignore this issue and use the arrow '→' of formal logic. So instead of 'If Charles is fat then Andrew is fat', we write:

Charles is fat → Andrew is fat.

And we define:

Conditionality: 'P → Q' is false if P is true and Q is false; true otherwise.

It is also useful to have:

Biconditionality: 'P if Q' is true if P and Q have the same truth value; false otherwise.

B. Quantifiers

The expression of generality is very complicated and messy in English, but we can for the most part ignore the complexity. Consider a statement that does not involve generality:

If Fido is a retriever then Fido swims.

A person saying this would presumably be relying on a certain background generalisation, which can be expressed in any number of ways, such as:

All retrievers swim.
Any retriever swims.
Every retriever swims.

In this book, we proceed as follows. First, we can express the above somewhat awkwardly as:

For every thing, if it is a retriever then it swims.

We think of this as comprising a quantifier – 'For every thing' – and an open sentence or matrix:

if it is a retriever then it swims

Then in place of the pronoun 'it', we introduce **variables**:

if x is a retriever then x swims

According to our policy with the conditional, we can rewrite it as:

x is a retriever → x swims

Then we restore the quantifier with the variable written in the place of 'thing', and put in a pair of parentheses for clarity:

For every x (x is a retriever → x swims).

Such is a **universal quantifier**; we could just as well have written 'For *each* x (x is a retriever → x swims)', or 'For *all* x (x is a retriever → x swims)'. Same thing. The important thing is that a sentence

> For every x ——

is true as long as the sentence written in place of '——' is true for every choice of x, and not otherwise. That is, the sentence above about swimming retrievers means that the open sentence:

> x is a retriever → x swims

is true no matter what we assume x to be. 'For every x (x is a retriever → x swims)' is a closed sentence, the universal closure of the open sentence 'x is a retriever → x swims'.

We will also have occasion to use the **existential quantifier,** which we write as:

> There is an x such that ——.

As in:

> There is an x such that (x is an albino & x is a tiger)

This sentence is to be understood as true if there is least one albino tiger, and false otherwise. Equally, we could say that *there exists an x such that* x is an albino x is a tiger, or *for some x*, x albino & x is a tiger. Same thing.

Once in a while we'll need more variables – 'y' and 'z' in addition to 'x'. For example:

> For every x, there is a y such that (x loves y)

That's our way of saying 'Everyone loves someone'. Or 'Some girl is loved by every boy' goes as:

> There is an x such that (x is a girl & for every y(y is a boy → y loves x))

This sort of example shows why we use variables instead of sticking with the ordinary pronouns: pronouns are hard to keep track of, and sometimes ambiguous, when there is more than one quantifier involved. And for those not averse to them, you can write the '∀' and '∃' of formal logic instead of our 'For every' and 'There is a', along with the variables.

C. Generalising at the level of singular terms and predicates

Occasionally, we will want to reason purely schematically, using *uninterpreted* singular terms and predicates. That is, we might want to say something that holds for 'Socrates taught Plato', but in such a way that it holds for any sentence comprising two singular terms joined by a two-place predicate. So we'll just write '*a*', '*b*' and so on for uninterpreted singular terms, and '$F\alpha$', '$G\alpha$' for arbitrary one-place predicates, and '$R\alpha\beta$' for an arbitrary two-place predicate. Then we write for example

> Fa

and

> Rab

– for atomic sentences (the more suggestive 'aRb' for the last one is out of fashion). This follows the standard practice in formal logic, which is itself modelled on mathematics.

• HISTORICAL NOTES

It's improbable that any actual person explicitly held the naïve theory of semantics exactly as presented here. Among ancient philosophers – primarily the Greeks – Plato (especially in his dialogue the *Cratylus*), Aristotle and the later Stoics explored some of the above ideas. The medieval and scholastic philosophers, Indian philosophers and the so-called modern philosophers of the seventeenth and eighteenth centuries – Locke, Leibniz, Hume and Berkeley – all wrestled at least occasionally with problems concerning language and meaning. Through a variety of factors, not the least of which was the development of logic in order to make good on the idea that mathematics is ultimately just logic, the philosophy of language became more explicit and central at the end of the nineteenth century. In particular, Gottlob Frege (1848–1924) in his *Begriffsschrift* of 1879, and Russell (1872–1970) especially in his *Principles of Mathematics* of 1903 (not to be confused with *Principia Mathematica* of 1910), subscribed to versions of the naïve theory; so did Ludwig Wittgenstein in his early book, *Tractatus Logico-Philosophicus* of 1921. An interesting precursor from our perspective is John Stuart Mill (1806–73); in his *A System of Logic* of 1843, Mill did not have the ideas that would propel Frege and Russell into greatness in logic – principally he lacked the idea of quantification – but he articulated the key naïve idea that proper names have denotation but not connotation, that, as it would be put much later by Ruth Marcus Barcan, they are just tags of their referents. As we'll see later, Russell never really departed from that idea, and it has its staunch supporters today. It was Frege who reacted in later work – especially 'On Sense and Reference' of 1892 (in Frege 1997) – to the apparent shortcomings of the idea by coming up with a new way of thinking.

• CHAPTER SUMMARY

Naïve semantics begins with atomic sentences, and breaks them up into predicates and singular terms. Each atomic sentence is composed of one n-place pure predicate and n singular terms. The meaning of a singular term is its referent, the object for which it stands; the meaning of a predicate is the universal or attribute that is its reference, that for which it stands. Universals comprise properties, binary relations, tertiary relations etc. corresponding to one-place predicates, two-place predicates, three-place predicates and so on.

The meaning of a sentence is the proposition for which the sentence stands. The meaning of an *atomic* sentence is a composite abstract object comprising the objects corresponding to its singular terms and the universal corresponding to its predicate. The truth-value of an atomic sentence is determined by its correspondence to reality or its lack of correspondence with reality: it is true if there is a fact composed as the sentence says, and false if there is not such a fact.

To cope with sentences that are not atomic sentences, we add (1) the devices of sentential logic – 'not', 'or', 'and' and 'if-then' – and (2) quantifiers corresponding to 'all' and 'some'. For simplicity, we understand the former as truth-functional, in terms of the truth tables in classical logic.

• STUDY QUESTIONS

1 The Vltava = the river featured in *By Night Under the Stone Bridge* by Leo Perutz. Does this fact represent a difficulty for naïve semantics? How is it connected with the distinction between simple singular terms and complex ones?

2 Take any newspaper or magazine article, and practise (a) identifying plausible examples of atomic sentences; (b) identifying the predicate in such sentences; and (c) writing the predicate with Greek letters, and then forming new sentences with the predicate, ensuring correct replacement. Note the relation between the predicates you identify and what is called the *main verb* in grammar.

3 According to naïve semantics, what, if anything, is the syntactical or semantic difference between the expressions 'redness' and 'α is red'?

4 Is it really true that there is no difference between a true atomic proposition and a fact?

5 According to the naive theory, 'Jane' refers to Jane, and 'smokes' refers to the property of being a smoker. Is it not possible, then, to merely refer to Jane, and refer to the property of being a smoker, by saying 'Jane, the property of being a smoker' – without expressing the proposition that Jane smokes? What more is required, in order to express the proposition?

• PRIMARY READING

Frege, G. (1997) *Begriffsshrift*, selections, in *The Frege Reader*, (ed.) Michael Beaney (Oxford: Wiley-Blackwell).

Mill, J. S. (1963ff) *System of Logic, Ratiocinative and Inductive*, volumes 7–8 of the *Collected Works of John Stuart Mill*, (ed.) J. M. Robson (Toronto: University of Toronto Press), Book I, Chapter II, 'Of Names'.

Russell, B. (1903) *The Principles of Mathematics* (Cambridge: Cambridge University Press), Chapter IV 'Proper Names, Adjectives and Verbs'.

• NOTES

1 This is denied by some; it is a complicated issue in metaphysics.

2 Again, we are leaving aside the worry about the inner structure of atomic proposi-tions, the difference in 'order' whereby *Mary kissed John* differs from *John kissed Mary*.

3 Actually Tarski regarded truth as a property of sentences rather than propositions. See Tarski 1969.

4 This is not to say that the idea of truth-as-correspondence-to-fact cannot be made to work. A good book that develops the idea is Barwise and Etchemendy 1987.

5 This should not be confused with the concept of Deep Structure or Universal Grammar first proposed by the great linguist Noam Chomsky (e.g. Chomsky 1965). Chomsky's own view of the matter was that the possibility of a universal grammar is a empirical hypothesis about the structure of the human mind, not a metaphysical hypothesis about the very possibility of language. So Chomsky is not concerned to generalise about language as such, but about human language. Perhaps surprisingly – due to the surface diversity of human languages – Chomksy's proposal has been partially corroborated by empirical research, especially Chom-sky's claim that only the reality of innate (genetically determined) structure, embodied in the brain, can explain the facts of human language acquisition.

2

˙fregean semantics

• 1 TWO PROBLEMS FOR NAÏVE SEMANTICS

The fundamental principle of naïve semantics is:

> **(NP1)** The meaning of every expression is its referent.

In what follows, we concentrate on two components of the principle, namely:

> **(NP2)** The meaning of a singular term is its referent.

> **(NP3)** The meaning of a (1-place) predicate is the property for which it stands. The meaning of a (2-place) predicate is the relation for which it stands; similarly for 3-place predicates etc.

Gottlob Frege (1848–1925) held something like the naïve theory in his early work. But in papers and notes written in the 1890s he formulated serious objections to NP2 (and to NP3) and came up with a more complicated theory that avoids them. The theory as a whole has a kind of overall symmetry that makes it very compelling, and its central components have been extremely influential, not only in the study of language but in the philosophy of mind and epistemology. In this chapter we describe the problems in the naïve theory that motivated Frege's theory, and then present a version of Frege's theory, or *Fregean semantics* as we will say.[1]

(A) The problem of cognitive value

We begin with Frege's famous example. The Evening Star – also known as 'Hesperus' – is the Morning Star – also known as 'Phosphorus'; the bright celestial object that appears in the western sky just after sunset is the very same object as the bright celestial object that appears, some months later, at the opposite season, in the eastern sky just before sunrise, namely the planet Venus. It is just one object appearing in different places at different times. Thus we have

> (1) The Morning Star = The Evening Star

According to the naïve theory, meaning is reference. In particular, the meaning of a singular term is its referent, namely the object for which it stands (NP2). Thus according to the naïve theory we have:

(2)   The meaning of 'The Morning Star' = the meaning of 'The Evening Star'.

Is this really correct? According to the principle of **compositionality**, the meaning of a sentence is determined by the meanings of its parts, together with the way it is constructed from those parts. It follows that if two sentences have the same structure, and each part at each location in one sentence has the same meaning as its corresponding part in the other, then the two sentences mean the same thing – that is, they express the same proposition (since the meaning of a sentence is a proposition). It follows, then, that the following sentences mean the same thing, express the same proposition:

(3)   The Morning Star is a planet.
(4)   The Evening Star is a planet.

According to naïve theory, then:

(5)   The proposition expressed by 'The Morning Star is a planet' = the proposition expressed by 'The Evening Star is a planet'.

But this seems obviously incorrect. Intuitively, (2) is *false*. (3) and (4) do not seem to say exactly the same thing. So (5) is false: the propositions expressed by (3) and (4) are not the same. If there is any doubt about this, remember that a proposition is supposed to be the object of propositional attitudes such as belief. Thus if (5) were true, then the belief that the Morning Star is a planet would be the *very same belief* as the belief that the Evening Star is a planet. But clearly they are not: one could coherently have one belief without having the other. This could happen if one did not happen to know that the Evening Star is the Morning Star (in fact, there was a time when people did not know this), or worse, if one positively denied that the Evening Star is the Morning Star. But if one could believe the one proposition but not the other, then they cannot be the same proposition. Likewise, if one kicks X but does not kick Y, then X and Y cannot be the same thing.

The matter emerges more dramatically if we consider the following:

(6)   The Morning Star = The Evening Star.
(7)   The Morning Star = The Morning Star.

As Frege puts it, (7) is knowable *a priori*, without any astronomical investigation at all. It is a triviality that does not 'extend our knowledge'. (6), on the other hand, is not a triviality, and is not knowable *a priori*; it required astronomical investigation to discover it, a discovery which *did* extend our knowledge. As Frege puts it, the **cognitive value** of (6) and (7) is not the same. In our terminology, the cognitive meaning of these must differ. Since the only difference between (6) and (7) is that one contains an occurrence of 'the Morning Star' where the other contains an occurrence of 'the Evening Star', the difference must be a difference in cognitive meaning between those two terms. Yet this cannot be a difference in reference; they refer to the same thing.

The examples have so far concerned *complex singular terms*, not simple singular terms, i.e. not *proper names*. Yet the same sort of thing arises in the case of proper names as well. For example, an ancient Babylonian name for the Morning Star is 'Phosphorus', and an ancient name for the Evening Star is 'Hesperus'. Thus an ancient Babylonian might have known that (8) is true, but not known that (9) is true:

    (8)   Hesperus = Hesperus.
    (9)   Hesperus = Phosphorus.

(B) The problem of empty singular terms

Empty singular terms are singular terms with no referent. For example, toward the end of the nineteenth century, many astronomers were convinced by the French mathematician Le Verrier that there must be a small planet between Mercury and the Sun, whose gravitational field caused the small perturbations observed in the orbit of Mercury. Le Verrier dubbed this purported planet 'Vulcan'. Thus any such astronomer would have believed the proposition expressed by:

    (10)   Vulcan is hot.

Yet according to the naïve theory, *there is no such proposition*. For, by the beginning of the twentieth century, it became apparent there was no such planet; and the apparent perturbations in Mercury's orbit can be explained by Einstein's theory of relativity. Thus if there is no such planet, then 'Vulcan' has no referent, and therefore, according to the fundamental principle of naïve semantics (actually NP2), no meaning. But how could there fail to be such a proposition? It was *believed* that Vulcan is hot; how can someone believe when there is no proposition believed? A belief, surely, must have some particular proposition that is the *content* of the belief. It is as if someone were to *eat* when there was *nothing that he ate*!

If there is any doubt about this, consider this sentence, where 'Nessie' is a purported name of the Loch Ness Monster, which we assume does not exist:

    (11)   Nessie is hot.

'Nessie' is a singular term without a referent. According to the naïve theory, it is therefore meaningless. Therefore (10) and (11) must have exactly the same meaning: they are both atomic sentences that attach the meaning of the one-place predicate α *is hot* to a meaningless singular term. But it seems clearly wrong to say that (10) and (11) mean the same thing.

• 2 THE SENSE-REFERENCE DISTINCTION

These considerations motivated Frege to conclude that associated with a singular term, in addition to its *reference*, is something else, which he calls its **sense**. Singular terms with the same reference may have different senses – or as we will put it more concisely, **co-referential** singular terms may have different senses.

That much, however, is only to *name* the problem; what we want is a *theory* that predicts the phenomenon we have noticed, and explains why it should arise. To do that, we have to answer the question: What *is* the sense of a singular term?

Frege characterises the sense of a singular term in two ways, only the first of which is prominent in the famous paper 'On Sense and Reference':

> ***Sense I***: The sense of a singular term is a *mode of presentation* of the referent.

> ***Sense II***: The sense of a singular term is *rule for determining* its referent.

According to I, the sense is like a perspective on a thing; it is a way the object is presented to us, a way of thinking of the object. This has a strong overtone of Kant, according to whom there is no such thing as perceiving or thinking of an object *directly*: we must always grasp it in some *manner*, think of it or perceive in some *way*. According to II, the sense is a way in which we find a thing; it is a way that we *go to* the object instead of a way that it *comes to* us. Two senses that lead to the same object are like different routes to the referent, different instructions for getting to the same place. But the two ideas can be brought together: one way in which an object can be presented to us is by its being the outcome of a search or procedure. *The sense presents the object as that which is determined by the rule.*

How is sense related to reference? It is tempting to represent the idea like this:

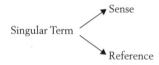

Figure 2.1 Sense and reference

As if all we had to do is to acknowledge that a singular term has two kinds or dimensions of meaning, namely sense and reference. This is not literally incorrect, but it fails to capture the relation that Frege envisages between sense and reference. The idea is that a singular term has a referent *by virtue* of the sense it expresses: the term expresses a rule for picking out an object, and the object is the term's reference because the rule picks out that object.

A more accurate and informative diagram would be this:

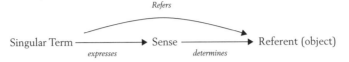

Figure 2.2 The relation of sense to reference

Reference, the relation between word and thing, emerges as a complex relation: to *refer* to x is to *express a sense* that **determines** x. It is defined as that complex relation, just as *x is the maternal grandfather of y* is defined as *y is the father of the mother of x*. The curved line should not be regarded as indicating a relation that is distinct from the compound relation *x expresses a sense which determines y*.

Now that we have distinguished sense from reference, what about *meaning*? Is the meaning of a singular term its sense, its reference, or both, or neither? Unfortunately, English translations of Frege have confused this issue; what we are calling reference (Frege: *Bedeutung*) has been translated both as 'meaning' and 'reference' (also as 'denotation', 'designation', 'nominatum'). Yet in English it is more natural to use 'meaning' for what we are calling 'sense' (Frege: *Sinn*). Nothing really depends on this, however; it is only a matter of words. When discussing Frege, it is best just to use the terms 'sense' and 'reference', and avoid 'meaning'; it is probably best also to think of Frege as proposing to split the ordinary concept of meaning into two aspects.

Some translations use 'meaning' for *Bedeutung*, and some use 'reference' for *Bedeutung*. But luckily none use 'meaning' for *Sinn;* they always use 'sense'. That makes it easy to avoid confusion when reading them: wherever you see the word 'meaning', think 'reference'.

● 3 THE DISTINCTION EXTENDED

Frege draws the sense-reference distinction for *all* expressions (we'll begin to see why a bit a later). For simplicity, we will confine the discussion to atomic sentences, hence to singular terms and predicates. Let us first consider sentences.

(A) Sentences

Remember the principle of compositionality: the meaning of a sentence is deter-mined by its parts, together with the way they are put together. (3) and (4), we said, express different propositions. But their corresponding *parts* all have the same referents. Thus the proposition expressed by a sentence is *not* determined by the referents of the parts of the sentence. The proposition expressed by a sentence, rather, is determined by the *senses* of its parts (along with the way the sentence is put together). Frege calls the proposition expressed by a sentence a *thought*. The *sense* of a sentence is a thought. We will mostly stay with the word 'proposition': the sense of a sentence is a proposition. Do sentences have reference as well as sense? Yes, but we will come back to this point in a moment.

(B) Predicates

Frege's actual view of predicates is a somewhat delicate matter. For now, we are going to work with a simplified scheme which respects important Fregean doctrines but is easier to work with. The *reference* of a predicate, we will say, is its **extension**. In the case of a one-place predicate such as 'is wise', this is simply the class (or set) of things that the predicate applies to, e.g. the class of wise things. The class of wise things is the class of things that the predicate is *true of*, or that **satisfy** the predicate. In the case of a relational (two-place) predicate, the extension can be understood as a set of ordered pairs. For example, the extension of the predicate 'loves' would be the set of all ordered pairs <x,y> such that x loves y:

> The reference of 'α loves β' = {<Victoria, David>, <David, Victoria>, <Charles, Camilla>, <Camilla, Charles>, and so on }

This is often called a 'relation-in-extension', since it is an object that stands to a two-place relational predicate just as an extension (set of objects) stands to a one-place predicate. For simplicity, we will speak of the reference of a predicate as its extension, whether the predicate is one-place or two-place.

The *sense* of the predicate is *rule*, or *criterion*, for whether or not an object or ordered pair goes into the extension of the predicate. The sense of 'α is mad', for example, is the criterion for whether or not something is mad; that is what we understand by the word 'madness'. Similarly, the sense of 'α loves β' is the criterion for love, and is what we understand by it.

• 4 COMPOSITIONALITY AGAIN; THE REFERENCE OF A SENTENCE

The sense of a singular term is a condition that an object must satisfy to be the referent of the term. The sense of a predicate is a condition that determines the extension of the predicate, which is its referent. In both cases, the sense is a *reference-determining condition*. Does not something similar hold in the case of sentences? Yes! Consider a simple atomic sentence:

> Socrates is wise.

We said that the sense of a sentence is not determined by the referents of its parts. But, since the reference of a singular term is an object, and the reference of a predicate an extension, there is something that is determined by the referents of the parts: the *truth-value* of the sentence.

For think about it: suppose a certain object O is the referent of the singular term '*a*', then if O is a member of the extension of the predicate 'β is *F*' then the sentence '*a* is *F*' must be true; if it is not, then the sentence must be false.

Thus the sentence is true if the referent of the singular term belongs to the extension of the predicate, and false if it is not. Furthermore, *if we replace the singular term with one with the same referent, the truth-value of the sentence will not change; similarly, it will not change if we replace the predicate with one with the same referent* (same extension). The analogous principle holds for atomic sentences whose predicate is a relational predicate.

Thus the truth-value of a sentence is determined by the referents of its parts. This leads Frege to say that the truth-value of a sentence is the referent of a sentence. This, in turn, enables us to bifurcate the principle of compositionality into two principles:

> **Compositionality of reference**: the truth-value of a sentence is determined by the referents of its parts (along with the way the sentence is composed).

> **Compositionality of sense**: the thought (proposition) expressed by a sentence is determined by the senses of its parts (along with the way the sentence is composed).

This enables us to say that the sense of *any* expression is a reference-determining condition. In particular, it enables us to say: *the sense of a sentence is its truth-condition.* It is the condition whose satisfaction makes the sentence true.

The theory has a certain architectonic quality, a certain symmetrical interdependence of parts, which many people find compelling. A diagram can illustrate:

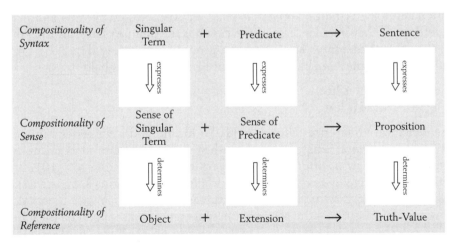

Figure 2.3 Fregean semantics for one-place atomic sentences

The idea is that when uttering a meaningful sentence, we express a proposition which is true or false depending on the referents of the parts of the sentence, which are themselves determined by the senses of the parts of the sentence.

Suppose, for example, that someone says 'Mikhail Gorbachev is brave'. The singular term 'Mikhail Gorbachev' expresses a *reference-determining condition* that determines a certain object, namely Gorbachev himself, the last premier of the Soviet Union. The predicate 'α *is brave*' expresses the condition under which an object is a member of a certain extension, which is simply the set of brave things. These two items of sense combine to form the proposition *that Mikhail Gorbachev is brave*. This proposition is true if and only if Mikhail Gorbachev is a member of the set of brave things. Thus, as expected, the truth condition of 'Mikhail Gorbachev is brave' is that Mikhail Gorbachev is brave.

• 5 APPLYING THE THEORY

How does the distinction between sense and reference solve the problems of cognitive value and empty singular terms?

Take the problem of cognitive value first. Pairs of co-referring singular terms, such as 'the Morning Star' and 'the Evening Star', may differ in sense. Thus (3) and (4) need not express the same thought, even if they must, given the truth of (1), have the same truth-value. Similarly, (6) and (7) need not, and do not, express the same thought. Since thoughts (propositions) are the objects of propositional attitudes, one might believe (7) without believing (6).

Now take the problem of empty singular terms. A singular term may express a sense that fails to pick out an object. For example, 'the largest natural number', or 'the present King of France', clearly expresses a reference-determining condition, but the condition fails to determine an object. A sense is also expressed by 'Vulcan': an object is the referent of that singular term just in case it is the unique planet orbiting the Sun inside the orbit of Mercury. Thus there is a proposition expressed by (10). Similarly for (11), and for something like 'The present King of France is bald'.

> (10)   Vulcan is hot.
> (11)   Nessie is hot.

So a sentence with reference-failure like (10) is meaningful – expresses a proposition – but is it *true* or *false*? The answer is neither. Since the sense of 'Vulcan' fails to determine an object, *no truth-value* is determined by the sense of (10). But the objection to the naïve theory was not that it fails to count such a sentence as (10) as having a truth-value, but that it fails to count it as meaningful. Frege's theory does so. It expresses a proposition – the sense of the sentence – and thus can be meaningfully asserted; one that can be believed, doubted and so on. And we get the right result that (10) and (11) express different propositions.

Unfortunately, Fregean semantics runs into trouble with respect to the closely related challenge presented by so-called **negative existentials**. Consider:

(12)   Vulcan does not exist.

That sentence not only expresses a proposition, that proposition is true. Vulcan does not exist, and it's true that Vulcan does not exist. But according to Frege, the non-existence of a referent for the singular term shows that the sentence *lacks* a truth value, *not* that it is true.

Frege did claim that existence is not to be expressed by the predicate 'α exists', but by the quantifier 'There exists an x such that …', which, as we noted in Chapter 1, can also be expressed as 'For some x, …'. To assert existence in the general case, for example 'Dolphins exist', we write 'There is an x such that (x is a Dolphin)'. To assert existence of an individual object, for example that the planet Jupiter exists, we write 'There is an x such that (x = Jupiter)'. Thus the sentence attributing *non*-existence to Vulcan should be written as:

(13)   Not: There is an x such that (x = Vulcan).

Famously, this manoeuvre purports to provide a sharp diagnosis of the invalidity of the ontological argument for the existence of God, along the same lines but perhaps more forcefully than that advanced by Kant. The argument tells us that the statement 'God exists' is true by the very meaning of the word 'God', and cannot be denied without contradiction. In particular, 'God' is defined as that being that satisfies the following predicates (presumably there are more predicates that serve to characterise God but we'll just stick to these three):

α is omniscient
α is omnipotent
α exists

So it is actually contradictory to deny the statement that God exists; to do so is like denying that a square has four sides. If we insist that existence is actually to be expressed as a quantifier, however, the last member of the list of predicates is ill formed. The statement that God exists must be written:

(14)   There is an x such that (x is omnipotent & x is omniscient)

One who denies this does not thereby get into logical trouble.

Yet this doesn't help with sentence (13), about Vulcan. For what we want is for (13) to say that the open sentence:

(15)   x = Vulcan

comes out *false* for every x – thus ensuring that 'There is an x such x = Vulcan' is false, hence that (13) is true. But according to Frege's theory, (15) comes out as *lacking* a truth-value, as *neither*-true-nor-false, for every x (on account of the presence of

'Vulcan'). Thus, 'There is an x such x = Vulcan' is neither-true-nor-false, and likewise (13) is neither-true-nor-false. It is still the wrong result.

Could not we get round this by pointing out that 'Vulcan' was introduced by means of a combination of certain predicates – 'α is a small planet between Mercury and the Sun, whose gravitational field causes the small observed perturbations in the orbit of Mercury', and then do the same trick we did with 'God'? That is, instead of (15), couldn't we write:

> (16)   Not: There is an x such that (x is a small planet between Mercury and the Sun, whose gravitational field causes the small observed perturbations in the orbit of Mercury)?

Yes, this solves the problem, but at a price; are all singular terms really equivalent to some combination of predicates? We'll come back to this in the chapter on Russell.[2]

• 6 SUBSTITUTIVITY AND EXTENSIONALITY

As explained in Section 4, Frege splits the principle of compositionality into two. The principle of compositionality of reference tells us that if we begin with a sentence S, and replace a part of S with an expression with the same reference, then the resulting sentence will have the same truth-value as S. More accurately, we can state:

> **The principle of substitutivity**: If sentence S contains expression e, and e* has the same referent as e, and S* results from S by replacing e by e*, then S* has the same truth-value as S.

In a word, substituting co-referring parts does not change a sentence's truth-value (replacement of co-referentials saves truth, '*salva veritate*'). It is important to appreciate how deeply founded this principle is in our understanding of language. Considering the following:

> (17)   Hesperus is a planet.
> (18)   Venus = Hesperus.
> (19)   Venus is a planet.

The truth of (18) shows us that 'Venus' and 'Hesperus' are co-referential: Venus and Hesperus are the same object. Therefore, (17) and (19) say the very same thing about the very same object. So they *cannot* differ in truth-value. What they say about the object is what is expressed by 'α is a planet', and the object they say this about is Venus, otherwise known as Hesperus. The principle of substitutivity seems to get to the root of the very idea of what it is to talk *about* an object, of *reference* itself. When we say something about an object, it doesn't matter by what means we refer to the object; it doesn't matter how we *pick out* the object. All that matters is whether that object is as we say it is; if it is, then what we say is true, and if not, then what we say is false.

The example we have just used concerns singular terms – 'Venus' and 'Hesperus'. But the principle of substitutivity is not restricted to any particular kind of expression. Thus consider predicates. Suppose that all and only the members of the club slept in the mansion on the night of the murder. Then if Smith is a member of the club, it follows that he slept in the mansion on the night of the murder; similarly, if Jones did not sleep in the mansion that night, then he is not a member of the club. Put in terms of the principle of substitutivity, this is to say that since 'α is a member of the club' and 'α slept in the mansion on the night of the murder' are coextensive, Smith's satisfying one predicate entails that he satisfies the other, and Jones' not satisfying one entails that he doesn't satisfy the other.

Co-extensive predicates are interchangeable in other contexts also, contexts in which the predicate does not occur in an atomic sentence. For example, the following predicates are co-extensive (assuming that so-called flying squirrels do not really *fly*; they only *glide*!):

> α is a bat.
> α is a flying mammal.

Their coextensiveness entails the truth of:

> For every x (x is a bat iff x is a flying mammal).

That is, something is a bat, if, and only if, it is a flying mammal. The following is true:

> For every x (x is a bat → x has sonar).

That is, all bats have sonar. The principle of substitutivity tells us that in any true sentence containing α *is a bat*, we can replace it with α *is a flying mammal*, and the result will be true. It follows, then, that

> For every x (x is a flying mammal → x has sonar).

That is, all flying mammals have sonar.

A language in which the principle of substitutivity holds generally is called an **extensional** language. A language in which the principle fails at least some of the time is a **non-extensional** language.

• 7 THE ANALYSIS OF PROPOSITIONAL ATTITUDES

The principle of substitutivity seems utterly axiomatic. Nevertheless, it might seem that there are counterexamples. Consider the following pair:

> (20)   Sally believes that Venus is a planet.
> (21)   Sally believes that Hesperus is a planet.

Clearly it would be possible for (20) to be true but (21) false, if Sally did not happen to know that Venus is Hesperus. (In fact, Sally could positively believe that Hesperus is *not* a planet yet believe that Venus is, without being irrational or illogical in any way.) Yet 'Hesperus' and 'Venus' are co-referential; so how could (20) and (21) differ in truth-value? Both (20) and (21), one might think, say the same thing about Venus: they both say of that object that it is *believed by Sally to be a planet*.

The answer in terms of Frege's theory is that (20) and (21) are not really *about* Venus at all (though it is about Sally). The predicate 'Sally believes that α is a planet' is not about planets. The truth-value of a sentence formed from it does not depend on what if anything is referred to by the singular term slotted into it. This is plausible because (21) could be true even if 'Hesperus' did not refer. Suppose that actually there is no such planet; the appearance of the supposed planet is actually a sort of hallucination that each of us happens to be subject to when looking at the sky. If the referent-determining rule expressed by 'Hesperus' did not happen to pick out an object, then still 'Hesperus is a planet' would express a thought, and Sally might believe that thought. As we saw, that is exactly what happened in the case of the French astronomer Le Verrier and the supposed planet Vulcan in the nineteenth century.

(20) and (21) then are not about Sally and Venus, but about Sally and the *proposition* that Hesperus is a planet; similarly for (20). This sort of fact is reflected in the difference between:

(22) Venus is a planet.
(23) that Venus is a planet.

Consider the thought expressed by (22). (22) *expresses* that thought, but (23) *refers* to that thought. (23) *is a singular term that stands for the thought expressed by* (22). In general:

> **Principle of that-clauses**: the result of prefixing a declarative sentence S by 'that' is a singular term whose referent is the sense of S.

Remember that the sense of a sentence is the proposition it expresses. What (20) says, then, is that Sally stands in a certain relation to a certain thought. In particular, she stands in the *believing* relation to the thought that Venus is a planet. At the first level of analysis, the sentence decomposes into a singular term standing for Sally, a two-place predicate 'α *believes* β', and a singular term standing for the thought that Venus is a planet. It is of the same form as 'Sally kissed John'. This is exactly what we should expect, given our earlier characterisation of the propositional attitudes: belief (in particular) is a certain relation between a believer and a thought. All of this carries over to the other propositional attitudes (fear, hope etc.).

That it should be possible for (20) to be true but (21) false is thus a counterexample to the principle of substitutivity. A language that has such devices as the sentence-operator 'that ___' is not, therefore, extensional. It is *non-extensional*: the referent of a that-clause does not depend on the *referent* of the sentence slotted in – a truth-value – but on the *sense* of the sentence slotted in. The role of 'Venus' and 'Hesperus' in (20) and (21) is not to refer to Venus; as philosophers sometimes say, that-clauses create an non-extensional *context*.

The referent of (22), 'Venus is a planet', is a truth-value, but the referent of (23), 'that Venus is a planet', is the sense of 'Venus is a planet'. The sense of the sentence becomes the referent of the corresponding that-clause; Frege also calls the sense of the sentence its *indirect referent*. What is the *sense* of 'that Venus is a planet'? It cannot be the same as the sense of 'Venus is a planet', for sense determines reference, and these have different referents. Frege calls the sense of 'that Venus is a planet' the *indirect sense* of 'Venus is a planet'. It is a higher-order, or level-2 sense. And this accounts for the difference of *sense* between (20) and (21), and thus accounts for their possible divergence in *reference*, their possible divergence in truth-value.

We'll return this topic in Chapter 7.

● 8 THE OBJECTIVITY OF SENSE

A sense of a referring term is both a *rule for determining* the reference of the term, and a *mode of presentation* of the reference. In an especially lucid passage in 'On Sense and Reference', Frege writes:

> The following analogy will perhaps clarify these relationships. Somebody observes the Moon through a telescope. I compare the Moon itself to the reference; it is the object of the observation, mediated by the real image projected by the object glass in the interior of the telescope, and the retinal image of the observer. The former I compare to the sense, the latter is like the idea or experience. The optical image in the telescope is indeed one-sided and dependent upon the standpoint of observation; but it is still objective, inasmuch as it can be used by several observers … But each one would have his own retinal image.
>
> ('On *Sinn and Bedeutung*' ['On Sense and Reference'] p. 155;
> translation slightly altered)

In 'The Thought: A Logical Inquiry', Frege again stresses that sense – what he calls the thought, what we are calling the proposition – is not mental, not experiential, not psychological, not of the same ilk as ideas. A proposition, as we said, is the kind of thing that can properly be said to be true or false. It is the objective meaning of a (non-context-relative) sentence, and is the object or content of a propositional attitude (belief, wish etc.). According to Frege, it follows from these considerations that propositions cannot be mental or psychological entities.

For what is a mental entity, an *idea* in the sense in which Locke and other earlier philosophers used that term? One example would be the sort of *mental image* we have when imagining something, or when we dream. Such a thing, as many philosophers have pointed out, is *private*. Suppose I am imagining my grandmother (now deceased). I have a vivid mental image in my mind's eye. It seems possible to describe to you what this image is like in such a way that you can generate your own image that is perhaps like it, but *you cannot perceive my mental image*. You cannot, in principle, verify that your image is like mine. Only I can perceive or experience my mental image: it is private. Likewise, only you can perceive yours. Mental images, and mental entities more generally, are *mental* in the sense that they are *in the mind*: the cash value of this seems to be that they are *private*, necessarily available only to the mind they are in. This is also, it seems, what is meant by calling something *subjective*: unlike objective entities like dogs and planets, a mental entity is immediately available only to one subjective point of view.

Consider now the hypothesis that the meaning of a sentence is a mental entity – an *idea* as Locke put it, or a *mental representation* as we might more elaborately put it. I say: 'Bologna is north of Florence'. What I mean is private to me, shut up in my mind. How can you understand me? How can you grasp *what I mean*? Well, you hear the words, and you are to respond somehow. They cause, in your mind, some kind of mental representation. But how are you to know that this mental representation has *anything at all* to do with mine? What could tell you that it is similar to mine? Well, you might try to describe your mental representation, asking me whether yours is like mine. But these are just more words: you attach a mental representation to them, and they cause a mental representation in me. How are we to find out whether *these* mental representations are at all alike? Clearly, there is no way: we can repeat the game forever, and never get any closer to finding out whether your thoughts are anything like mine. As Frege put it, language on this model would not amount to mutual understanding at all; utterances would merely be caused by mental states, not properly expressing a meaning at all.

If there is to be communication at all, meaning must be something 'out there' in some way: instead of being private, it must be something public, something that is no more my possession than yours. Of course, there are mental states, there is such a thing as the psychological process of thinking; there are mental processes that go on when we mean something by what we say. Nevertheless, a sentence like 'Bologna is north of Florence' has a public meaning: when uttered in the normal way, there are *linguistic rules* that determine it as meaning that a certain city stands in a certain geographical relation to another. The individual person, when hearing it spoken, may understand it – recognise the proposition it expresses according to compositional rules – or fail to understand it. This holds even when we are talking about inner states. If Sally says 'I am hungry', then according to linguistic rules, this sentence is true if and only if the speaker is in a certain physiological state at the time of utterance. If she says 'I am sad', then it is true if and only if the speaker is in a certain mental state at the time of utterance. The sentence is *about* a mental state, but its *meaning* is not a mental state.

Fregean sense, then, is not mental or psychological. Of course, it isn't physical either: senses such as propositions are not physical objects. They are reference-determining rules associated with expressions. Sense, then, inhabits the strange world of the *abstract*: senses, like mathematical objects, are non-spatial objects with no causal powers.

Finally, it is important to be clear that *sense*, in Frege's terminology, *has nothing to do with the senses*, e.g. seeing and hearing. Also, it has nothing to do with **sense-data**, which Russell and others regarded as the immediate objects of perception. There is absolutely no presumption that a word with sense has to appertain to something *sensible*, something that can be sensed or perceived. For example, '2 + 2 = 4' expresses a sense, namely the proposition that two and two are four.

This should strike one as perfectly natural: we do ordinarily speak of the *sense* of a sentence, and describe meaningless talk as *nonsense*.

• 9 FREGE'S THEORY OF THE REFERENTS OF PREDICATES, AND THE CONCEPT HORSE PROBLEM

Frege's view of the *senses* of predicates is intuitive: for example, to understand the sense of the predicate 'α is a horse' is to understand the rule or criterion for whether or not the predicate applies to an arbitrary thing. If one does grasp that sense, and also grasps the sense of the singular term 'Red Rum', then one grasps the proposition expressed by 'Red Rum is a horse'. One understands that sentence.

The *reference* of predicates is another matter. Earlier, I said that for the sake of simplicity we would assume that Frege thought of the referents of predicates as their extensions, the set of things that the predicate applies to. Frege's real view is more complicated (the classic reference is 'On Concept and Object').

Consider:

(24)   Red Rum is a horse.

We can't really take the referent of 'α is a horse' to be the set of horses, for that set is merely an *object*, nameable by a singular term, i.e. 'the set of horses'. What is so special about those particular objects which makes them suitable for references of predicates, for making propositions? Why those, and not, say, numbers, or pencils? If one says 'Red Rum, my pencil!', one lists things, one doesn't express a proposition; similarly with 'Red Rum, the set of horses'! If we try saying (26) is really

(25)   Red Rum *is a member of* the set of horses

we thereby launch an infinite regress: that sentence mentions Red Rum and the set of horses, but it *also* includes the words 'is a member of'. If we explained that expression, like the original 'α is a horse', as itself referring to set, the same issue would arise. We'd get something like the monstrous

(26)   Red Rum the set of horses the set of ordered pairs such that the first is a member of the second.

This, again, is a list, not a sentence. *The moral is that a sentence must have something whose role is not merely to stand for an object.*

Instead, Frege holds that a predicate denotes a *function*. Just as the value of the function denoted by '$\alpha + 2$' when applied to 3 is 5, and the value of the denotation of 'the mother of α' for a person is the person's mother, the value of the function denoted by 'α is a horse' for Red Rum is either of the two truth-values, depending on whether or not Red Rum is a horse. Since, in fact, Red Rum is (or was) a horse, the truth-value of the sentence is truth.

Frege calls functions whose values are truth-values **concepts**. The terminology is unfortunate because it seems more appropriate to call the *senses* of predicates by that word, as indeed did the great Fregean, Alonzo Church. But in the remainder of this chapter we'll stick with Frege's way of speaking.

Fregean concepts and functions in general are not objects, and cannot be referred to by singular terms. They are 'second-level' entities. Objects comprise the **first-level**, and entities that can be applied to objects are **second-level** entities.[3] Ignoring functions like that denoted by '$x + 2$' which are not concepts, we can say equally that first-level entities, objects, can be the inputs for second-level entities, the concepts, which yield truth-vales as outputs. Functions are like arrows, pointing from one entity to another; concepts are the special case where the entities pointed to are the truth-values, truth or falsity. Predicates denote them, such as:

α is green
α is a friend of the Dalai Lama
$\alpha + 2 = 7$

But Frege now perceives a riddle. The reference of a predicate such as

(27) α is a horse

is a concept. Now consider:

(28)   'α is a horse' refers to the concept horse.
(29)   'the concept horse' refers to the concept horse.

(28) seems unobjectionable. And (29) seems inevitable – surely the sentence "'A' refers to A" will be true no matter what referring term we put for 'A'. Thus the two terms 'α is a horse' and 'the concept horse' should be thought of as referring to the same entity. Therefore, at least in extensional contexts, they should be intersubstitutable. Wherever one occurs (extensionally), it should be possible to replace it with the other without changing the truth-value of the whole in which it occurs. Continue with an empirical truth:

(30)   Red Rum is a horse.

Thus, from the point just made that 'α is horse' and 'the concept horse' being intersubstitutable, we infer:

(31)   Red Rum the concept horse.

This not only fails to be true, it is nonsense! It is grammatical or syntactically ill formed. Yet it gives the appearance of following from true premises.

The problem, in Frege's view, is with the phrase 'the concept horse'. (28) is *not* true. 'α is a horse' has a gap in it indicated by the Greek letter, whereas 'the concept horse' does not. It isn't the sort of thing that can play the role of a predicate; predicates are necessarily *incomplete* or *unsaturated* as Frege puts it, and concepts by their nature are incapable of being referred to by terms that are complete, saturated, or gapless.

What should we write in place of (28)? Nothing. For Frege, *predicates only refer when they are performing their normal roles in complete sentences*. Indeed, it seems that any attempt to *say* what predicates refer to is doomed to failure – since grammar itself seems to require that the space in 'E refers to __' is replaceable only by a singular term, which thus refers to an object, a first-level entity, not a concept, a second-level entity. It is an extremely paradoxical situation, which has inspired many, many responses. Frege himself was well aware of the situation, and begged the reader to grant him a 'grain of salt'.

Concepts, then, are absolutely, categorically different from objects; nothing you can say about the one can be said about the other, in the sense that if you say something about the one, any attempt to say it about the other will be ill formed nonsense. For example, we can say that singular terms are inter-substitutable if and only if they each refer to the *same object*. The concept of identity is only applicable to objects. It makes no sense to assert or deny it of the referents of predicates, of concepts. But there is an analogue for concepts: two predicates are intersubstitutable if they are *co-extensive*, namely if they have the same extension.

Note again that speaking with Frege in this way of concepts is rather strained. For example, the predicates 'α is a flying hippo' and 'α is a round square' are co-extensive, because they each fail to apply to anything. Their extensions are the same, the empty set. But surely, we want to say, the concepts are different! We want to speak with Alonzo Church, that they express different concepts, different senses. But just be reminded that when Frege speaks of concepts, he means functions whose values are truth-values.

• HISTORICAL NOTES

Frege was not well known until long after he died in 1925 – although philosophers Bertrand Russell, Rudolf Carnap and Ludwig Wittgenstein were all keenly aware of him while he was alive, and Edmund Husserl had some contact with him; and amongst leading pure mathematicians, Giuseppe Peano and David Hilbert corresponded with him. Most people say he was without a doubt the unsung inventor or discoverer of modern logic, the symbolic logic which handles inferences such as 'Every mollusc is an animal; therefore all who eat molluscs are eaters of animals'. The key – which is now standard in logic – is the integration of propositional logic with variables, predicates and quantifiers. This advance was modestly but firmly announced in *Begriffsschrift*, which appeared in 1879. The logic was vastly more powerful than anything that existed before, and it made the thesis plausible that arithmetic is really logic – a thesis that he sketched informally in the *Foundations of Arithmetic* of 1884, and attempted to prove rigorously in the *Basic Laws of Arithmetic* of 1893 and 1903. The proofs and presentation were impeccable, except for one detail: his assumption that every predicate determines an extension, a class or set, was inconsistent. Famously, Russell wrote to Frege informing him of this fact, just as Volume 2 of the *Basic Laws* was to be printed. Frege arguably never recovered from what he described as the 'shock' of having received the news from Russell; it was for Russell, along with A. N. Whitehead, to make the case in a more complicated way for the reducibility of arithmetic to logic, in *Principia Mathematica* of 1911.

The exact connection of Frege's work in logic and the foundations of mathematics to his ideas in the philosophy of language has been the subject of some dispute. But among the undisputed elements is that an explicit distinction between sense and reference was announced in 1892, with 'On Sense and Reference'. It enabled him to maintain rigorously that pure mathematics delivers knowledge, despite its consisting of logical true equations. No less important in Frege's eyes was 'On Concept and Object', also from 1892; the central idea of that piece had been active in his thought since at least 1884, but the power and precision of his analysis on such an abstract topic was almost without precedent. After 1903, little was heard from Frege until 1918 when he published 'The Thought: A Logical Inquiry', in which he makes the case for the 'third realm', the objectivity and abstract nature of propositional content. Russell thought Frege's sense-reference distinction unnecessary. In a way Wittgenstein agreed with Russell on that point, but there is no mistaking Wittgenstein's debt to Frege in his early work the *Tractatus Logico-Philosophicus* (Wittgenstein says that Frege 'quite wiped the floor' with him during his 1912 visit to Frege, on the recommendation of Russell). Carnap (1891–1970) developed Fregean themes in his *Introduction to Semantics* (1942) and *Meaning and Necessity* (1956 [1947]); he had attended courses with Frege in the early 1910s. Michael Dummett (1925–2011) did the most to establish Frege's name at the top of analytic philosophy with a series of great books about him starting with *Frege: Philosophy of Language* (1973).

• CHAPTER SUMMARY

Frege begins with a two-pronged attack on naïve semantics, focusing on **(NP2):** the meaning of a singular term is its referent.

1 The first prong concerns co-referential singular terms. For example, since the Morning Star = the Evening Star, the meaning of 'the Morning Star' = the meaning of 'the Evening Star', according to the naïve theory. But that conflicts with the evident fact that the two sentences 'The Morning Star is a planet' and 'The Evening Star is a planet' do *not* mean the same. The two sentences do not have the same

cognitive value, as Frege puts it; discovering that one is true is not the same as discovering the truth of the other. It also conflicts more dramatically with the observation that whereas 'the Morning Star = the Morning Star' is *a priori*, 'the Morning Star = the Evening Star' is empirical, *a posteriori*.

2 The second prong of the attack concerns non-referring singular terms, such as 'Vulcan' or 'The Loch Ness Monster'. According to naïve theory, their lacking reference entails that they lack meaning; but this flies in the face of the evident difference in meaning between 'Vulcan is hot' and 'Nessie is hot', as well as the fact that a person can believe the content of 'Vulcan is hot' while disbelieving that of 'Nessie is hot'.

Frege responds to this by postulating that each meaningful expression expresses a sense, which is a rule for determining the referent of the expression, if it has one. If the sense does determine a referent, then the sense acts as a mode of presentation of the referent. The distinction is drawn across the board: a singular term expresses a sense that purports to determine an object as its referent; a one-place predicate expresses a sense that purports to determine an extension (in fact a *function*) as its referent, and similarly for two-place predicates and so on, and a sentence expresses a sense (a proposition, what Frege calls a thought) that purports to determine a truth-value as its referent. Thus the principle of compositionality is split in two, one for reference and one for sense.

Thus (1) 'The Morning Star is a planet' and 'The Evening Star is a planet' have different senses despite their saying the same thing about the same object. And 'Sally believes that the Morning Star is a planet' and 'Sally believes that the Evening Star is a planet' need not coincide in truth-value, for the two relate Sally to different propositions. (2) 'Vulcan is a planet' is neither true nor false, because of the non-existence of Vulcan; but it expresses a proposition despite lacking a truth-value. Therefore 'Sally believes that Vulcan is hot' has a truth-value. However, Frege still has the problem of negative existentials: there appears to be no non-arbitrary way of explaining how 'Vulcan does not exist' is true; Frege's view gets the wrong answer that it is neither true nor false.

Frege argues that there is no coherent alternative to the objectivity of sense; propositions are not in anyone's mind, but are public abstract entities.

Frege takes predicates to refer to unsaturated entities he calls 'concepts'. Any sentence – take 'Jane smokes' as a representative – must have among the entities to which it refers an unsaturated or incomplete entity in addition to Jane; for taking the rest of the sentence to denote another saturated or complete entity – an object – would have it as only a list of objects, not a sentence. Therefore the sentence must be taken to have the referents Jane and the unsaturated referent of 'α smokes', a Fregean concept. This latter entity is for Frege a function: it has its value the truth-value truth if Jane smokes, and falsehood if Jane does not smoke. The Fregean puzzle of the concept horse arises because of the apparent reasoning from a true statement to something that does not even express a proposition: Red Rum is a horse (suppose true); 'α is a horse' refers to the concept horse; therefore Red Rum the concept horse. Frege diagnoses the problem as that "'α is a horse' refers to the concept horse" is, strangely enough, not true; 'the concept horse', in being a saturated expression, refers at most to an object, not to an unsaturated entity, a concept.

• STUDY QUESTIONS

1 Assume that Johnny sincerely exclaims: 'Santa Claus is in the department store!' Suppose that there is a man dressed up in a red suit etc. in the department store. Is what Johnny says false? True? Does Johnny falsely believe that Santa Claus is in the department store? What is the meaning of 'Santa Claus' in terms of Fregean semantics?

2 For Frege, except in cases where the expression fails to determine a referent, the sense of an expression is a mode of presentation of its referent. If we accept this, do we say that psychological acts of thinking necessarily involve senses, and not necessarily referents? Compare these ideas with the idea that the content of a perception is never simply an object, but either (a) an object *from-a-particular-point-of-view*, or (b) a collection of sense-data, which could be exactly the same if it were a case of hallucination, and the object did not exist.

3 It is plausible to say that 'bought' and 'purchased' are synonyms – that they express the same sense. Is the following therefore a valid argument? Why or why not?

> Sam bought a turnip.
> Therefore, Sam purchased a turnip.

What about:

> Susie believes that Sam bought a turnip.
> Therefore, Susie believes that Sam purchased a turnip.

Discuss the relation between:

> that Sam bought a turnip.
> the sense of 'Sam bought a turnip'.

4 *Conceptual analysis* is, in Fregean terms, the search for statements like:

> (a) x *knows* that p if and only if x *has a justified true belief* that p,

where the parts italicised express the very same sense. If it is successful, then apparently such a statement is the same statement as

> (b) x *knows* that p if and only if x *knows* that p.

But (b) is a triviality, which cannot extend our knowledge; (a), even if it does represent a successful analysis, seems not to be. This is known as the *paradox of analysis*; what should a Fregean say in response?

5 What do you think of the following strategies for avoiding the problem of negative existentials within Fregean semantics? (A) Introduce the expression 'It's true that P', which says of a *proposition* P that it's true: if P is false, *or defective in such a way as to be neither true nor false*, it yields a falsehood; and P is true, it yields a truth. Then analyse 'Vulcan does not exist' as 'Not: It's true that (there is an x such that x = Vulcan)'. (B) Suppose that there is an ordinary first-level predicate 'exists'. Now suppose that when we say such things as 'Vulcan does not exist', we are saying: 'Imagine that Vulcan really exists; that state of mind is mistaken' (for a much more careful presentation of such a view, see Gareth Evans 1982, Ch. 10).

6 How could words come to acquire their senses? If there were no language-users, would there still be senses?

7 For Frege, concepts are a subclass of functions (remember that in Fregean language, concepts are the referents of predicates, not their senses). Therefore just as the function '$\alpha + 5$' has the value 7 for the argument 2 – i.e. '$2 + 5$' is a singular term denoting 7 – 'α is white' has the value true for the argument snow – i.e. 'Snow is white' is a singular term denoting truth. Are all true sentences thus singular terms denoting truth values? Are truth-values objects, alongside the Eiffel Tower? Is there no logical difference between sentences and singular terms? Does that mean that one can assert something by saying 'Truth!'? Can you think of reasons for doubting this?

• PRIMARY READING

All relevant sources for Frege are included in *The Frege Reader*, edited by Michael Beaney (Oxford: Wiley-Blackwell, 1997); the main ones are 'On *Sinn und Bedeutung*' ['On Sense and Reference'], and 'On Concept and Object', 'Thought'; see also 'Function and Concept', the letter to Husserl, the comments on *Sinn und Bedeutung*, the *Grundgesetze der Arithmetic* Vol. 1 Selections, Letter to Russell 13/11/1904, and Letter to Jourdain January 1914. Beaney has finessed the delicate matter of whether to translate 'Bedeutung' as 'reference' or 'meaning' by not translating it.

Although it was written well before he had the idea of distinguishing sense from reference, no set of recommendations for reading Frege would be complete without mentioning Frege's wonderful *Foundations of Arithmetic*, translated by J. L. Austin, (Oxford: Basil Blackwell, 1974).

• SECONDARY READING

There are now many books about Frege, but certainly the most substantive is M. Dummett, *Frege: Philosophy of Language*, second edition (Cambridge, MA: Harvard University Press, 1993). The book is outstanding, but you may want to begin with two essays by Dummett: 'Frege's Philosophy' and 'Frege's Distinction Between Sense and Reference', in Dummett's collection, *Truth and Other Enigmas* (Cambridge, MA: Harvard University Press, 1978).

A much shorter and more accessible book is H. Noonan, *Frege: A Critical Introduction*, (Cambridge: Polity, 2001).

• NOTES

1 Experienced Fregeans will recognise a number of places in which I simplify or omit. Some Fregeans doubt that his theory was meant to apply to *natural language*, that his remarks were only to explain his artificial symbolic language, his 'Begriffsschift' (Concept-script). I think he thought that his Begriffsscrift more exactly mirrors what goes on more vaguely in natural language, namely the expression of thoughts, of propositions.
2 Frege himself, in his great work the *Basic Laws of Arithmetic*, accommodated this shortcoming by stipulating that in such cases, in effect, the referent is actually the empty or null set. But as Frege himself allows, this is plainly artificial. At any rate, we don't want to say that Vulcan is the empty set, or that Vulcan = the present King of France.
3 There are also third-level entities, and fourth-level entities, and so on. Quantifiers, since they take second-level entities (concepts) as arguments, are third-level. There are even mixed-level entities, such as the referent of 'α falls under the concept-ϕ'.

3

russellian semantics

• 1 THE TASK FOR RUSSELL

Two families of problems motivated Frege's distinction between sense and reference. We can sum these up by calling them problems of:

1 Existence
2 Identity/Substitutivity.

Existence problems include the question of how to explain the evident meaningfulness of sentences like:

> The man who killed the Kennedys worked for the Mafia.
> Vulcan is hot.[1]

– despite the fact that there is no such man as the man who killed the Kennedys (no single person killed both Bobby and John) and no such planet as Vulcan, in which case the singular terms 'The man who killed the Kennedys' and 'Vulcan' are empty, i.e. do not refer to anything. Note that such a sentence as this could be true:

> Jones believes that Vulcan is hot.

– which implies that there is such a proposition as that Vulcan is hot, in which case 'Vulcan' must be meaningful, despite not having a referent.

Identity problems concern the fact that co-referring singular terms may differently affect what Frege called the *cognitive values* of sentences in which they occur. The most glaring examples are such truths as:

> Venus = Venus.
> Venus = the Evening Star.

This is the most glaring kind of case because the first sentence is so unlike the second in cognitive value. But also a case like this shows that sentences can say the same thing about the same object but differ in cognitive value:

> Venus is a planet.
> The Evening Star is a planet.

These are not identity statements – not of the form 'x = y' – but since Venus is identical with the Evening Star, a theory that tries to explain meaning in terms of reference alone, such as the naïve theory, appears to have a problem.

Because of this, sentences that ascribe propositional attitudes may present *apparent* failures of the **substitutivity** principle, as in:

> George wondered whether Scott = the Author of *Waverley*.
> George wondered whether Scott = Scott.

According to the example due to Bertrand Russell (1872–1970), the Prince Regent George, later King George IV, did wonder whether it was the poet Scott who wrote the famous Scottish novels; but he did not, of course, wonder whether Scott is Scott.

Similarly, the following sentences need not have the same truth-value:

> George believes that Venus is a planet.
> George believes that the Evening Star is a planet.

But Russell does *not* accept Frege's distinction between sense and reference. He thinks there is a better and more economical way to solve the existence and identity problems. Russell accepts the main principle of naïve semantics, that, essentially, meaning is just reference; he finds ways round the apparent need to postulate sense.

• 2 THE THEORY OF DEFINITE DESCRIPTIONS

We can distinguish between *simple* singular terms and *complex* singular terms. Simple singular terms are proper names such as 'Paris', 'Michaelangelo' and so on (this includes names such as 'Winston Churchill', which comprise more than one word; for now we ignore this complication and regard all proper names as simple singular terms). Complex singular terms include such examples as:

> the capital of France
> Alexander's father
> the most intelligent human being.

An important fact is that *all* complex singular terms can be rewritten in the form

> the F

where F is some predicate. For example, the singular term 'Alexander's father' can be written as 'The father of Alexander'.[2]

A singular term of the form 'the F' is what Russell calls a **definite description**. Russell's theory of descriptions is a theory of the word 'the'. According to what we have said about singular terms generally, what remains when we remove a singular term from a sentence is a predicate. Thus any sentence containing a definite description can be understood as having the following form:

(1)   The F is G.

– for some possibly complex predicate 'α is G'.[3] Thus consider an example:

(2)   The present King of France is wise.

According to Frege's theory, this sentence is meaningful – that is, it expresses a sense – but it is neither true nor false, since 'the present King of France' does not have a referent. But Russell thinks that that cannot be right. For a meaningful sentence, a sentence expressing a sense as Frege would put it, expresses a *truth-condition*: a way that the world must be if the proposition is to be true. Either the world is that way, in which case the sentence is true, or it is not, in which case the sentence is false. (2) *does* express a truth-condition: therefore, since it is not true, it must be false. For what could it mean to say that a sentence is false, than that it is meaningful (expresses a proposition), but is not true?

The truth-condition of (2) is clear. It may be expressed as a conjunction of three propositions – the *existence*, *uniqueness*, and *categorical* clauses:

(2a)   There is a King of France.
(2b)   There is not more than one King of France.
(2c)   Whoever is King of France is wise.

A little reflection shows that (2a)–(2c) are jointly sufficient and individually necessary for the truth of (2); their conjunction is necessarily equivalent to (2). We can put the point more generally by saying that (1) is necessarily equivalent to the conjunction of:

(1a)   There is an x such that Fx.
(1b)   Not: (there is an x and y such that ($x \neq y$ & Fx & Fy)).
(1c)   For every x (Fx → Gx).

(1) can be understood as saying 'There is exactly one F, and it is G'. In fact the conjunction (1a–1c) is logically equivalent to the more compact:

(1*) There is an x such that (Fx & for every y (Fy → y = x) & Gx).[4]

You might find the sub-formula: For every y (Fy → y = x) not very transparent. It is equivalent to:

For every y ($y \neq x$ → not: Fy)

which says 'everything besides x is non-F'. Russell's claim is that sentences of the form (1) are analysed, say the same thing as, sentences of the form (1*).

Russell stresses the affinity between 'The F is G' and 'There is an F that is G' ('Some F is G'): whereas the former, in Russell's view, says that exactly one F is G, the latter says that *at least* one F is G. In other words, 'The' should be considered a quantifier, along with 'There is' or 'Some' – and also alongside 'All' and 'An' and so on. If we consider the phrases

The F
Some F
An F
All F
Each F

and so on, it is clear that any one of them forms a sentence when joined to a predicate '… is G', and that each has a meaning irrespective of whether there are any objects for the predicate F to denote. A way to put it is that they are all *descriptions*, but the first is a *definite* description and the rest are *indefinite* descriptions.

This observation helps to dislodge the naïve idea that 'The F' is a genuine singular term, i.e. a referring expression like the name 'Sigmund Freud', despite the fact that they slot into the empty place in a one-place predicate to form a sentence. 'The F is G', as shown by its analysis as the conjunction (1a)–(1c), has nothing like the simple form of 'Fa'; unlike the conjunction (1a)–(1c), 'Fa' is the simplest possible sentence, an atomic predication. The *logical form* of 'The F is G' is very different from its *surface form*, i.e. its grammatical or linguistic form.

Crucially, Russell's way of explaining the word 'The' is what he calls **contextual definition**, or *definition-in-use*. An **explicit** or **direct** definition substitutes a given symbol with another that is grammatically of the same category (the defined expression is a simple symbol, the defining expression normally is complex). For example, we can define 'bachelor' as 'unmarried man': these are equivalent expressions of the same grammatical category:

df: For every x, x is a <u>bachelor</u> if and only if x is an unmarried man.

Wherever the predicate 'unmarried man' occurs, the definition licenses one to replace the symbol with 'bachelor' (or vice versa). By contrast, the technique of contextual definition of a symbol gives a rule for transforming *whole sentences* containing that symbol into whole sentences that do not contain the symbol. So Russell does not give us a form of words or symbols that is equivalent to 'The' or to 'The F'. Rather, he explains how to re-express the content of any sentence of the form:

The F is G,

without substituting some other kind of singular term for 'The F' (or some symbol for 'The'). The result, is (1*) – for which (1) is shorthand.

Thus: (1*) *does not contain a symbol (simple or complex) that has simply been substituted for* 'The F'.

In the case of what Russell called a *logically proper name*, sentences containing the name are fully meaningful only if the bearer of the name exists. So if 'a' is a logically proper name, then 'Fa' is not meaningful if 'a' lacks a referent. It is clear, on Russell's analysis, that it is not a presupposition of the meaningfulness of (1) that The F exists: if The F does not exist, then (1) is false, and therefore not meaningless. This is obvious, since the meaning of (1) is given more explicitly by (1*). *This is the point of saying that definite descriptions are not referring expressions* (or that they 'have no meaning in isolation'), and that is why Russell says that the relation between 'The F' and the F, when the F exists, should not be called the relation of reference or meaning; he calls it the relation of 'denoting' (but we will not follow him in that point of usage).

Note finally that since 'The King of France is wise' is *false* on Russell's theory, its *negation* is true. That is, 'It is not the case that the King of France is wise' is true. Thus for Russell we have to distinguish the **internal** from the **external negation** of 'The F is G'.

> The F is not-G (internal)

means 'there is exactly one F and it is not G', whereas

> Not: the F is G (external)

means merely that it is false that the F is G. An *internal* negation can be false when the corresponding external negation is true. Consider the following example:

> The Loch Ness Monster is not swimming. (internal, false)
> Not: the Loch Ness Monster is swimming. (external, true)

The first requires for its truth the existence of the monster but who is not swimming, whereas the second requires *either* that the monster exists but is not swimming, *or* that the monster simply doesn't exist. Internal negations always entail their corresponding external negations, but not vice versa.

Spelled out quasi-symbolically, these are:

> *Internal negation*:
> There is an x such that (Fx & for every y (Fy → y = x) & not: Gx)

> *External negation*:
> Not: There is an x such that (Fx & for every y (Fy → y = x) & Gx)

This distinction is just where the negation sign is. In the internal negation, the negation sign is *within* the **scope** of the definite description, which takes **wide** scope with respect to negation. In the external negation, the description takes **narrow** scope with respect to negation.

● 3 APPLYING THE THEORY OF DESCRIPTIONS

I–II deal with existence issues; III–IV deal with issues of cognitive value and identity.

I. In Frege's theory,

> (3) The man who killed the Kennedys is Cuban.

is not true, and not false either: it is meaningful, but neither true-nor-false. The reason as we saw in Chapter 2 is this: for Frege, this sentence is of the form

Fa.

It ascribes the predicate 'is Cuban' to the referent of the singular term 'the man who killed the Kennedys'; the sentence is true if the predicate applies to that thing, and false if it does not apply to that thing. That is, it is false if and only if its negation is true. Since the singular term lacks a referent, this procedure never gets started, so no truth-value is determined. In Russell's theory, as explained above, the sentence is false; in Russell's theory, (3) is *not* of the form *Fa*, and the 'the man who killed the Kennedys' is not a singular term at all.

II. Consider this sentence (and assume that 'the Loch Ness monster' is a definite description, meaning 'the (unique) monster who lives in Loch Ness'):

(4)   The Loch Ness monster does not exist.

As explained in Chapter 2, it's plausible that there are two ways to interpret the word 'exists'. First, we can take it as an ordinary *first-level predicate*, like 'is fat' or 'is wise'. In that case, it is true of every object, and not false of any object. Thus, the 'nonexistence' predicate 'does not exist' is false of every object. In that case, how could (4) be true? Take again Frege's theory. To determine the truth-value of (4), we must first find the referent of 'the Loch Ness monster', and ask whether the nonexistence predicate is true of it. Suppose 'the Loch Ness monster' does have a referent. Then it exists, so 'the Loch Ness monster does not exist' is false. So if (4) were false, then Frege's theory would have no problem. But (4) is true. How can Frege's theory determine it to be true? If 'the Loch Ness monster' has no referent, then (4) comes out *neither-true-nor-false*, and *not* true – for the same reason that (3) came out that way on Frege's theory.

On Russell's theory, (4) comes out true, if we take 'exists' to be an ordinary first-level predicate. However, neither Frege nor Russell take that view of 'exists'. They both take existence to be expressed by the *existential quantifier*. We can attach it to a predicate like 'is a dog' to say that dogs exist – 'There is an x such that (x is a dog)' – but it cannot meaningfully be attached to a singular term; that is, we cannot write 'For some x (Fido)'. That is ill-formed nonsense. What then of (4)? The trouble for Frege is that he has no direct way to express the content of (4): if 'the Loch Ness monster' is a singular term, then (4) simply doesn't contain a predicate to which the existential quantifier might be attached, to become a sentence which can then be negated. The difficulty is not ameliorated if we suppose that the real form of (4) is

(4*)   Not: There is x such that (x = The Loch Ness monster).

This does now contain a predicate – 'β = The Loch Ness monster' – but the predicate still retains the empty singular term 'The Loch Ness monster', and thus is not true and *not false* of any object; there is no object such that the predicate is satisfied depending on whether or not a given object is identical with it. The problem lies with

Frege's theory of the semantical functioning of terms such as 'The Loch Ness monster' as referring terms.

For Russell, again, (4) presents no problem, since definite descriptions already contain quantifiers. If we take F as meaning 'is a monster who lives in Loch Ness', then (4) comes out simply as:

(4**)   Not: There is an x such that (Fx & for all y (Fy → y=x)).

(Of course, this would not be true if there is more than one Loch Ness monster).

III. How does the theory of descriptions solve problems of identity, cognitive value and substitutivity? From Russell's example of George IV, we can write:

(5)   George IV wondered whether Scott = the author of *Waverley*.
(6)   It is not the case that George IV wondered whether Scott = Scott.

Both of these are true. If we assume that 'the author of *Waverley*' is a referring expression, then from (5) and

(7)   Scott = the author of *Waverley*.

which is true, we could infer

(8)   George IV wondered whether Scott = Scott.

– which contradicts (6). That is, (7) seems to tell us that we can substitute 'the author of *Waverley*' for 'Scott' wherever 'Scott' appears, in which case we can move from (5) to (8). The contradiction is evaded by the theory of descriptions in the following way. The theory of descriptions tells us to recast

(9)   Scott = the author of *Waverley*.

as

(10)   There is an x such that [x wrote *Waverley* & for every y (y wrote *Waverley* → y=x) & x=Scott].

(This is still of the form 'The F is G', where 'F' is 'wrote *Waverley*' and 'is G' is '= Scott'). Thus (5) becomes

(5*)   George IV wondered whether: There is an x such that [x wrote *Waverley* and for every y (y wrote *Waverley* → y=x) and x=Scott].

(5*) does not contradict (6). Notice that the only singular term (besides 'George IV' and '*Waverley*') in (5*) is 'Scott', so we cannot use (9) to get (8) from (5). The definite description 'disappears on analysis'; what is revealed is that, despite initial appearances, there is no singular term for which 'Scott' can be substituted.

There is a final complication. Suppose we have:

(11)   Mary believes that ghosts ≠ goblins.

Since neither ghosts nor goblins exist, the two predicates are co-extensive, and each can be substituted for the other. So it looks as if we have 'Mary believes that ghosts ≠ ghosts'! In other words, if Russell accepts that predicates with the same extension are co-referential (as Frege did), then it seems that he's got trouble. So he'll have to accept that co-extensive predicates may refer to different entities – for example, properties or universals. We'll see more of this doctrine below.

• 4 NAMES AS DISGUISED DEFINITE DESCRIPTIONS

Russell was well aware that existence and identity problems arise for ordinary proper names as well as for definite descriptions. For example,

> (12)   Pegasus does not exist.

is seemingly both meaningful and true, and the following triad is seemingly consistent:

> (13)   John believes that George Eliot is an author.
> (14)   It is not the case that John believes that Mariane Evans is an author.
> (15)   George Eliot = Mariane Evans.

Russell's response is to suppose that ordinary proper names are not *really* referring expressions at all, but *disguised definite descriptions*. For example, the meaning of 'Pegasus' is really the same as that of 'the winged horse', or some such thing. In that case, the meaning and truth-value of (12) can be explained as above using the theory of descriptions, whereas Frege, as we learned in Chapter 2, could not. Frege's theory has it that (12) is meaningful, but that it is neither true nor false – not, as according to Russell's theory, that it is true, which is the correct answer.

What about 'George Eliot' then? In fact, it is implausible to say that there is precisely *one* definite description that gives the meaning of that name. For example, A might know George Eliot only as the author of *Middlemarch* and *Daniel Deronda*, when B knows her only as the author of *Silas Marner* and *The Mill on the Floss*. Yet surely both A and B may be credited with understanding such a sentence as 'George Eliot was interested in German philosophy'. So Russell does not claim that each ordinary proper name is equivalent to some *one* definite description. Rather, he claims that on each occasion whereby one *uses* or *understands* an ordinary proper name, the name is equivalent in the person's thought at that moment to a definite description. Thus for any sentence '… a …' containing a proper name a, the claim is:

> For any subject B, any proper name *a*, and any occasion whereby B understands or meaningfully uses *a* in a sentence '… *a* …', there is a description 'The F' such that '… *a* …' is synonymous for B on that occasion to '… the F …'.

That is to say, whenever you think something you would express as '*a* is G', what you are really thinking is given by 'The F is G', for some uniquely identifying predicate F. Each *use* of an ordinary proper name serves to abbreviate a definite description.

• 5 KNOWLEDGE BY ACQUAINTANCE AND KNOWLEDGE BY DESCRIPTION

Suppose I know a man called 'Mr Wiggins' only as the village baker, and do not know that he has a daughter. Suppose you know the self-same 'Mr Wiggins' only as the father of your friend Esmeralda, and do not know about the business he is in. Thus according to Frege, if I say to you 'Mr Wiggins is ridiculous', you, knowing Mr Wiggins, will respond as if you understand my statement. But I will understand the statement as 'The village baker is ridiculous', and you will understand the statement as 'Esmeralda's father is ridiculous'. But then, what is the basis for saying that we communicate? There is no proposition that we both understand.

Frege responds to this apparent difficulty merely by saying that for ordinary, non-scientific purposes, we simply tolerate such cases of non-overlapping knowledge of the referents of proper names. So long as the referent is the same, then normally we don't get into trouble, and we can say that we communicate in a kind of downgraded sense of 'communicate'.

Russell has more or less the same difficulty, but has a more painstaking response. Suppose we ask: if ordinary proper names actually abbreviate definite descriptions, then are *any* singular terms genuine referring expressions? Are there any *logically proper names*, as Russell puts it?

It would be strange if there were not. For in that case, there would be no atomic sentences at all! (And no truth-functional compounds of them, such as 'Fa & Rab'.) And there had better be. For suppose there were not. Then all sentences would be generalisations, that is, sentences of the form

> For every x (... x ...)
> There is an x such that (... x ...).

(or truth-functional compounds of these, but set those aside). What do generalisations mean? What does it mean to say that every x is F? It means that for each object *x*, F*x* is true. That is to say, our understanding of a generalisation 'For every x, ... x ...' is by virtue of our understanding that it is true just in case *each instance* of it is true. 'For every x, Fx' means 'Fa and Fb and Fc and ...', where *a*, *b*, *c* and so on, are all the objects that exist. So our understanding of generalisations seems to be based upon our understanding of their instances – atomic sentences. And by definition, atomic sentences contain genuinely referring singular terms, i.e. logically proper names.

What was the reason for supposing that ordinary proper names are not logically proper names? There were two reasons: first, the existence of a bearer of the name is not a presupposition of the meaningfulness of a sentence containing the name. Second, if *n* is an ordinary proper name and *n** some other terms such that *n* = *n** is true, *n* is not thereby interchangeable with *n** in all sentences *salva veritate* (that is, without changing the truth-value of the sentence). Substitution failure occurs, for example, in sentences about propositional attitudes: John might believe that Hesperus is a planet but not that Phosphorus is a planet despite the truth of 'Hesperus = Phosphorus', and so on.

How do we *know* that a sentence containing an empty proper name, like 'Pegasus flies', is meaningful? Plausibly, we know this because we recognise that someone could take an attitude towards the content of 'Pegasus flies'. It could be true that John believes that Pegasus flies, so long as he believes that Pegasus exists. Since belief is an attitude towards a proposition, there must be such a proposition as that Pegasus flies. So the reason that 'Pegasus' is meaningful yet empty is that it is possible that one could be mistaken as to whether Pegasus has a bearer. So plausibly: a *logically proper name* must be a name such that one *could not be mistaken* as to whether it has a referent.

Similarly, how do we know that, despite the truth of 'George Eliot = Mariane Evans', 'George Eliot' and 'Mariane Evans', do not have the same meaning? Answer: because someone could disbelieve that George Eliot = Mariane Evans. So plausibly, a logically proper name must be a name such that one could not be mistaken as to which object is its bearer.

Putting these points together: if there is a name such that one could not be mistaken as to the *existence* of its bearer, and one could not be mistaken as to the *identity* of its bearer, then the reasons that Russell cites for denying that such-and-such term is a logically proper name will no longer be in force.

Are there such names? Yes. For there are things about whose existence and identity we are never mistaken (or so Russell thought). These things include:

     I   Sense-data
     II   Universals
     III   The Self

We will ignore III, as Russell himself is not sure about this, and it raises issues that go too far beyond the philosophy of language. As for the other two:

(A) Sense data

If you are experiencing a patch of red in your visual field, or a tickle in your throat, then it seems literally absurd to suppose you might be mistaken, or mistakenly suppose the sense-datum to be identical to another. For such things, 'to exist is to be perceived', as Berkeley put it; 'to be this one rather than that one is to be perceived to be this one rather than that one', he might have added.

Now, of course, we don't give names to our sense data like 'Sigmund' and 'Elizabeth'. Russell's idea is really this. We do, of course, in a certain sense talk about things in the world such as tables. Suppose then that I see my cluttered table, and say 'The table is cluttered'. According to Russell, what I really do in such a case is to talk about the table *via* my sense data of it. I could conceivably be mistaken as to the existence of the table, but not about the sense impression I am having. So what I do is to think:

> *The external cause of THIS (table-shaped batch of sense-data) is cluttered.*

I don't say the word 'this', but I so to speak use it in thought to refer *directly* to my sense data; so I am using it as a logically proper name. But the table itself is only 'denoted' in Russell's sense (by the definite description 'the external cause of THIS'), and not referred to directly. And, of course, the definite description is to be analysed in the Russellian way.

(B) Universals

Suppose I think that the Earth is round. (Pretend for simplicity that 'the Earth' is a logically proper name.) Of course, I can imagine being mistaken as whether there are any objects that instantiate the property; there are surely properties about which human beings have been mistaken in that way. But that is not the issue; could I be mistaken as to the very existence of the property roundness? It hardly seems possible. Could I be mistaken as to whether or not roundness is identical with some other property? Well, this might be imaginable. For example, perhaps someone might think that *being equiangular* and *being equilateral* are the same property when they are not. But set that aside: let as assume that when we refer to or mean a property such as roundness in such a proposition as *The Earth is round*, we think of the property of roundness in such a way that we could not be mistaken as to either the existence or identity of the property. Likewise for any universal, as it enters into thought when we think a thought whose content is an atomic proposition.

As Russell puts it, the proper *subjects* of an atomic proposition are sense-data, the entities that we *perceive*. The entities meant by the *predicates* of an atomic proposition are universals, the entities that we *conceive*. Universals are creatures of thought, sense-data creatures of perception, and this is reflected logically in their differing roles in the structure of propositions. These are things with which we have a special epistemic relation, to wit, that we cannot be mistaken about either their existence or identity. Russell calls this the relation of *acquaintance*, and leads him to formulate his famous

> **Principle of acquaintance**: any proposition we can understand must be composed entirely of entities with which we are acquainted.

We use such knowledge of items of acquaintance to form propositions. Since we are not acquainted with tables and trees, it follows that we cannot understand atomic propositions about, or which 'contain', tables and trees. But how then do we talk about, and communicate about, such things?

Russell's answer is somewhat perplexing but not obviously incorrect. Suppose there is a table before us, and I say 'The table is round'. I denote the table *via* a description containing reference to my sense data and notion 'the external cause of …'. Call this description 'the external cause of φ'. You understand what I say by means of your own sense-perceptions, using some description 'the external cause of ψ'. But if all goes well, the external cause of φ = the external cause of ψ. So the situation is:

I think: The external cause of φ is round.
You think: The external cause of ψ is round.
The external cause of φ = the external cause of ψ.

Neither one of us can think that the external cause of φ = the external cause of ψ, since we're not acquainted with each other's sense-data; we lack what Russell calls **knowledge by acquaintance** of the table. But, since I know that the external cause of φ exists, and you know that the external cause of ψ exists, we both know that *there is* an object x (the table) by virtue of which the thing you are thinking of is the thing I am thinking of. We both have **knowledge by description** that there is such a table. Thus we both know that there is a **singular proposition**

a is round

which is equivalent in this context to the proposition that I think, and to the one that you think. Neither of us can grasp this proposition (because neither of us is directly acquainted with a, but we both know that there is such a proposition).

The resulting picture of the relation of empirical thought to reality is very similar to that of Locke and perhaps Hume. For that reason Russell is generally regarded as an empiricist.

• HISTORICAL NOTES

In his book *The Principles of Mathematics* (1903) Russell thought of language as more-or-less transparent, that one could 'see' through it the entities meant, and that the logical form underneath – of facts, universals and objects etc. – corresponded closely with the outer form of its linguistic expression. He held many elements of naïve semantics – with the clearest departure from it represented by his theory of 'denoting concepts', which in some ways aligned him with Frege. The view encouraged him to think that questions of language could often be ignored; one is talking directly about the subject-matter of language, not language itself. That view gradually changed, most decisively with the theory of descriptions announced in 'On Denoting' (1905), according to which logical form may be very different from the grammatical form. Analytical philosophy is often said to date from this article, because Russell discovered the vein, as it were, which logically trained philosophers are uniquely equipped to mine: beneath the hubbub of ordinary language, there lays hidden the crystalline realm of propositions in their purity. The time-slice of Russell that we have presented here is the Russell of his book *The Problems of Philosophy* (1912; it was also the time when he wrote with A. N. Whitehead the magnificent *Principia Mathematica* – 1910, 1912 and 1913 – which developed the thesis that mathematics is founded on logic).

That view rapidly gave way to his 'logical atomism' (1918, 1924), according to which, very roughly, ordinary material objects are identified with classes of sense-data, and are not the causes of them. The young Ludwig Wittgenstein (1889–1951), who began studying with Russell in 1910, came out with his *Tractatus Logico-Philosophicus* in 1921; and Rudolf Carnap (1891–1970) delivered a rigorous development of a view that is in various ways similar to Russell and Wittgenstein's logical atomism, in his *The Logical Structure of the World* (1928). Another figure who accepted the basics of Russell's logical atomist view was Alfred Ayer (1910–89). W. V. Quine (1908–2000), of whom we'll hear much more of in Chapters 7 and 9, was profoundly impressed by Russell's work in the foundations of mathematics as well as by the theory of descriptions, but also famously presented an alternative to the picture of knowledge purportedly shared by Carnap and Ayer, named 'holism'.

• CHAPTER SUMMARY

Russell sets out to solve the puzzles addressed by Frege's theory of sense and reference, without positing the category of sense in addition to reference. There are fundamentally two such problems: that of nonexistence, and substitution within propositional attitude contexts.

First, Russell sets out his theory of definite descriptions. All complex singular terms can be written as 'The F', and – except for certain cases – any sentence containing 'The F' is of the form 'The F is G' for some (possibly complex) predicate 'α is G'. 'The F is G' is equivalent to 'There is an x such that Fx, and there is not a y such that Fx and Fy and x ≠ y, and Gx' – which is 'There is one and only one thing such that it is F, and it is G'.

Second, he claims that all ordinary proper names are really definite descriptions in disguise; they abbreviate them. For example, on a particular occasion of use, one's use of 'Bob' might mean, in sense of being strictly equivalent to, 'the man standing before me'.

Thus '*a* is G', where there is no such thing as *a*, is analysed as of the form 'The F is G', which according to the above is false – unlike Frege's account, according to which it is neither-true-nor-false. Furthermore, if there no such thing as *a*, '*a* does not exist' comes out as 'Not: There is exactly one x such that Fx', which is true; Frege's scheme runs into trouble in getting the right truth-value in such cases, called *negative existentials*.

The key to solving the puzzle of propositional attitudes is again to analyse definite descriptions in the same way, whether they are explicit or disguised; once analysed, Russell believes, the puzzle disappears. For example, Granted that Scott = the author of *Waverley*, the conjunction 'George IV wondered whether Scott = the author of *Waverley*' and 'It is not the case that George IV wondered whether Scott = Scott' looks to be inconsistent. But the apparent inconsistency disappears when the definite description 'the author of *Waverley*' is analysed.

For Russell, the only genuine logically proper names – ones that cannot be analysed as disguised definite descriptions – are ones standing for sense-data (and possibly for the self). More generally, Russell propounds his famous distinction between knowledge by acquaintance and knowledge by description; the crucial principle is his principle of acquaintance: any proposition we can understand must be composed entirely of entities with which we are acquainted.

• STUDY QUESTIONS

1 Could Frege borrow Russell's strategy of distinguishing internal from external negations in order to cope with true negative existentials?

2 Use Russell's distinction of scope to show why 'Ludwig thought that the cookies were bananas' admits of two readings, differing according to the sort of error imputed to Ludwig.

3 One might think, upon encountering the theory of descriptions, that *numerals* are really quantifiers. Explain this thought.

4 Alexius Meinong (1853–1920) held that existence *is* (more or less) a predicate – that such things as Pegasus or Santa Claus may fail to exist, but nevertheless they are *objects of thought*. Russell held something similar at one time, but dropped it when he came upon the theory of descriptions. Was he right to? Is not Meinong's theory better just because it does not involve a distinction between surface grammatical form and deeper logical form?

5 Does Russell think we genuinely communicate about ordinary things such as tables and trees?

• PRIMARY READING

Russell, B. 'On Denoting,' *Mind*, 14, 479–93. Reprinted in his *Essays in Analysis* (London: George Allen and Unwin, 1973), pp. 103–19, and in *Logic and Knowledge*, (London: George Allen and Unwin, 1956), pp. 41–56.

——'Knowledge by Acquaintance and Knowledge by Description', *Proceedings of the Aristotelian Society*, New Series, Vol. 11 (1911), pp. 108–28; reprinted in his *Mysticism and Logic and Other Essays* (London: George Allen and Unwin, 1918).

● SECONDARY READING

Hylton, P. (2005) *Propositions, Functions, and Analysis: Selected Essays on Russell's Philosophy* (Oxford: Oxford University Press). Contains several essays that are accessible yet penetrating, including a comparison of Russell with Frege.

Neale, S. (1993) *Descriptions* (Cambridge, MA: MIT Press). A searching but lucid exploration of Russell's theory of descriptions.

Sainsbury, M. (1979) *Russell* (London: Routledge). A broad introduction to the main aspects of Russell's philosophy.

● NOTES

1 At one point many astronomers erroneously believed there to be a planet orbiting the sun within the orbit of Mercury, and called it 'Vulcan'; see Chapter 2, Section 1.

2 It's actually a little more complicated. Examples such as 'Sally's teacher' do not imply uniqueness in the way that 'Sally's father' does. Indeed, the uniqueness of Sally's father is not determined by semantics but by the facts of biology, and 'Sally's teacher' in the context 'Sally's teacher was talking' is equivalent to 'A teacher of Sally's', hence not a singular term. We can think of such expressions as 'Sally's teacher' or 'Sally's father' to be ambiguous, implicitly awaiting transformation with a quantifier into forms such as 'The teacher of Sally', 'A teacher of Sally' or 'Any teacher of Sally'. Normally the context clarifies which quantifier is meant.

3 This also is actually more complicated; we ignore apparent counterexamples involving modal vocabulary and the propositional attitudes.

4 In fact, it is equivalent to the yet more compact: 'There is an x such that for all y, $((Fy \leftrightarrow x=y) \ \& \ Gx)$', or '$\exists x \forall y ((Fy \leftrightarrow x=y) \ \& \ Gx)$'.

4

·kripke[1] and putnam on naming, necessity and essence

• 1 THE DESCRIPTIVIST PARADIGM

Both Russell and Frege can be regarded as having held a *descriptivist theory of proper names*. For ordinary proper names, such as 'Aristotle' or 'Madonna', both figures hold that on each occasion of using or understanding the name, what the speaker or understander means or understands by the name can be expressed by a definite description.[2] In this sense, (ordinary) proper names are strictly equivalent to definite descriptions: they *abbreviate* them; they function as *shorthand* for them. Thus suppose that Beethoven reads the following sentence:

> Mozart is dead.

What he grasps, when he reads and comprehends this sentence, will be something like: *The composer of Don Giovanni is dead*. If so, then at that moment, the following two sentences will for Beethoven be *synonymous*; they will express the very same proposition:

> Mozart is dead.
> The composer of *Don Giovanni* is dead.

True, Russell and Frege differ on how a definite description such as 'the composer of *Don Giovanni*' is to be explained; Frege holds it to be a genuine singular term whose job is to *refer*, whereas according to Russell's contextual definition of definite descriptions, it contains a quantifier – 'the' means 'exactly one' – and therefore does not strictly speaking refer; but this difference will not matter for what follows. The view seems to answer the question: in virtue of what facts about one's understanding does one talk about an object by using a name?

• 2 NECESSITY, POSSIBILITY AND POSSIBLE WORLDS: A PRIMER

It seems to be a *necessary truth* that 2 + 2 = 4: it could not have been false. Other seeming necessary truths: that everything is identical with itself, that if x is bigger than y and y bigger than z then x is bigger than z.

We know that ice cream exists. But it is *possible*, in the sense that it might have been the case, that ice cream didn't exist. Ice cream might not have existed. It is a truth, but not a necessary truth, that ice cream exists.

What are necessity and possibility? For our purposes, we are going to assume what is most convenient, namely the interpretation of these concepts in terms of **possible** worlds. A necessarily true proposition is a proposition that would have been true *no matter what*. It *could not* have been false: however the world had gone, the proposition would have been true. That is: the proposition is true in *every possible world*. Similarly, a possibly true proposition is one that *might have been the case*. That is, there is some way the world could have gone in which the proposition would have been true. That is, the proposition is true in *some possible world*. So we have:

> A proposition is **necessary** if it is true at every possible world.
> A proposition is **possible** if it is true at some possible world.

If *p* is a proposition that is possible but not necessary, then *p* is **contingent**; if it is true, like the proposition that ice cream exists, then we can speak of it as *a contingent truth*.

The words 'possible' and 'necessary' are not always used in this way, especially not outside philosophy. So let us be clear. We are talking about what in philosophy is standardly called *metaphysical modality*, which is a **metaphysical** notion, not an **epistemological** notion. In speaking of a proposition being possible we mean either it *is* true, or it *could have been* true. We don't mean, 'I don't know whether or not it's true'. For example, we *know* with certainty that the highest mountain on Earth is not in Tahiti, but it *could* have been. In some possible world, Earth's highest mountain is in Tahiti. It *might have been the case* that the highest mountain on Earth is in Tahiti, even though it isn't, and we know that it isn't.

Similarly, by 'necessary' we don't mean 'it is certain'. Outside philosophy, we do say 'not necessarily', meaning 'we can't be certain that it is so', but that is not the sense we have in mind. This is clear from the fact that some necessary truths are not certain, not even known. For example, truths of mathematics are standardly taken to be necessary truths, but not all of them are known.

The traditional epistemological analogues of necessity and contingency are *a priori* – knowable by reason independently of experience – and *a posteriori* or *empirical*, knowable only through experience.

For convenience, we sometimes write:

'Nec (p)' for 'It is necessary that p'.
'Pos (p)' for 'It is possible that p'.

'Nec' or 'It is necessary that'is a *sentential operators* (a sentential connective), like 'It is not the case that'. Unlike 'It is not the case that', 'Nec' is not *truth-functional*; it is *non-extensional*, in the sense introduced in Chapter 2 – and in particular an intensional operator. The truth-value of

Nec (p)

is not determined by the truth-value of p. For example, the truth-value of 'Nec (the Earth is round)' is not settled by the fact that the Earth is actually round. 'Nec' thus differs from truth-functional sentential operators such as those appearing in

it is not the case that p
p and q
p or q

In these cases, the truth-value of the whole is determined by the truth-values of the constituents – by that of p in the first example, and by those of p and q in the others.

Possibility and necessity are generally held to be *inter-definable*, in the sense that each can be defined in terms of the other:

A proposition is necessary if its negation is not possible.
A proposition is possible if its negation is not necessary.

One of the most interesting possible worlds is the *actual world*. The actual world is the way things actually are (a noted saying from Ludwig Wittgenstein's *Tractatus Logico-Philosophicus* was 'The world is all that is the case'). Note that everything actual is possible, since nothing actual can be impossible, else it would not be actual.

What *is* a (non-actual) possible world? Is it like the actual world except for being spatio-temporarily discontinuous from it, as David Lewis famously held? Or are they unlike the actual world in being abstract rather than material or concrete? Or are we to take the phrase 'possible worlds' merely as a heuristic, that they are just a 'manner of speaking' and don't *really* exist at all? It is best not to worry too much about this (you can worry about it in your metaphysics class). A possible world is simply a way things might have been, a way things could have been. If you don't like the air of science fiction attending the phrase 'possible world', you may call them possible *situations*, or *counterfactual circumstances* (except you cannot call the actual world a counterfactual circumstance, since the actual facts are not contrary-to-fact). The air of science fiction should be measured against the sheer ordinariness of speaking of *ways that things might have been*.

We can take any proposition and possible world – any way things could have been – and ask whether the proposition would have been true *at* that world. This just means: consider these possible circumstances; would that proposition have been true under those circumstances? Consider the proposition that some apes are carnivores, and consider a world in which there are no animals. Is the proposition true at that world? No; since apes are animals, and there are no animals at that world, there are no carnivorous apes at that world. And presumably there are possible worlds in which apes exist, but only vegetarian ones.

Possible worlds make it straightforward to interpret not only 'Nec' and 'Pos' but also **counterfactual conditionals** (subjunctive conditionals). Consider:

> If Jones had been wearing a seat belt, he would have survived the collision.

We can say this appropriately only if the antecedent is false – Jones was *not* wearing a seat belt. Thus, if we interpreted this as a material, truth-functional conditional, it would automatically come out as true. As would:

> If Jones had been wearing a seat belt, he would not have survived the collision.

For the truth-table for the material conditional – '$\rightarrow$' – has it that such conditionals are true whenever the antecedent is false. So how do we determine whether it is true that if Jones had been wearing a seat belt, he would have survived the collision?

Easy: consider a possible world that is just like the actual world except that Jones, contrary to fact, was wearing a seat belt at the moment of the collision. Keep everything else, or as much as possible, the same. This is, as David Lewis puts it, the *nearest* possible world to the actual world. Does Jones survive in that world? If yes, the counterfactual conditional is true; if not, it is false.

• 3 KRIPKE'S OBJECTIONS TO THE DESCRIPTION THEORY OF PROPER NAMES

Suppose you understand 'Mozart' as *the composer of Don Giovanni*. In that case, you will understand the following sentence as *analytic*, true by virtue of meaning:

> (1)   Mozart is the composer of *Don Giovanni*.

In fact, this sentence, understood in that way, will be strictly synonymous with both of the following:

> (2)   The composer of *Don Giovanni* is the composer of *Don Giovanni*.
> (3)   Mozart is Mozart.

Kripke points out that since all analytic truths are necessary truths, (1) must be a *necessary truth* (at least those analytic truths that do not contain indexicals are necessary truths – a topic for later).[3] It is also *a priori*: since obviously (3) and hence (2) are *a priori*, and (1) expresses the same proposition as (2), (1) is *a priori*.[4]

The problem is obvious: (1), Kripke observes, is *not* a necessary truth! It might have been the case that Mozart never wrote that magnificent opera; he did write it, but he *could have* stuck to instrumental music; he could even have been run over and killed by a carriage as a small child, and never written any music at all. There are possible worlds in which (1) is false.

Nor is (1) *a priori*: that (1) is true is a piece of *empirical knowledge*. Of course, we can know (3) with perfect certainty, but we can intelligibly doubt the truth of (1) – we have very good evidence that it is true, but we don't know it with *perfect* certainty, not in the way that we know the truth of (3). So (1) and (3) must have different *cognitive value*, and hence do not express the same proposition. The very sort of argument – from cognitive value – that Frege used to gainsay the naïve theory can be used against his alternative. Nor is (1) *analytic*: it is not because of the *meanings of words* that (1) is true. It is no triviality like (2) or (3), or like 'Every square has four sides'.

The descriptivist idea seems wrong from the point of view of *metaphysics* – because it entails wrongly that propositions such as (1) are necessary rather than contingent; seems wrong from the point of view of *epistemology* – because it wrongly entails that propositions such as (1) are *a priori* rather than *a posteriori* (empirical); and seems wrong *semantically*, because it wrongly entails that propositions such as (1) are analytic rather than synthetic.

There is another kind of objection, a devastating one. Consider the name 'Josef Haydn'. Suppose you know that this is the name of a composer, around the time of Mozart. But suppose you don't know anything more than that; you can't name any of his compositions, and so on. In short, you lack an *individuating* description, a description that would pick out the name's bearer from everything else in the world: you cannot formulate *any* sentence of the form:

Josef Haydn is the F.

– which you know or believe to be true. But if so, then according to the description theory of names, *you cannot succeed in referring to Haydn*, not even by using the name 'Josef Haydn'. In that case, if you were to say or think, 'Josef Haydn was a composer', then *you do not succeed in saying or thinking something about Joseph Haydn!* But that seems quite wrong: it seems perfectly clear that you do possess some information *about Haydn* – you know him to be a composer who lived around the time of Mozart.

We can call the argument of the last paragraph the *argument from ignorance* against descriptivism. The argument is closely related to the *argument from error*. Suppose George is like most people in knowing just one fact about Dante: he wrote the *Divine Comedy*. According to descriptivism, then, 'Dante = the author of the *Divine Comedy*' is analytic for such people. Suppose that in fact it was written by the humble Adriano; he wrote in absolute secrecy until discovered by Dante, who then strangled Adriano and took credit for the great poem. The descriptive theory has 'Dante wrote the *Divine Comedy*', as understood by George, wrongly coming out as true, and about the wrong man; surely Dante is the referent of 'Dante', not Adriano. The fact that propositions such as (1) are contingent and empirical shows up dramatically in this sort of case. The assumption that referring to an object by means of a proper name depends on the ability to pick out the object by means of a uniquely identifying description seems to be false, since we often succeed in using proper names to talk about objects apparently without possessing such a description.

The conclusion of these lines of argument may be put by saying that proper names are **directly referring expressions** (following Kaplan; this is not exactly Kripke's conclusion). That is to say, they do *not* refer by means of some kind of *conceptual representation* of the object such as a Fregean sense (mode of presentation). Proper names, on this view, have only reference, and not sense. In another vocabulary due to Mill, they only *denote* their objects, do not *connote* anything. This anti-Fregean line is often called 'direct reference theory' (confusingly, direct reference theory is often called 'Russellian', despite its denial of what Russell said about ordinary proper names).

• 4 RIGID DESIGNATION

A contingently true sentence is true in the actual world, but false in some non-actual possible worlds. For example, 'The Beatles sold more records than the Rolling Stones in 1965' is true in the actual world, but false in some non-actual worlds.[5] A necessary truth, by contrast, is true in all possible worlds.

Just as some sentences vary in truth-value from world to world whereas others don't, some singular terms designate different things depending on what world we are talking about, whereas others don't. Consider:

(4)   the number of Martian moons
(5)   the number of positive integers less than 3.

Assume that the truths of arithmetic are necessary truths. Both these expressions designate the number 2 (the moons of Mars are Phobos and Deimos). However, that is because in the actual world, there happen to be two moons orbiting Mars. Had things been different, Mars might have had more moons (or fewer). Thus, with respect to other possible worlds, (4) designates a different number: in certain coun-terfactual circumstances, there would have been six moons round Mars, or fourteen, etc. (5), however, designates the same number, *whatever possible situation we are considering*. Since it is a necessary truth that there are exactly two positive integers less than three, (5) designates the same object with respect to all possible worlds.

A singular term such as (5), whose referent remains constant from world to world, is what Kripke calls a *rigid designator*. (4) is *non-rigid* (or 'flaccid').[6]

Careful: of course, the *words* 'the number of positive integers less than 3' might have been *used* differently. If the history of English had been different, they might have had different meanings. In that case (5) might have designated a different object. In the same sense, the *words* 'Bachelors are unmarried' might have meant something else – if 'bachelors' meant *porcupines* and 'unmarried' meant *hairless* then those words would have expressed a false proposition. But when we ask whether 'Bachelors are unmarried' expresses a necessary truth, we mean that, *given what the sentence means*, could *the world* have been such that it was false? Could the *proposition* that 'Bachelors are unmarried' men have been false? Of course, the answer is no, since 'Bachelors are unmarried' means 'Unmarried men are unmarried'. Likewise, when we ask whether (5) is a rigid designator, we are asking whether, *given the meaning of the words*, the world could have been such that it designates something other than the number 2. The answer, assuming that arithmetic truths are necessary truths, is no.

Now consider:

    (6)   Nixon
    (7)   the 37th US president

Nixon was in fact the 37th president of the United States. Now consider that man, Nixon. Are there worlds in which not him, but someone else, is the 37th president? Yes. So (7) is not rigid. What about (6)? Consider its referent, Nixon. Are there worlds in which not he, but some other man, is Nixon? No! The following is *true*:

    (8)   The 37th US president might not have been the 37th US president.

For this says: take the man who (actually) is the 37th US president (Nixon); there are possible worlds in which *that man* is not the 37th US president.

But compare:

    (9)   Nixon might not have been Nixon.

That's false! We cannot take Nixon, and then find a possible world in which he is not Nixon. There is no world in which *that man* is not Nixon. What is going on is that 'Nixon' is a rigid designator: 'Nixon' designates the same object with respect to all possible worlds. Sentences of the form of (9) constitute a *test* for rigidity: for any term put in both blanks, if '__ might not have been __' comes out true, then the term is rigid; if not, not.

Again, of course, the term 'Nixon' could have been *used* differently; Nixon might not have been called 'Nixon'. There are possible worlds in which Nixon is not called 'Nixon'. We are not denying that obvious fact. The idea rather is that when *we* use the word 'Nixon', using it according to its customary meaning, and talk about some possible world or conceivable situation, we are always talking about the same man, namely Nixon, the man actually called 'Nixon'.

The Kripkean points in this section can be summed up as:

(a) Genuine proper names are rigid designators. (The reverse does not hold, as (5) shows).

(b) Genuine proper names refer directly.

(c) Directly referring terms are rigid designators, but not all rigid designators refer directly (again consider (5)).

• 5 FIXING THE REFERENCE I: CAUSAL CHAINS

If the descriptivist theory is false, then what theory of reference is true? If you can refer to Haydn by means of 'Josef Haydn' without being able to pick him out with a description, how do you do it?

Kripke proposes a theory that is so simple and plausible to common sense that it's bizarre that it took so long for anyone to think of it. In our imagined example, when you use 'Haydn', you have an implicit intention like this: 'By "Haydn" I mean the person *they* mean by it", where 'they' are people from whom you've heard the name – authors of books or magazine articles, friends, people on the radio or television etc. For convenience let us represent those people as a single person, A. Now who did A mean by it? Well, A heard the name from someone else, say B; and thought, 'By "Haydn" I mean the person they mean by it'. And who did B mean? They got it from someone else, say C. And C got it from D, D from E, and so on. There is a **historical chain** of users of the name reaching *backwards in time* from your use of it back to … what? Well, eventually we get to people who actually knew Haydn, knew him *in person*. They were introduced to the man, or the boy, and were told 'And this is Josef Haydn'. The *first* users of the name were (presumably) his parents: they stood over the gurgling baby and said, 'Let's call him "Josef"'; together with the convention that the child takes the surname of the father, this amounted to a *dubbing*, a ceremony of *naming*. From that point on, the parents used the name with the intention to refer to *that boy*; people who acquired the name from the parents then undertook to refer to the boy to whom the parents referred, and thus the chain got started. In the economic phraseology that is sometimes used, the parents are the *producers* in the name-using practice, those who inherit the name are the *consumers*.

This theory has the advantage that it explains how it is that even if unbeknownst to you some other person is called 'Josef Haydn', you refer to the composer, not to that other person: who you refer to depends on which chain of communication you intend, perhaps only implicitly, to connect with.

• 6 FIXING THE REFERENCE II: DESCRIPTIONS

But have we really got away from the use of descriptions? Isn't 'the person they were referring to by N' a description? Yes, but it does not *give the meaning* of the name N. The arguments against the description theory still apply: it is *not* a necessary fact about Haydn that he came to be talked about in the way he has been by means of that name.

Thus, assuming still that it was A from whom you got the name, consider the sentence:

(10)   Josef Haydn = the person A refers to by means of 'Josef Haydn'.

This sentence is true, so the two singular terms 'Josef Haydn' and 'the person A refers to by means of "Josef Haydn"' in fact have the same *referent*. But they don't have the same *meaning*. They are not *equivalent*: they are not *necessarily equivalent*, not *epistemically equivalent*, and not *conceptually equivalent*. In Fregean terms, they don't have the same cognitive content. Of a possible world where he is not called 'Josef Haydn', (10) is false: that man is *not* the person who A refers to by means of 'Josef Haydn'.

According to Kripke, the role of such a description as 'the person A refers to by means of "Josef Haydn"' is not to give the meaning of the name but to **fix the reference** of the name. Roughly, Frege (and Russell) held that there must be some sort of explicit intention in the mind of the language-user that determines the referent of a name, and that the *content of that intention* constitutes the meaning of the name. Kripke sees that last move as the crucial mistake: what fixes the reference of a name need not enter into the meaning, the cognitive content, of the name. The description may be used to fix the reference of the name, but the name does not abbreviate the description.

Actually, we can go further. When successfully using a name, is it necessary to have an explicit intention that fixes the name's reference? No! Once we give up the idea that names must have some kind of expressible cognitive content, all we are interested in is to what the name refers. All we need in the theory of reference, then, is an account of what facts do determine the referent of a name. Put like that, we needn't assume that among these facts must be explicit intentions in the mind of the speaker. Thus, we can say posit a pair of *semantic rules*:

1 If A dubs a given object with the name NN, then when A uses the name NN, A refers to that object by means of NN.
2 If C uses a name NN, and C acquired the name NN from B, then C refers by NN to whatever B referred to by NN.

Such semantic rules might simply determine what a speaker refers to by means of a name, even though the speaker is unable to formulate the rule. (However, the precise extent to which a speaker may be ignorant of such rules or conventions is unclear.)

Once we recognise how reference-fixing works, we recognise that the referents of proper names *can* be fixed in something very close to what Frege and Russell envisaged. For example, we might, by the name 'Homer', *stipulate* that that we shall refer to the author of the *Iliad*. But what we do, in such a case, is merely specify the object that is to be the referent of the name. We do not thereby specify a *meaning* for the name; we do not accept the name and the description we use as *synonymous*, as equivalent in meaning. We thereby accept that the following is a straightforward contingent truth, not in any sense a necessary truth:

(11)   Homer is the author of the *Iliad*.

So definite descriptions can be used to fix reference: a dubbing or baptism ceremony is not necessary. The description, in such a case, is like a *pointing-device*.

There are examples that seem to cause trouble for Kripke's picture. First, some names plausibly do fit the descriptivist theory. One might think that whatever the facts of pre-historical Greece, 'Homer' is actually intended to *mean*, be *synonymous* with, 'The author of the *Iliad*' – it is not merely, as was just suggested, that that description is used to *fix the reference* of the name. Similarly with names like 'Jack the Ripper'; perhaps the name really abbreviates a certain description – perhaps it *is* plausible to say that Jack the Ripper might not have been Jack the Ripper (whereas it is false that Nixon might not have been Nixon). Second, we've said nothing about proper names for *fictional* entities such as 'Superman' or 'Santa Claus'; it is plausible to say that these are only *pretended* to refer, they don't really. Since these terms are not meaningless, apparently the associated descriptions must enter into an account of their meaning.

It's unclear that these represent a problem for Kripke. His claim is that *normal* cases of proper names – what we called in the box above at the end of Section 4 *genuine* proper names – don't fit the descriptivist theory, not that none do. A more serious problem arises in cases such as that raised by Gareth Evans.[7] Legend has it that the island of Madagascar was not originally so-called – that owing to a mistake by European explorers and map-makers, the name which was originally the name of part of the African coast got transferred to the large island offshore. Unlike the 'Homer' case, one does not feel tempted to think that 'Madagascar' is a descriptive name. Surely it's a genuine proper name, subject to all the Kripkean arguments that show it to be so. Many subtly different variants of this sort of case are possible, but all have in common that the object denoted by the contemporary users of the name fails to match that of the original producers of the name. How precisely to handle such cases has proven a big topic; but presumably a solution has to do with the fact that the historical chain of communication gets *disrupted* in such cases, that at some point in history the users have begun passing along a piece of *misinformation*.

• 7 NATURAL KIND TERMS AND ESSENCE

Putnam's famous 'Twin Earth' argument runs as follows (in 'The Meaning of "Meaning"', Putnam 1975). Water, as you know, is H_2O. Suppose there were a planet that is exactly like Earth in every respect, down to the smallest detail, except that the clear liquid in rivers and streams is some other chemical compound XYZ. But for all ordinary purposes XYZ is indistinguishable from water; behaves exactly as water does – it boils at the same temperature, sustains life, and so on. Would that stuff *be* water, or not? Putnam says not. So long as it is not H_2O (or H_3O), it is not water, no matter how exactly similar it is in other respects to water.

Why? According to Putnam, when we use a term such as 'water', we are using what he calls a 'natural kind' term. In fact, it functions almost exactly as a proper name does according to Kripke. Idealising somewhat, we define it – fix its reference – by pointing to some water and declaring: by 'water' I mean *that stuff* (just as the parents might fix the reference of 'Josef Haydn' by declaring 'by this name we mean this child'). Similarly, to fix the reference of 'Tiger' we point to an animal and decide that that word shall apply to all and only animals of the same species as *that animal*.

Natural kinds include substances like water and gold, and species like tigers. More generally, we introduce a natural kind term by pointing to a sample of the kind and intending that the word shall denote whatever is the same kind as the sample. The role of 'same natural kind' with respect to these sorts of predicate is the exactly the same as that of 'same object' with respect to proper names.

It follows that a descriptive definition of such a term as 'gold' cannot be correct. One might try to define it as a 'shiny, malleable yellow metal'; we may suppose this description would be *true of* gold and only of gold, but it does not give a *synonym* for 'gold'; it does not actually give the meaning. For consider:

(12)   Gold = the shiny, malleable yellow metal that is widely used for jewellery.

This is perhaps true, but it is only contingently true. It is obviously only contingent that it is used for jewellery. And in other possible worlds there are other shiny, malleable yellow metals.

What is it for something to be the *same kind* as another thing? In the case of elements, such as gold, one thing is the same kind as another if and only if they have the same atomic number (this is the number of protons in the nucleus of the atom). In the case of chemical compounds such as water, it is the composition of molecules; in the case of water each molecule comprises one atom of oxygen and two of hydrogen: H_2O. In the case of species, it is perhaps less clear, but one account might be: being a member of a certain genealogical type; another might be, having a certain DNA configuration; another might be, capacity for mating to produce fertile offspring.

Natural kind terms are not descriptive like 'muddy' or 'vermin', but certain descriptions do have a privileged status with respect to natural kinds. If we are pointing to some water, then necessarily, something is *that stuff* if and only if it is H_2O; or rather, something is the same stuff as that stuff if and only if it is H_2O. That is because *having the same molecular constitution* is the criterion of identity for compound substances. Therefore:

(13)   Necessarily, water = H_2O.

So it seems we can say: H_2O is the *essence* of water; H_2O is just what water *is*. But this is not something we know *a priori*, and it is not the case that 'water' and 'H_2O' are synonymous. A person who does not know that water is H_2O lacks scientific knowledge, but does not thereby lack linguistic knowledge: for he too can point to water and say that 'water' means that stuff.

Thus, contrary to what many philosophers had thought (Hume, Kant): *some necessary truths are empirical (a posteriori).*

• 8 INDEXICALITY

Putnam's point about natural kinds can be summed up by saying that terms for natural kinds typically function as *indexicals* such as 'this', and are not equivalent to any context-free description such as 'big orange stripy carnivore'.[8] What reference gets fixed by introducing such a term depends on the nature of the animal or whatever that is *actually pointed to* when the term is introduced.

In fact, that is very much what is going on with Kripke's explanation: proper names are plausibly thought to be indexicals, since the bearer is determined by the identity of the object pointed to at the starting point of the causal chain, when someone says 'Let's call him "Josef"' etc.

Just as in the case of ordinary proper names, one can introduce a natural kind term by means of a reference-fixing description: one might say, 'By "water" I mean the stuff that *actually* flows in rivers and falls as rain', without thereby deeming 'water' and 'the stuff that actually flows in rivers and falls as rain' synonymous. This does not make them any less indexical, since the meaning determined by this procedure depends on what liquid actually flows in rivers and falls as rain. This is reflected in the truth of the following:

> (13) The stuff that actually flows in rivers and falls as rain might not have flowed in rivers and fallen as rain.

That is, consider the stuff in the actual world that flows in rivers and falls as rain; are there possible worlds in which that stuff does not flow in rivers and fall in rain? Yes, there are.

• 9 IS MEANING IN THE HEAD?

From a Fregean point of view, it would be natural to suppose that the proposition one expresses by means of a sentence such as 'Daphnia live in water' is determined by one's internal psychological state – ultimately by the state of one's brain. It follows from Putnam's indexical view that this is false. If Twin Earth is really just like Earth, then your doppelganger lives there: your exact duplicate except that he or she has XYZ in his or her body where you have H_2O. If so, then when you and your duplicate say 'Daphnia live in water', you mean different things. Since you refer to H_2O, and your duplicate to XYZ, the truth-condition of what you say is that Daphnia live in H_2O, and that of what your duplicate says is that Daphnia live in XYZ. Since you and your duplicate must be in the same brain-states (assume that the identity of brain-states does not depend on whether it's water or XYZ that's inside the body), it follows that the meaning of what you say is not determined by your brain-states. It depends also on the environment, on the physical context in which you live. What we know as 'water' is not the same as what those on Twin Earth know as 'water'. Thus if you were presented with a glass of XYZ and said, 'Ah, water!', you'd speak falsely, even though Twin Earthlings call it 'water'; the words 'water' on Earth and 'water' on Twin Earth would be homonyms – words that sound the same – but not, strictly speaking, synonyms. Such is the basic argument for *semantic externalism*: you and your duplicate refer to different things despite there not being a difference in what concepts you grasp, or there not being a physiological difference between you. Semantics does not supervene on physiology or, more generally, on one's internal states.

• 10 A WARNING AND A BIG PROBLEM

An important warning: a common mistake is to overreact to Kripke and Putnam, and to think that what has been shown is that *all* terms are natural kind terms or that all terms refer directly to their referents or are rigid designators. As intimated above in Section 8, that's not so. Not even all nouns are directly referential or are rigid designators. The concept of a *ruin* or *mud*, for example, cannot be defined in terms of the nature of a substance, or in terms of the nature of the things that actually realise the role marked out by the word; unlike 'water' or 'tiger', the terms express concepts of the roles themselves, not the realisers, let alone adjectives (like 'stupid', 'difficult'), verbs ('shake', 'thwart'), or adverbs ('busily', 'centrally'). Much of language comprises descriptive words, and is not directly referential or rigid (a good question concerns terms for *artefacts*; is the concept, say, of a *book*, a concept of a certain artefactual essence – are there *artefactual kinds* – or is it a descriptive concept?).

There are similarities between Putnam's account and John Locke's old discussion of real and nominal essence. For Locke, the nominal essence of K is the rule we use to pick out instances of K, normally comprising observable properties. So the nominal essence of gold might be 'shiny, yellow malleable metal'. The real essence of K is underlying nature; Locke thought we could not know real natures, but surely he'd be glad to know that he's been proven wrong.

Russell believed that ordinary proper names are not really proper names at all. They are abbreviations for definite descriptions, which according to his theory are not singular terms but quantifiers. The only logically proper names are names of sense-data, universals and perhaps the self. Logically proper names in his view have no descriptive content, contrary to Frege; they don't express a rule for determining a referent and they do not express a mode of presentation of the referent.

For these reasons, direct reference theory is Russellian, because it sides with Russell as against Frege on the question of the descriptive content of proper names: they haven't any. It departs from Russell, however, in accepting ordinary proper names as genuine proper names, that is, as logically proper names.

It's true, Kripke's arguments against Frege and Russell's descriptive view of ordinary proper names is very powerful. What then of the epistemological reasons that led Frege to the theory of sense, and which led Russell to hold that only 'items of acquaintance' can be the referents of logically proper names? How is a direct reference theorist to explain the following sort of possibility:

> John believes that Hesperus is a star.
> John does not believe that Phosphorus is a star.
> Hesperus = Phosphorus.

For it now looks as if 'Hesperus' and 'Phosphorus' have the same meaning after all, in which case these three sentences cannot all be true. And what of names for the non-existent, such as 'Vulcan'? This is not a fictional name, and was intended for all the world as a normal proper name; but since it has no referent, it appears that Kripke's account gets the wrong answer that the name is meaningless.

There seem to be three possibilities. One might try to come up with some sort of grand unification theory, one that accounts for the cognitive dimension of language that exercised Frege and Russell but which accommodates the facts about reference and necessity that Kripke points out. Or one might be able to rebut Kripke's arguments. Or one might advocate Kripke's arguments, but propose, *contra* Frege, that questions of *reference* should more sharply be distinguished from questions of cognition, which are matters for *epistemology*, the *philosophy of mind*, or *psychology*. We'll return to this in Chapter 7.

• HISTORICAL NOTES

Until the 1960s, many well known philosophers – Hume, Ayer and Carnap being conspicuous examples – accepted that the three distinctions – *a priori* versus *a posteriori* or empirical, necessary versus contingent, and analytic versus synthetic –aligned; moreover, the first two distinctions could be explained as, or reduced to, the third. There is no need for a queer faculty of *a priori* knowledge, and there is no mystery of how truths can be necessary: all of that can be explained in terms of semantics, of how we speak; what can look like metaphysically or epistemologically substantive matters are unsubstantive matters concerning language. The logical positivists, armed with the much more powerful logic of Frege and Russell, undertook from late 1920s through the 1950s to develop the view, seeking an end to metaphysics and new clarity to epistemology. Carnap's *The Logical Structure of the World* (1967 [1928]) and 'Empiricism, Semantics and Ontology' (1950, in Carnap 1956) and Ayer's *Language, Truth and Logic* (1936, revised edition 1946) were clear and influential statements of such views. Kripke published his paper 'Identity and Necessity' in 1971, and the book that made him and his views famous, *Naming and Necessity*, in 1980 (actually it was first published in 1972 in *Semantics of Natural Language*, eds D. Davidson and G. Harman). Contra Ayer and Carnap, the three distinctions are actually all quite separate, and examples of propositions were given that are *necessary* but *empirical*, and *a priori* but *contingent*. It is difficult to overestimate the effects of Kripke's views had, not only on philosophers of language but epistemologists, meta-physicians and philosophers of science. In general, the views were liberating: after years of nay-saying by Carnap and his ilk, philosophers could now openly advance metaphysical theories without the supporting proviso that the claims are implicit in our concepts, that they are analytic. Like many significant changes in intellectual history, however, Kripke was only the most visible of the revolutionaries; David Kaplan, Peter Geach, Keith Donnellan as well as Hilary Putnam were writing things in the 1960s very much within what was often called the 'new theory' of reference, and the idea is present in the work in modal logic of Ruth Barcan Marcus dating from 1947, in her characterisation of names as descriptionless 'tags'. The key event was a meeting of the Boston Colloquium for Philosophy of Science in 1962, at which Barcan Marcus presented the results of her paper of 1961, 'Modalities and Inten-sional Languages'. In the audience were W. V. Quine, Alfred Tarski and the young Saul Kripke, who had made a name for himself at age eighteen with an important paper of 1959 on modal logic. What happened that day, what precisely was under-stood by whom, and how much was retained by Kripke, remains controversial. What is relatively clear is that if Barcan Marcus did discover the idea, she did not pursue its implications nearly so far and so penetratingly as Kripke did.

• CHAPTER SUMMARY

Possibility, in the sense we have in mind, is a metaphysical notion: to say that p is possible to say that, even if in fact p is not the case, and even if it is known that p is not the case, it might have been the case that p. In this sense, that *the ancient Greeks developed nuclear power* is a possible but not actual truth. Possibility is inter-definable with necessity: p is possible if it is not necessary that not-p; p is necessary if it is not possible that not-p. At worst, the notion of a *possible world* is a very useful heuristic; it is a way that things could or might have been.

Frege and Russell can be thought of without too much violence as having agreed that for any ordinary proper name N, it means on the particular occasion of its use or understanding some definition description of the form *the F*. Kripke poses no fewer than four objections: (1) If N means the F then it is *necessary* that N is the F; typically that is not so; (2) if N means the F then it is *a priori* that N is the F; typically that is not so; (3) if N means the F then it is *analytic* that N is the F; typically that is not so; (4) one can understand sentences containing N without accepting *any* proposition of the form 'N = the F'. One can refer to a thing by means of a name without possessing descriptive knowledge of the thing.

Kripke provides a *causal-historical* alternative to the descriptive theory of what deter-mines reference: one uses a name N. What do I refer to by N? One acquired N from language-user A; and what did A refer to by N? A acquired N from B; and what did B refer to by N? We follow the chain back in time until we reach a person who fixed its reference by either dubbing – saying 'this object shall be named "N"', or some equiv-alent – or by description, as in 'I shall name the F "N"'. It is crucial that in the latter case, the description merely points to the object; it is not to be understood as synon-ymous with the name, and the name does not thereby acquire any conceptual content. Furthermore, the criteria for the reference of a name do not have to enter into one's understanding of the name; there is no need to know how the chain links one back in time to a reference-fixing act.

Rigid designators are terms which always refer to the same object in every possible world (except those in which object does not exist). Others are called non-rigid or flaccid designators; an example of the former as 'The number of sides in a square'; of the latter 'The 42nd US president'. Ordinary proper names are rigid designators; thus 'Charles Dodgson = Lewis Carroll' is a necessary truth, whereas 'Lewis Carroll = the author of *Alice in Wonderland*' is true but not necessarily true. 'Charles Dodgson might not have been Charles Dodgson' is false, but 'The author of *Alice in Wonderland* might have not been the author of *Alice in Wonderland*' is true.

This picture extends very naturally to what are called *natural kind terms*, such as 'water' and 'tiger'. If something is water, then it necessarily is water. But no true description in terms of observable or surface properties *necessarily* holds of water. However, a description in terms of what does distinguish water from other substances – H_2O – does refer to the same substance with respect to any possible world. Thus 'water = H_2O' is a necessary truth, despite its being *a posteriori*, and despite its not being analytic. Thus substances *do* have essences.

Some uses of indexical referring expressions refer rigidly. If one points at some water, and says 'that is water', one utters a sentence that expresses, on that occasion of its use, a necessary truth. Indeed, the phenomena of rigidity is at its clearest in such cases; one feels that it is *that stuff*, unmediated by concepts, that one refers to.

It is entirely possible there should be pairs of possible situations such that one cannot tell which one is in 'from the inside', but which differ in that one contains, for example, H_2O, whereas the other contains an indetectably distinct substance XYZ. A linguistic community that has always been in the first situation will refer to H_2O by the phoneme 'water', whereas a linguistic community that has always been in the second situation will refer to XYZ by the same phoneme. These are two words – homonyms – that look and sound the same. These considerations support the thesis of semantic externalism: the reference of at least some words is determined by the nature of the surroundings, not by internal conceptual resources available to language-users.

• STUDY QUESTIONS

1 Think further about the suggestion, made on behalf of the descriptivist theory of proper names, that there *is* a description that any user of the same N can supply

which will refer to the right object: 'the object that the linguistic community *actually* refers to by N'. Run through each of Kripke's four objections to the descriptivist theory. Do they apply here? Does the suggestion involve one in a circle?

2 Does a person not need *any* conceptual resources to refer to an object? It seems one must, in order to do something more than just making sounds. What then must a language-user understand or intend in order to refer my means of a proper name or indexical to an object? What about referring to a kind, or species?

3 Shakespeare, let us assume, wrote *Macbeth*, *King Lear*, and so on. If that is a fact, is it really a contingent fact? Or is it more plausible that in, say, academic or critical discussions of a play, 'Shakespeare' should be understood as 'the author of the play'? Does that spell significant trouble for Kripke's view?

4 Suppose Mrs Smith goes to the hospital and gives birth to a boy. The squiggling thing is handed to her; she says 'I dub him "Roger"'. He is taken away to be weighed, checked over and cleaned up. But while undergoing this procedure he gets mistakenly switched with another boy who was born at same moment, called 'Sam' by his mother. Nobody ever knows that there was a mistake. Brought to Mrs Jones, the boy who was dubbed 'Sam' grows up happily, being called 'Roger'. What is the boy's name? Years later, if the mistake is detected, does the boy learn that he is not Roger, but Sam?

5 To what extent should we be semantical externalists? Assuming we accept the Kripke-Putnam line on 'water' etc., should we also be externalists about the concept of a *table*? What about the concept of *food* – for does not it have a nature underneath our ordinary experience of it? What about *pain*, for which one might think that it has a nature in physiology that until recently was unknown?

6 There is a piece of platinum held in France that used to be regarded as the ultimate criterion for one metre. But Kripke says that even so, it was never *a priori* and necessary that the length of the standard metre is one metre; it was at most *a priori* but contingent that the length of the standard metre is one metre. Why would he say this? Do you agree?

• PRIMARY READING

Kripke, S. (1980) *Naming and Necessity* (Cambridge, MA: Harvard University Press).
Putnam, H. (1975) 'The Meaning of "Meaning"', *Minnesota Studies in the Philosophy of Science*, 7, pp. 131–93.

• NOTES

1 Legend has it that the main idea behind Kripke's view of proper names was first hatched in the pioneering work in modal logic by Ruth Barcan Marcus; see the Historical notes at the end of this chapter.

2 Not everyone accepts that Frege accepts this. In my view, he did. But this does not matter so far as Kripke is concerned: Kripke's attack is directed at the descriptive theory itself, whoever held it.

3 A sentence like 'I'm here' is analytically true – the conventions of language are such that no utterance of it can ever be false – yet the propositions expressed by it are contingent. For example, suppose one is at Wembley Stadium; thus an utterance of 'I'm here' expresses the proposition that one is at Wembley. But it is not a necessary truth that one is at Wembley, for one could have been somewhere else. We'll investigate further in Chapter 5.

4 Actually that is debateable; if Mozart were never born, then would not 'Mozart = Mozart' fail to express a truth? To allow for that possibility, we could write 'If Mozart exists, then Mozart = Mozart'. But that would complicate the discussion unnecessarily.

5 'True' in this sense is a relation between a proposition and a world. But 'true' as ordinarily used means 'true at the actual world', namely 'actually true'.

6 To be more precise, we can say that a rigid designator designates the same object *in every world in which that object exists*. What Kaplan calls an *obstinately rigid designator* designates the same object in every world, period – in which case the object is a *necessary existent*.

7 For this and many other examples, see G. Evans, 'The Causal Theory of Names', in his *Collected Papers* (Oxford: Oxford University Press, 1985), pp. 1–24; for 'Madagascar' see p. 11.

8 Some natural kind terms are not indexicals. For example, elements such as *Berkelium* were defined and supposed to exist before any examples had been found or synthesised.

5

possible worlds: semantics, context and indexicality

• 1 POSSIBLE WORLDS AND INTENSIONALITY

The 44th US president is the first black US president. The two definite descriptions happen to pick out the same individual, but they don't mean the same. This is reflected in the fact that the two don't *necessarily* pick out the same individual: at other possible worlds, for example, the 36th US president is the first black US president, not the 44th.

The only mammals that fly are bats (assuming that flying squirrels don't really *fly*, that they only *glide*). Therefore the predicates 'α is a bat' and 'α is a flying mammal' are co-extensive; the set of bats is exactly the same as the set of flying mammals. But the two predicates are not synonymous; their meanings differ. And this is reflected in the fact that although in the actual world the set of bats is the same as the set of flying mammals, there other possible worlds where there are creatures that are the one but not the other.

Impressed by this correspondence, many philosophers have proposed that the meaning of linguistic expressions should in some sense be identified with this behaviour across possible worlds. We can speak of each expression as having an **intension,** which determines, at each possible world, its extension at that world. So the intension of 'the first black US president' determines Barack Obama as its extension in the actual world, but someone else, say Jesse Jackson, at another possible world, and others at others. The intension of 'α is bat' determines the same extension as 'α is a flying mammal' in the actual world, but determines a different extension at other possible worlds, such as one with flying dolphins.

Similarly, propositions can be identified with the intensions of whole sentences: the intension of a sentence, the proposition it expresses, determines the *truth-value* of the sentence at each world (remember that for Frege the referent of a sentence is its truth-value). Thus the truth-value of 'Barack Obama is the 44th US president' is the same as that of 'Voltaire wrote *Candide*'; but the equivalence is only an actual one; in other possible worlds the two have different truth-values. For our purposes, we can think of the intensions of sentences – propositions – as sets of possible worlds or possible circumstances, namely the ones at which the sentence is true. This fits with Frege's characterisation of the sense of a sentence as its truth-*condition*: to say that the sense of a sentence is its truth-condition is arguably to say that the intension of a sentence is the set of circumstances under which it is true.

This, or variants of this, have for the past 60 years been a popular approach for explicating meaning. It's very intuitive. One's grasp of the meaning of the word 'red' seems to entail that one knows not just what counts as red in the actual world, but also what would be red in other situations, other possible worlds. The most reliable and familiar technique to convince yourself that one expression's meaning differs from another's is to engage in hypothetical reasoning: in the actual world, A and B stick together, but are there possible situations in which they fall apart? If so, then A and B have different meanings. But the other way round – that if A and B stick together in every possible world, then their cognitive meanings coincide – is not true. For if P and Q are *themselves* necessary truths – say '2 + 2 = 4' and 'Any kangaroo is a kangaroo' – we don't want to say that P and Q thereby mean the same. Intensional equivalence cannot entail cognitive equivalence, not just like that. Similarly, there are predicates that are cognitively inequivalent but necessarily have the same extension: 'α is a round square' and 'α is an animal that lived before animals existed' have the same extension – namely the empty or null set – but obviously don't mean the same. For singular terms, the obvious cases are those definite descriptions built of the predicates just mentioned: 'the round square' and 'the animal that lived before animals existed'; these are intensionally equivalent, since they denote nothing in every possible world, but they are not cognitively equivalent.

There are many, many responses and approaches to this set of problems, beginning with the Frege-based Carnap and Church in the late 1940s, through Montague, Kaplan, Lewis, Stalnaker and many others up to the present. The approach often has to do with the compositional structure of sentences. 'The round square' and 'the animal that lived before animals existed' necessarily have the same extension, but it's not the case that they are built in the same way from parts which are themselves intensionality equivalent. That they should be is Carnap's requirement of *intensional isomorphism*: synonymous sentences – sentences that are cognitively equivalent – must be intensionally isomorphic.

But this and others like it are too complex for this book, as well as there not being one that dominates the scene in the ways that the ideas of Frege, Russell and Kripke have. Instead, in this chapter, we focus on a particularly interesting aspect of intensional semantics, namely its interface with the topic of indexicals.

• 2 INDEXICALS AND DEMONSTRATIVES

Consider the following words:

I, me	tomorrow
you	today
he	yesterday
she	now
here	there
they	him, her
this, that	then
we	mine

These are all indexicals (or each has an *indexical use*, as will emerge). Take the word 'I'. It is a singular term, but it would be wrong to say that the *word* 'I' has a referent; it is not like 'Rotterdam', always having the same referent on each occasion of use. Rather, each *utterance* of the word has a referent. Its referent is the speaker, the one who happens to be saying it.

Take the word 'today'. Each utterance of the word refers to a day, namely the day containing the moment at which it is uttered. The word 'here' refers to the place at which it is uttered (although 'here' also has a *demonstrative* use; see below). And so on.

In general, the reference of an indexical depends on the context of utterance. Arguably, this is not so of an expression like 'the Sun' or 'Rotterdam', which always refers to the same thing, irrespective of the context of utterance.

Thus the *linguistic meaning* of an indexical is a *rule* (an intension) that determines the referent of a token of that indexical at each possible context of utterance. For each possible context of utterance, the rule specifies what the referent of an utterance of the indexical would be at that context.

Tense also represents indexicality with respect to time. When one says 'It's snowing here', one means that it's snowing here *now*. For the past or the future, one says 'It was snowing' or 'It will be snowing'.

Some indexicals are demonstratives. Take the word 'that'. In its demonstrative use, the speaker must, in order to refer to something, point or otherwise gesture towards the intended referent. If, in a pine forest, a speaker says 'That's a very beautiful tree', but doesn't point or otherwise indicate which tree he means, then it seems he has not succeeded in expressing what he meant to say. In order to do so, he must point to or otherwise indicate the tree he means. However, the pointing-gesture may be *implicit* rather than *explicit*. If we are walking through open country, and there is just one tree to be seen, and it right there in front of us, then I needn't point out which tree I mean when saying 'That's a very beautiful tree'. You'll know which tree I mean.

The gesture needed to complete a demonstrative is called a demonstration. Indexicals that do not require a demonstration – tacit or overt – are called **pure indexicals**. The referent of an utterance of a pure indexical is determined simply by the context of utterance.

The context of utterance is roughly the situation in which an utterance is made or could be made. It includes, but is not restricted to:

> (identity of) speaker, hearer, time, place.

Unlike 'I', 'now' and the like, which are simple, many indexical expressions are **compound** – for example, 'my horse', 'that big red house', 'the day before yesterday', and so on.

Many words have both an indexical and a non-indexical use. Consider:

> Every man who owns a donkey beats it.
> Lady Ottoline Morrell met Ludwig Wittgenstein, but didn't like him.

'It' and 'him' in these contexts are reflexive pronouns, devices of *cross-reference*. Someone using these words in these ways is not relying on the context of utterance to determine their referents. 'It' in the first example works like a bound variable 'x' in logical notation, and 'him' in the second case could without loss be replaced by another occurrence of 'Ludwig Wittgenstein'; in the first case, there is no particular donkey being referred to at all, but in the second, the referent of 'him' is determined by a so-called **anaphoric** connection to the occurrence of 'Ludwig Wittgenstein'.

In the following cases, however, those same words do function as indexicals:

> (One surfer to another, as they watch an incoming wave): It's a big one!
> (One prison camp guard to another, as a prisoner is seen escaping through the barbed wire): Shoot him!

The fact that, unless we are talking long-distance on the telephone or something like that, we do not normally say 'It's snowing *here*', but just 'It's snowing', shows that indexicality, or as we will sometimes say **context relativity** or **context-sensitivity**, is often *implicit*. Frequently, it simply goes without saying that that is what one is talking about; our intended hearers will understand.

The use of quantifiers is especially striking in this regard. It's rare that by 'Every' we really mean 'Everything whatever'. For example if one says 'Everything's cooked' just before a dinner party, one doesn't mean that *everything that exists in the universe is cooked* – or that *everything that exists, has existed, or will exist, is cooked*. One merely means that the food that one has actually prepared for the upcoming dinner party is cooked. Technically, one *implicitly restricts the domain of quantification*, relying on the hearer's knowledge of the situation to interpret what one said. That is, one interprets 'Every x is –' as if it meant 'Every x which is F is –', where F is a predicate delimiting the range of the quantifier.

• 3 THE ACTUAL WORLD AS A CONTEXT

Suppose Jones exists in a possible world W. His dog is Fido. Jones says 'My dog has fleas' at exactly 1.00 p.m. What he says is true just in case Fido has fleas at 1.00 p.m. If Jones utters the very same sentence again at 8:00 p.m., then what he says is true just in case Fido has fleas at 8.00 p.m., not 1.00 p.m. *What he says* depends on the context of utterance: the proposition he expresses on the second occasion is different from the one he expresses on the first, because on each occasion the present tense of the verb 'to have' indicates that he means that the dog has fleas *now*, i.e. at the time of utterance, which changes.

Now consider Jones in an alternative possible world W^*, in which Jones has a different dog, namely Spot. He says 'My dog has fleas' as before. Clearly, what he says is true just in case Spot has fleas at the time of utterance.

Now return to the first world W, where Jones' dog is Fido. Suppose now that Fido doesn't have fleas, but Jones says 'My dog might have had fleas'. What he says could be explained in either of two ways:

(1) In some possible world, Jones has a dog, and it has fleas.
(2) In some possible world, Fido has fleas.

It seems clear that (2) is correct. When Jones says 'My dog might have had fleas', he is talking about his *actual dog*, the dog he has at W. He means that *it* might have had fleas: that there is some possible world in which that very dog, Fido, has fleas. He does not mean merely that in some world he has some-dog-or-other that has fleas.

Now back over to W^*. Assume that Spot does not have fleas in W^*. If Jones had said, in *that* world, 'My dog might have had fleas', then he is talking about Spot, not Fido. Which dog Jones is talking about using 'my dog' depends on which world he is in; in W he talks about his dog in W, in W^* about his dog in W^*, and so on. So we have to add the *world* of utterance to our list of indices that make up the *context* of utterance:

Contextual indices: time, place, speaker, audience and *world*.

Of course, no sentences are *actually* uttered at non-actual possible worlds. But sentences are uttered at such worlds (just as other things happen: apples fall from trees, wolves howl and so on). So the context of utterance is not *necessarily* the actual world, even though the context of every actual utterance is the actual world.

• 4 TWO-DIMENSIONALISM: CONTEXT OF UTTERANCE VERSUS CIRCUMSTANCE OF EVALUATION

If all goes well, an utterance of a declarative sentence expresses a proposition, something that can be true or false. The proposition is the meaning of the utterance; it is *what is said*. We have just said that among the contextual parameters that determine what is said is the *world* in which the utterance takes place (along with time, place, identity of speaker and so on). We have also said, however, that we can take any proposition, and evaluate it *at*, or *with respect to*, a possible world: ask whether it is *true* at that world. The proposition has a *truth-value* at each world. That was what Section 1 of Chapter 4 was chiefly about.

Thus, following David Kaplan, we must distinguish sharply between context of utterance and **circumstance of evaluation**:

> Sentence-meaning + context of utterance ⇒ proposition
> Proposition + circumstance of evaluation ⇒ truth-value

A *sentence* meaning is a linguistic rule for determining the proposition expressed by a given sentence for each possible context of utterance: the **character** of a sentence determines, with respect to a given context of utterance, what **content** is expressed, what proposition is expressed. We say more generally that the character of a sentence is determined by the characters of the expressions it comprises, including its indexical expressions. For instance, the character of the indexical pronoun 'here' is wherever the utterer happens to be; its content, for a given utterer at location L, is L.[1]

We may then ask whether that proposition (that content) is true at a given possible world. When we say that a proposition is true, we normally mean truth at the actual world; but we may also ask, of the proposition expressed, whether it is true with respect to other worlds. Truth, in this way of picturing things, is not absolute, not simple a property of propositions: it is a relation between a proposition and a world.

Certain consequences of this scheme are striking. Consider the sentence:

> I am here now.

No actual utterance of this sentence could ever be false: the proposition expressed by any actual utterance of that sentence is true with respect to the actual world.

This might lead one to suppose that since it could not be false, 'I am here now' expresses a necessary truth. That would be a mistake. For Jones says it at a certain time, in a certain place. What he says is that *Jones is in that place at that time*. Is what he says a necessary truth? No! Jones *could* have been in a different place at that time. In other possible worlds, he is not in that place at that time. So the proposition is false at such worlds.

We might, however, want to say that 'I am here now' is a kind of *analytic truth*: for linguistic rules – conventions of language – ensure the truth of what it expresses on each occasion of its use. Yet what it expresses on each occasion is a contingent truth, not a necessary truth. This flies in the face of the traditional philosophical view that analytic truths are necessary truths, but it appears that they just aren't.

Suppose I say:

> I do not exist.

Although the proposition I express is false, there *are* circumstances with respect to which the proposition is true, namely worlds in which I don't exist. So it is not a necessary falsehood, even though every utterance of the sentence is true. This perhaps explains the wonder of Descartes' *cogito*: according to linguistic rules, every utterance of 'I exist' expresses a proposition that is true at the world of utterance; but even so, that proposition may be false at other words. So the sentence 'I exist' is an analytic truth but the propositions it potentially expresses are not necessary truths.

In short, the context of utterance determines the proposition expressed by the utterance; the circumstance of evaluation determines the truth-value of the proposition at a given world. The context of utterance is a situation with respect to which we are asking: what is the proposition that would be expressed by this sentence? The circumstance of evaluation is a possible world with respect to which we are asking: is this proposition true with respect to this world?

This picture addresses one itch you may have felt during the discussion of Kripke and Putnam. Suppose we grant that water is indeed necessarily H_2O. Still, you might think, surely in some sense water *could have turned out* not to be H_2O, but XYZ. That is surely imaginable, surely *conceivable* in some sense. *If* the XYZ-world *had been actual*, then water *would have been* XYZ – though, in actual fact, water is necessarily H_2O.

The picture, generalised, grants this. We can think of two kinds, or *two dimensions*, that determine the modal characteristics of any sentence: context of utterance, and circumstance of evaluation. The contingency of 'water = H_2O' is contingency along the first dimension, as we consider alternative contexts of utterance of the sentence. The necessity of 'water = H_2O' is necessity along the second dimension, as we consider alternative circumstances of evaluation.

Many people find the following sort of table helpful. Let 'watery stuff' be a non-rigid designator for whatever at a given world satisfies the stereotype that is actually satisfied by H_2O – a clear liquid that boils at 100 degrees Celsius, etc. Each horizontal row represents a possible context of utterance (or 'world considered as actual', as it sometimes put), abbreviated '*CU1*' or '*CU2*'. Each vertical column represents a possible circumstance of evaluation (a possible world), abbreviated '*CE1*' or '*CE2*'.

Table 5.1 Two-dimensional diagram for 'water = H_2O'

	CE1: watery stuff = H_2O	**CE2**: watery stuff = XYZ
CU1: watery stuff = H_2O	'water = H_2O' is true 'water =XYZ' is false	'water = H_2O' is true 'water = XYZ' is false
CU2: watery stuff = XYZ	'water = H_2O' is false 'water = XYZ' is true	'water = H_2O' is false 'water = XYZ' is true

The top row – **CE1/CU1** and **CE2/CU1** – are what Kripke and Putnam were primarily concerned with. Are there worlds with respect to which the proposition actually expressed by 'water = H_2O' is false? The answer to that *metaphysical* question is no. The left column – **CE1/CU1** and **CE1/CU2** – indicates the imaginability or conceivability of alternative scenarios. Is it conceivable that 'water = H_2O' could have turned out false? The answer to that *epistemological* question is yes.

Especially interesting are **CE1/CU1** and **CE2/CU2**, the situations represented by the left-to-right diagonal. The first represents simply the actual non-modal proposition expressed by 'water = H_2O'; the second represents what *would have been* expressed by the non-modal sentence expressed by 'water = H_2O', *had XYZ been actual*. In general, a location on the diagonal represents the non-modal proposition that would have been expressed by a sentence had that situation been actual. Had the XYZ world been actual, then in that world it would have been *necessarily* false to say 'water = H_2O'; in particular, it would have been false to say 'water = H_2O' with respect to a world in which the watery stuff = H_2O. That is what is shown by **CE1/CU2**.

• 5 FURTHER DISCUSSION: RIGID DESIGNATION AGAIN

Consider the following sentences:

(1) The world record holder in the 100 metres is Jamaican.
(2) In 1990, the world record holder in the 100 metres was American.

Given the actual context of utterance, namely 12 March 2012, (1) is true: the definite description 'The world record holder in the 100 metres' denotes the *present* (the time when I was writing this) record-holder, Usain Bolt of Jamaica. But the description as it occurs in (2) does not pick out Bolt; (2) does not say, of Bolt, that *he* was American in 1990 (which would be false). The description picks out the record-holder in 1990, namely Carl Lewis, and says truly of him that *he* was American. Compare:

(3) In 1990, the present world record holder in the 100 metres was American.

It is plausible to say, strictly speaking, that (3) says falsely of Bolt that he was American in 1990. It says: the present world record holder in the 100 metres is such that, in 1990, he was American. If someone were to utter (3) with the intention of expressing the proposition expressed by (2), he would be misusing the word 'present'.

Such a definite description as 'the world record holder in the 100 metres' is normally used in a way that is called *temporally* non-rigid. This means that when we talk about different times, the object it denotes depends on what object satisfies the description at *that* time. So the description picks out Bolt in (1) but Lewis in (2).

Contrast this with 'the *present* world record holder in the 100 metres'. This description is *temporally* rigid. The denotation of the description is fixed by the context of utterance (namely, the time), irrespective of the time being talked *about* –

irrespective, that is, of the presence of such phrases as 'Next year...' or 'In 1990...'. That is why (2), as I utter it now, is true, but (3) false: in the present context, Bolt is the men's world record holder in the 100 metres, so the definite description in (3) denotes Bolt, and (3) says something false about Bolt. The identity of the present record-holder is *irrelevant* to (2), however its truth-value depends only on the nationality of whoever was the record-holder in 1990. In the non-rigid use, so to speak, the description doesn't care about the time of utterance, only about the time that is being talked *about*.

Just as we can distinguish between temporally rigid and non-rigid terms, we can distinguish between modally rigid and modally non-rigid terms (recall that in the philosophy of language and metaphysics, modality has to do with necessity and possibility). Consider a variant on a previous example:

(4) That dog has fleas.

Imagine someone saying this of Fido, i.e. Fido is the dog demonstrated (pointed at) by the speaker. Now imagine someone pointing at Fido and saying:

(5) It might have been the case that that dog has fleas.

(5) is true just in case in some possible world, the proposition expressed in (5) by the clause 'that dog has fleas' is true. Suppose we are checking a world to see if that proposition is true at that world. Which dog do we check for fleas? Clearly, we check *Fido*, the dog actually demonstrated in the context of utterance of (5). No *other* dog is relevant.

The expression 'that dog', as it occurs in (4) and (5), is a modally rigid designator, or rigid designator for short. What this means is that the context of utterance determines the referent of the expression, and even when we are talking about counterfactual circumstances, non-actual possible worlds, the referent remains the same; we keep talking about Fido, the dog determined by the context of utterance.

Compare:

(6) The winner of best-in-show at Crufts in 1966 had white hair.
(7) It might have been the case that the winner of best-in-show at Crufts in 1966 had black hair.

Both are true. But unlike 'That dog' as encountered in (4) and (5), 'The Crufts winner of best-in-show in 1966' is a non-rigid designator. The winning dog in 1966 was in fact Oakington Puckshill Amber Sunblush, a white toy poodle. What makes (7) true is that irrespective of that, in some possible world a dog with black hair wins the title – it could be that a different dog, say a giant schnauzer, wins Crufts in 1966 and had black hair. Now compare:

(8) It might have been the case that the actual winner of best-in-show at Crufts in 1966 had black hair.

Unlike (7), (8) can be read as being about OPAS: it instructs one to find the dog that actually won Crufts in 1966, and to find a world in which *that* dog is black. So it appears the word 'actual' does with respect to modality what 'present' does with respect to temporality: it tells us to use the actual context of utterance (time, world) to find the referent; it rigidifies what might otherwise be a non-rigid singular term.

6 THE RIGIDITY OF INDEXICALS

You may have noticed that in Section 4, when introducing the idea that the possible world in which an utterance takes place is part of its context, we said that our example 'My dog' is both an indexical and a rigid designator. It is an indexical since it means 'the dog that belongs to me', the rule for which is *the dog that belongs to the speaker*. It's being rigid was why, in evaluating 'My dog has fleas' at other worlds, we were asking the question about the *same dog* in each world.

This is not to deny that there are also non-rigid uses of phrases like 'my dog'; for example, we can say 'I wish he were not my dog', without thereby wishing he were not the dog that he is; such uses are equivalent to non-rigid descriptions such as 'the dog that belongs to me'. Whether or not such an expression is being used rigidly sometimes depends on the intentions of the speaker. Thus assume that my dog is a beagle, and consider:

> If I had chosen a different dog, then my dog would have been a French Bulldog.
> If I had chosen a different dog, then my dog would have belonged to someone else.

In the first sentence, 'my dog' is used non-rigidly (I am not saying that my beagle might have been a French Bulldog!); in the second sentence, it is being used rigidly (I am not saying that a dog might have been both mine and someone else's).

7 INDEXICALITY IS ESSENTIAL

It is tempting to suppose that indexicals, in theory, are optional. In principle we could get with only singular terms that are *purely conceptual* – their meanings composed entirely of descriptive concepts so that the way in which the singular term acquires its referent does not depend on the context of utterance. Such a picture, however, is very hard to sustain. First, consider the case of a simple, pure indexical such as 'here'. Suppose, standing somewhere in a forest, I say 'There are no mushrooms growing here'. It is perfectly clear that I succeed in referring to the place where I'm standing, even if I have no other way to refer to it: even if I cannot *individuate* it, *pick it out*, by describing it using only general concepts, or without exploiting the context of utterance. I might even say this when I am *lost*, so I have no way at all of describing where I am, except perhaps 'somewhere in the New Forest', which would fall far short of picking out the much smaller region I designate by saying 'here'.

Second, there is a more systematic philosophical point. Many terms we use for times and places seem non-indexical, such as 'the solar system', 'California', '4.00 p.m.', 'January 12 1986'. But there are a great many stars with orbiting planets; when we speak of 'the' solar system, what we really mean is *this* solar system. More generally, think of what is involved in locating things on a map. If I draw a map with a spot I label as 'My house', does that tell you where it is? No! It tells you where it is *only if you know where you are on the map*. That is, you have to know where on the map is *here*. Knowing where something is requires relating it spatially to where you are.

Similarly with times. Suppose you visit the planet Zog, and are told that such-and-such happened in the year 34909 in the Zog calendar. This doesn't tell you when it happened unless you know what year it is *now* in the Zog calendar (you'd also need to know how long a Zog-year is). The situation is the same with our own calendar, but we are so used to it that it isn't quite as obvious. If you are told that the date of a certain event is 12 January 1986, what you are immediately told is that the date is exactly 1985 years and 12 days after the (supposed) birth of Jesus Christ. But that doesn't tell you *when* the event happened; strictly speaking, it doesn't even tell you whether the event is in the past, the present or the future. What you need to know is what date it is *now*. Thus what being told the date of a past event really tells you is that it took place a certain number of days before *now*, i.e. the present. So it seems you can't make use of these supposedly non-indexical descriptions of things without turning them into indexical ones.

An even more striking case concerns first-person pronouns, as was pointed out by John Perry. Suppose you are told that a certain person is going to be tortured. The person is described as 'the person who is X, Y and Z'. You don't know who it is that is uniquely identified as being X, Y and Z. Your worry, naturally, is this: is the person who is X, Y and Z *me*? Your attitude towards the upcoming torture depends on this; no further descriptions of the person to be tortured, no descriptions of the form 'The person who is such-and-such', will tell you what you want to know unless you can determine whether or not the person who is such-and-such is *you*.

Indexicals are thus essential to our understanding of language and ability to refer to things. Context-dependence is not a shortcoming or fault of language.

• 8 INDEXICALS AND FREGEAN SENSE

Frege was well aware of indexicals, and tried to incorporate them into his sense-reference theory. Speaking of the present tense (which implicitly contains what is expressed by *now*), he wrote:

> If a time-indication is conveyed by the present tense one must know when the sentence was uttered in order to grasp the thought correctly. Therefore the time of utterance is part of the expression of the thought ... The case is the same with words like 'here' and 'there'. In all such cases the mere wording, as can be

preserved in writing, is not the complete expression of the thought; the knowledge of certain conditions accompanying the utterance, which are used as means of expressing the thought, is needed for us to grasp the thought correctly. Pointing the finger, hand gestures, glances may belong here too.

('Thoughts', in Frege 1997, p. 332)

Remember that a sense can be understood as either a mode of presentation of the referent or a rule that picks out the referent. Frege's idea here seems to be that the linguistic meaning of an indexical is a rule that determines the sense expressed on each possible occasion of its use; the sense thereby expressed determines the object. So the mode of presentation involves the context of use. The rule for determining an object by an utterance of, say, 'the present temperature', is something like 'the temperature at time T location L', where T and L are the time and location of the utterance.

Frege also says, indeed in the very same passage: 'If someone wants to say today what he expressed yesterday using the word "today", he will replace the word with "yesterday".' (ibid.).

But Frege is running into trouble here. The trouble is that according to the longer quotation above, successive utterances of 'today' and 'yesterday', even if they do refer to the same day, present it in different ways. The 'conditions accompanying the utterance' are different. In that case 'today is Tuesday' spoken on Tuesday must differ in sense from 'yesterday was Tuesday' spoken on Wednesday. So once yesterday has passed, we *can't* express today what we expressed yesterday.

Frege's remark about 'today' and 'yesterday' is probably the wiser one. For the picture he sketches in the longer passage above is too restrictive. A bit later in connection with the first-person pronouns 'I' and 'me' he says 'everyone is presented to himself in a special and primitive way': the thought one expresses by using 'I' can only be grasped by oneself; for that thought, the listener must substitute a thought expressed using 'he' or some such. If so, then surely something analogous goes for 'now' and 'here': more than one person can be presented with a given moment and grasp it as *now*, but once that moment has passed, that moment cannot again be presented *in that way* again. Similarly with 'here': only actually being in a place can one understand it has *here*.

If that is so then the thoughts expressed by utterances of 'I am hungry', 'It is raining here', 'It is raining now' and the like become unavailable if one is not the speaker, if one is not present or the moment has passed. Yet this hardly seems to matter, as Frege observes in his remark about 'yesterday' and 'today': so long as we know we are referring to the right object, we don't care about the mode of presentation. If so, then the notion of sense does not seem to be relevant to an account of communication, at least where indexicals are concerned. We'll return to this in Chapter 7.

• HISTORICAL NOTES

Elements of intensional semantics are found in Frege and Russell, and the general idea goes back much further. Modern attempts to carry out the idea began perhaps with Carnap's *Introduction to Semantics* (1942) in which he employs the notion of an '*L*-state' with respect to a semantical system as doing duty for possible worlds. The theory of indexicals also had its precursors in the work of Frege, and more substantively in Russell's theory of what he called 'egocentric particulars' in his *Inquiry into Meaning and Truth* of 1940 (published in 1950). Until Kaplan's work officially appeared in 1989 in the form of his 'Demonstratives', various people contributed to the topic, including Tyler Burge, Hector-Neri Castañeda, Gareth Evans, David Lewis, Barbara Partee and Frank Vlach. But with the appearance of Kaplan's work, activity on the topic exploded (actually manuscripts of 'Demonstratives' circulated much earlier than 1989). John Perry has been enormously influential in epistemology and the philosophy of mind; his main works specifically about indexicals are 'Frege on Demonstratives' (1977) and 'The Problem of the Essential Indexical' (1979).

• CHAPTER SUMMARY

Intensional semantics is an attempt to explain meaning via the concept of possibility; such observations as that knowing its meaning enables one to determine, for any possible world, whether a sentence is true, encourages one to identify meaning with modal truth-conditions. The trouble is that it is implausible to say that knowledge of its truth-value in every possible world is sufficient for knowledge of the meaning of a sentence, since for example not all necessary truths are synonymous.

However, the approach is very fruitful, especially when it comes to indexicals. Indexicals are referentially context-dependent expressions such as 'now' and 'here'. Each has a character that determines, for each context of utterance, a referent, in such a way that the referent shifts with context. Some indexicals are demonstratives, requiring a demonstration, which may be implicit, to secure a referent.

The context of utterance includes, in addition to the time and place of the utterance, the possible world in which the utterance takes place. And from Kripke and Putnam in Chapter 4, we're familiar with the idea of asking whether, irrespective of its actual truth-value, a proposition would be true at alternative possible worlds. Thus we can distinguish between the context of utterance and circumstance of evaluation: the character of an expression – its linguistic meaning – plus the context of utterance yields the content expressed by an utterance of the expression; in turn, the content plus the circumstance of evaluation yields the truth-value, extension or referent of the utterance. The difference between character and content is obvious in the case of explicit indexicals, but interesting also in the case of natural kind terms such as 'water', which Putnam suggests contain an implicit indexical component. Given the actual world as context, 'water' has the content H_2O – it tracks H_2O across possible worlds (as circumstances of evaluation); but in other contexts, it tracks for example XYZ. This 'two dimensionalism' captures the idea that despite its being (actually) necessary that water = H_2O, things might have turned out that it is necessary that water is XYZ.

The modal issues have their ready temporal analogues; in particular the distinction between modal rigidity and modal non-rigidity is analogous to that between temporal rigidity and temporal non-rigidity. For example, 'the present F' is the temporal analogue of 'the actual F'.

It does not appear possible to regard indexicality as a mere convenience; it appears that any map or calendar, for example, is useless unless one has an indexical anchor – similarly and strikingly, descriptions of the doings of human beings can never have the same force without the item that one of the people is *you*. To find that 'The F is G' is not intrinsically meaningful in the way that 'You are G' is.

Indexicality puts pressure on Frege's ideal of communication, according to which perfect communication involves you and I grasping the *same sense* (the same thought). For example, the mode of presentation of a time signalled by 'now' passes instantaneously; it cannot later be presented in the same way. But that hardly seems to detract from one's ability to communicate at a later time about the time indicated.

• STUDY QUESTIONS

1 Consider 'Snow is white' and 'Snow is white and all kangaroos are kangaroos'. Do these have the same intension? What can be said from the point of view of intensional semantics to reconstruct the strong intuition that they do not mean the same?

2 If one says 'My car is parked in a garage', is the phrase 'My car' an indexical, whose job is to refer to an object, or is it a Russellian definite description, or both, or neither? Spell out the implications of each hypothesis.

3 Suppose we accept Kripke's account of proper names. Suppose Brown says: 'I am not dead'; does this mean the same as 'Brown is not dead'? What if we accept the description theory of proper names?

4 Can the distinction between (7) and (8) of Section 5 be displayed with the scope of definite descriptions instead of the word 'actual'? For example: 'It might have been the case that the F is G' versus 'The F is such that it might have been the case that it is G'? Use examples.

5 Especially once we've observed that *tense* is a kind of indexical, should we conclude that all actual sentences contain indexicals? Which do not?

• PRIMARY READING

Kaplan, D. (1989) 'Demonstratives: An Essay on the Semantics, Logic, Metaphysics, and Epistemology of Demonstratives and Other Indexicals', in *Themes from Kaplan*, (eds) J. Almog, J. Perry and H. Wettstein (Oxford: Oxford University Press).
Perry, J. (1979) 'The Problem of the Essential Indexical', *Noûs*, 13, pp. 3–21.

• NOTE

1 We are exploring Kaplan's celebrated theory of indexicals, but with a simplifying change: we are pretending as if the theory is one of *utterances*, but actually Kaplan's theory assigns what he calls 'contents' – objects, extensions and propositions – to *expressions-relative-to-contexts*.

6

pragmatics

Philosophers often talk as if the stating of facts or the conveying of factual information were the sole purpose of language. Of course, it isn't; there are also questions, commands, predictions, greetings, jokes, narrations, and many others, only some of which can appropriately be assessed as true or false. But this territory was relatively uncharted until the past 40 years or so, when some philosophers – especially J. L. Austin, H. P. Grice and John Searle – sought a theoretical framework in terms of which to describe it. Perhaps motivated by Wittgenstein's emphasis on the practical dimension of language – on its *use* for certain *purposes* – these figures have been so successful that the basic framework that emerged from their work has for over 30 years now served as a touchstone for mainstream philosophy of language and theoretical linguistics. In this chapter we will explore its initial forms and motivations, and consider some applications.

• 1 MOOD AND FORCE REVISITED

In the Introduction we distinguished *meaning* from *force*. Semantics concerns the former, and pragmatics is largely concerned with the latter. The following three sentences, we said, *express the same proposition*, but would normally be used to express it with different *force*. The grammatical differences are differences of *mood*:

Table 6.1 Mood and force

Sentence	Mood	Force (that would standardly be expressed by that mood)	Proposition
You are going to eat raw fish.	Indicative/ Declarative	Assertion	that you are going to eat raw fish
Are you going to eat raw fish?	Interrogative	Question	that you are going to eat raw fish
Eat raw fish!	Imperative	Command	that you are going to eat raw fish

It is natural to think that force is at least partly a psychological matter: in central cases, a person asks a question or makes an assertion only if they *intend* to (exactly what the intention must be, and whether it is *always* necessary or sufficient, are further questions; we will say more below). By contrast, the role of mood is clearly a matter of *convention*: for example, there is a convention whereby the use of the interrogative mood indicates to the listener that the speaker is asking a question, i.e. expressing the proposition with interrogative force. In English, the interrogative mood is typically accomplished by reversing the order of subject and verb.

But the relation of mood and force is somewhat fluid. The use of mood is not the only way to indicate force. The mere uttering of a sentence in a given mood is not sufficient for saying something with the force standardly conveyed by that mood. One can utter 'Eat raw fish!' without commanding or enjoining anything, especially if one is alone. It is also not necessary. We can ask a question by using the indicative mood, usually by varying our tone of voice, using a rising intonation. That too is a convention: there is a convention according to which if you utter 'you are going to eat raw fish' with that sort of rising intonation, you are to be understood as asking a question, not making an assertion. In written English, we can indicate a question by attaching a question mark to a sentence in the indicative mood, as in 'You are going to eat raw fish?'

• 2 SPEECH ACT THEORY

Yet another way is to say something like:

> I ask you whether you are going to eat raw fish.

Indeed, instead of the rather complicated conventions in English by which we express force, we *could* eliminate distinctions of mood entirely from the language, and employ a set of operators like 'I ask you whether...':

> I assert that you are going to eat raw fish.
> I ask you whether you are going to eat raw fish.
> I command that you are going to eat raw fish.

In his famous paper 'Performative Utterances' (1961), John Austin noticed that such forms do exist in English, and furthermore that their grammatical structure can be misleading, at least to a philosopher. Consider the second one, 'I ask you whether you are going to eat raw fish'. Superficially, one might say that this is really an *assertion*, namely an assertion *that the speaker is asking the listener whether he or she is going to eat raw fish*. But this, Austin held, is a confusion. The purpose of 'I ask you' is not to *describe the speaker*; when you utter 'I ask you whether you are going to eat raw fish', your aim is not to describe yourself. For it if it were, it looks as if you would be describing yourself falsely, and a wag could rightly say: 'No you're not!' The purpose of such an utterance, obviously, is to *bring it about* that the speaker asks a question whose content is expressed by the words that come after. This is clear from the fact that someone making that utterance, in the right circumstance, does *thereby* succeed in asking a question.

Austin's idea is that there are certain sorts of words such that, in saying them, one *thereby performs a certain kind of act* – the act which, on a more superficial view, they might seem to describe or announce. The point is clearer from examples like this:

> I apologise.
> I hereby bequeath my cigar case to my nephew.
> I promise to do that.
> I name this ship the *Queen Elizabeth*.

Provided that the circumstances of utterance are of the right sort (they are not uttered in the performance of a play, the person is empowered to name the ship etc.), to utter such words is to *perform* the act of apologising, bequeathing, promising, dubbing. In committing the verbal act of uttering them, one does not *report the fact* that one performs the act – as if the act itself consisted in some other, perhaps non-verbal act. Rather, performing the act is actually *constituted* by the utterance. Austin, then, called these forms of words – I apologise, I bequeath, I promise, I name – *performative* verbs. The word 'hereby' is perhaps a good clue as to what is going on.

When he wrote 'Performatives', Austin was thinking that linguistic utterances can be divided into performative and non-performative: a distinction between utterances that – according to some conventions – *do* something (perform an act), and those that say something, or more accurately *state* or *assert* something. In practice, however, it proved difficult to describe this difference. One problem is that *I assert, I ask* and so on seem to be performative verbs; but since saying 'I assert that my client is innocent' and 'My client is innocent' seem equally to serve for an assertion that the client is innocent – for saying that the client is innocent – what are we to say of the distinction between doing and saying? What this suggests is that saying should *not* be distinguished from doing; for saying *is* a kind of doing, even if a specially important kind. This idea is reinforced by the observation that there are *many* kinds of acts that are acts of stating, of saying: reminding, telling, informing, describing, criticising, alerting and so on.

Accordingly, Austin soon devised the theory he is most famous for, and which is now more or less the standard theory of what he called *speech acts*. A normal speech act comprises three main sub-actions (there is also a fourth, namely the *phonic* act of uttering certain phonemes; but we will pass over this). Sticking with our example of the question concerning the eating of raw fish, the picture looks like this:

Table 6.2 Force distinctions within a speech act

Locutionary act	The expression of content (meaning, cognitive and/or expressive)	Expressing the proposition that the intended audience is going to eat raw fish
Illocutionary act	The act performed *in* speaking (especially the expression of *force*, aka illocutionary force)	Asking whether the proposition is true
Perlocutionary act	The acts performed by the speaker *by means of* the illocutionary act that is an effect on the audience	For example, getting the listener to say whether or not he or she is going to eat raw fish

This is the central framework of speech act theory as pioneered by Austin and developed by John Searle. Thus take the question, *Are you going to eat raw fish?* The speaker performs the **locutionary act** of expressing the proposition *that you are going to eat raw fish*. He expresses it by means of a sentence in the interrogative mood. Assuming the circumstances are appropriate – for example, the listener was in a position to hear – he thereby performs the **illocutionary act** of *asking the listener* whether he or she is going to eat raw fish. The **perlocutionary act** depends on the listener; if he or she is agreeable then it will be something like *getting the listener to say* whether or not he or she is going to eat raw fish.

Semantics is concerned with locutionary acts, with classifying sorts of expressions according to their meaning, and with describing the meaning of types of expression. Locutionary acts *are not* confined to sentences that express propositions. There is a convention, for example, according to which 'Ouch!' expresses pain on the part of the speaker; but the meaning is non-propositional, and wholly expressive rather than cognitive. The meaning expresses a state of the speaker, but does not describe anything. Similarly for 'Oops', 'Rats!', and the like. Yet these are not simply *noises* that are *caused* by pains and errors, as when a cat shrieks when you step on its tail. That 'ouch' expresses pain is a convention of English, as you will quickly appreciate if you step on a foreigner's toe.

Pragmatics is concerned in the first instance with illocutionary acts. As we have seen, illocutionary force is largely conventional. Yet it remains surprisingly difficult to specify under exactly what conditions a speaker performs a given type of illocutionary act. Return to the case of promising. Clearly, one who promises thereby incurs an obligation to bring about the truth of a certain proposition. Yet we can ask various further questions about promising that are not easy to answer:

• Is it necessary, in order to make a promise, that one use the word 'promise' (or assent to the question 'do you promise?')?

- Is it sufficient? Aside from play-acting, singing a song etc., can one say 'I promise to do such-and-such' without actually promising?
- Must promises be to the effect that the *promiser* will do or refrain from doing something?

Similar questions arise in connection with other speech acts, including assertion. The point remains, however, that in a few cases it remains compelling that merely uttering a certain form of words – so long as the speaker is responsible to the convention in play – is sufficient for having performed a certain speech act. Saying 'I promise', in certain circumstances, is one case; saying 'I apologise', in certain circumstances, is another. In these cases, the conventions are such that if the utterance took place under the requisite circumstances, one cannot claim not to have performed the action on the grounds that one did not 'mean it', i.e. did not have such-and-such intentions. Apologising by saying 'I apologise', for example, is a bit like bowing: one can do it while feeling nothing but resentment, but one does thereby apologise or bow all the same.

There are a great many illocutionary acts besides the basic ones mentioned so far. One can *admonish, describe, warn, order, request, criticise, censure, welcome, reprove, compliment, greet, berate, plead, chastise* and so on (of course, some types will include others as sub-varieties). The study of *per*locutionary acts would not be an enquiry into the conventions of language so much as the psychology and social features of actual linguistic episodes. The *per*locutionary act performed by means of an illocutionary act involves an effect on the audience. It must be describable in terms of a transitive verb, where the subject of the verb is the speaker and the object is the audience. Thus for example. 'In speaking that way, General Patton roused the troops' would be a description of a perlocutionary act; one can also *anger* one's audience, *persuade, interest, frighten, bore* them and many others.

Perlocutionary acts do not have to be *intentional*, but they do have to be describable as things that the speaker *did*. Thus, for example, Patton may have intended by his speech to rouse the troops, but succeeded only in *frightening* them. Though not intentional, *frightening the troops* would still be something that General Patton *did*, and did by speaking as he did. Obviously, there is no end to the variety of possible perlocutionary acts, and they are not in general governed by convention in the way that illocutionary acts are. But they are essential to an understanding of language nevertheless, because speaking is an *intentional activity*. We don't just speak for the hell of it; we speak to people for reasons, namely in order to have some effect on the people we speak to. A perlocutionary act is typically the end, or goal, we are shooting for in speaking as we do, even if we fail and end up performing some other perlocutionary act or none. The illocutionary act, in such cases, is merely the means towards that end.

• 3 IMPLICATURE

Suppose that Jones' parents ask Headmaster Smith how Master Jones is getting on at the boarding school. Smith replies, 'Well, he hasn't been expelled'. Mr and Mrs Jones would naturally take Smith to intend the message that Master Jones is not doing well at school, not well at all. But Smith did not *say* this, and what he says does not *logically entail* it either. It is perfectly possible that what Smith said should be true, when Master Jones *is* doing well at school.

Nonetheless, it would be reasonable to understand Smith in the way indicated. In the mid 1960s H. P. Grice (1913–1988) introduced the term **conversational implicature** for this phenomenon, one of intended perlocutionary force.[1] In particular, Smith did not say that Master Jones is not doing well at school, and what he did say did not logically entail it; instead, Smith's statement *implicated* that Master Jones is not doing well at school.

In general:

> A statement P *implicates* the proposition Q if: P does not logically entail Q, but a well-informed, competent speaker would take the speaker to be intending to convey Q.

Thus if Smith were to say: 'Well, he hasn't been expelled' when he knows that Master Jones is doing well, he would not be saying anything false. So it would not be *semantically* improper for him to say this. What he says, however, would be *pragmatically* improper. In fact, it is precisely because it would be pragmatically improper for him to say this under such circumstances that it would be reasonable for the listener to understand him to be conveying that Master Jones is not doing well.

The reason, according to Grice, is that there exists a certain general maxim of conversation that he calls the **cooperative principle**. This principle is hard to sum up in detail, but it comprises several sub-maxims. These include:

- maxims of quality: do not say what you believe to be false; do not say anything for which you lack adequate evidence;
- maxims of manner: be brief; avoid obscurity, ambiguity, vagueness;
- maxims of relation: be relevant;
- maxims of quantity: make what you say neither more nor less informative than is required for the purposes at hand.

These are, in a certain sense, conventions, but they are not conventions like those of politeness. They are more like the rules of a game. Just as intentional adherence to the rules of chess is a necessary condition of what it is to *play the game of chess*, so intentional adherence to these rules is a necessary condition of what it is to engage in *conversation*. Conversation is, in this sense, a *practice*, that is, a practical activity partly defined by certain rules. For this reason, such rules are often known as *constitutive* rules, as opposed to *regulative* rules such as moral rules or rules of etiquette. Of course, unlike the case of chess, adherence to these rules is not all-or-nothing; they can be obeyed or flouted in various ways and to varying degrees. Conversation is not a tightly defined activity, and different forms of conversation – banter, theoretical discussion, rowing, debate, arguments, heart-to-heart talks, chat and so on – each have their own weightings of these rules, along with rules or principles of their own.

The bottom line is that people in conversation of various kinds understand each other to be cooperative, as trying to help one another. Thus, the reason that conversational implicature works is that speakers understand each other to be trying to obey the sub-maxims of the cooperative principle (in very much the same way that game players understand each other as trying to obey the rules, and as trying to win the game). Thus Jones' parents would normally understand Smith to be trying to be informative. Thus, if Master Jones were doing well, Smith would have said so: not being expelled is a necessary condition of doing well, but it is far from sufficient, and if Master Jones were doing well, there would be far more to say about it than that. So it would be natural and justified for Mr and Mrs Jones to reason: Smith is trying to be informative and truthful, but he is also trying to be polite, or avoid hurting our feelings; so he is saying the most positive thing he can say; since that is the most positive thing he can say, he must be trying to convey that our boy is not doing well.

● 4 SOME APPLICATIONS OF THE CONCEPT OF IMPLICATURE

The notion of **implicature** can help to explain a number of phenomena that would otherwise obstruct or complicate the logical analysis of language. For example, according to the standard truth-functional analysis of the conditional 'if-then' of English, the following statement would be true:

> If mares are smaller than fleas, then mares are larger than cats.

The reason is that according to the truth-functional analysis, a conditional with a false antecedent is *true*.[2] This is bizarre, since the conditional seems quite wrong, especially since *nothing* is smaller than a flea but larger than a cat; this is the reason we refrained in Chapter 1 from simply advocating the truth-functional account.

The impropriety of such a conditional, however, can now be explained in pragmatic rather than semantic terms. It would indeed be wrong to *say* it. But what makes it wrong to say it is not its failure to be true.

Of course, everybody knows the obvious fact that mares are not smaller than fleas. Therefore the conditional is *not informative* to anyone. One knows that mares are horses, bigger than fleas; one therefore knows that a case when the antecedent is true, and the consequent is also true, will never happen, just because the antecedent is always false. Since, according to the truth-functional analysis, the falsity of the antecedent entails the truth of the conditional (but not the other way round), an assertion of this conditional violates the maxim of quality, which is the rule of informativeness: a person cannot learn anything from it. Thus the conditional is true but **pragmatically improper**.

In general, an assertion of a conditional statement is appropriate (i.e. informative and relevant) only if the truth-value of both antecedent and consequent are *unknown*, or can reasonably be presumed so by the speaker. Thus a conditional whose antecedent's truth-value is known to be false is *never assertible*. So no wonder the donkey-conditional looks so weird.[3]

But if it is not the truth-values of the constituents that justify the statement, what does? Answer: some other kind of *connection* between them, often but not always a causal connection. For example, one might say 'If the pork was off, then the dog will throw up' – not being certain whether the pork was off or whether the dog is going to throw up, but believing that dogs usually vomit bad meat. If one accepts the conditional, then if one finds the antecedent to be true, then one can infer the consequent (or if one accepts the conditional, and finds the consequent false, one can infer the falsity of the antecedent). However, not every case is as simple as this; for our purposes, we can rest with the idea that in general, an assertion of a conditional is proper only if the speaker reasonably assumes the truth-values of its antecedent and consequent are unknown to both speaker and hearer, but has some other grounds for asserting the conditional. Otherwise, the cooperative principle is violated.

This is why we have jokes like 'If that's a jackdaw then I'm a monkey's uncle', said by someone who knows that it's not a jackdaw. Since he isn't a monkey's uncle, and everyone knows this, everyone understands him to be saying that it's not a jackdaw. The possibility of such jokes shows that we do implicitly understand the conditional truth-functionally; part of the humour is that we do not normally assert a conditional purely for truth-functional reasons.

Violation of the cooperative principle – in particular the maxim of quantity – explains why, if one knows, for example, that Marie's car is a Fiat, it would be wrong to say 'Marie's car is a Fiat or it's a Volkswagen', despite the fact that the disjunction is true. It would be misleading, suggesting that one holds the two options open.[4] Likewise, to say that 'All mammals bigger than blue whales are nocturnal' is, according to the classical account of quantification, true, because there are no mammals bigger than blue whales; but to say so would be misleading, since one could assert the more informative 'No mammal is bigger than a blue whale'. And there are many other examples where the Gricean strategy promises to remove the apparent tension between intuition and orthodox semantics or logic.

It is largely because we do implicitly rely on cooperativeness – especially the maxims of relation and quantity – that we are able to convey so much information with so few words. For example, given the information jointly available in the context, one could convey that one won't come to this evening's party by saying: 'I'm in Edinburgh' (the party is London, too much hassle to come just for a party etc.). However, this points to a complication with the Gricean point of view. So far, one might think that the conversational maxims come into play only once one knows what propositions are expressed by an utterance; the maxims are triggered by the need to discover the implicatures of an utterance, not by the need to identify the proposition literally expressed by the utterance. But it seems that semantics and pragmatics do often necessarily interpenetrate; in such cases the two must work together, as a team. For example, suppose your roommate says:

> The landlord said on Tuesday he would fix the window.

The sentence is ambiguous: is the proposition that the landlord's statement that he'd fix the window happened on Tuesday, or is it that the landlord said that Tuesday is the day that he'd fix it? Typically, one would rely on information about the context, including information relevant to the speaker's likely beliefs and purposes to disambiguate such an utterance, to find out which proposition it expressed. You might be in a position to reason: 'My roommate and I both know that the landlord works full-time, and never comes to us except on weekends; so the first interpretation is more likely'. That reasoning assumes something like Grice's maxim of quality: the speaker would not express anything he believes to be false.

So perhaps the identification of the propositions expressed by an utterance and of the implicatures of the utterance is better thought of as different aspects of a single process of interpretation, one which takes stock of all interpretation-relevant information.

• 5 STRAWSON'S AND DONNELLAN'S OBJECTIONS TO RUSSELL'S THEORY OF DESCRIPTIONS

According to Russell's theory of definite descriptions (Chapter 3), definite descriptions – expressions of the form 'The F' – do not have the semantical function of referring, because their significance does not depend on the existence of a unique F or of Fs generally. Instead, a sentence such as 'The King of America is rich' says that there is a unique person who is the King of America, and that he is rich. The proposition expressed by the sentence is therefore false, since there is no such thing as the King of America.

P. F. Strawson (1919–2006), in his famous 'On Referring' (1950), voiced the following objection. If someone were actually to say 'The King of America is rich!', we would not react by saying that what he said is *false*. We would not say 'No, the king of America is not rich!' We would say something like, 'No, no, you're under a misapprehension; America has no king.' The whole business of saying something truth-evaluable has not got started. Such a person, according to Strawson, has attempted to *use* the phrase 'The King of America' to *refer*, but failed, as if he were aiming blindfolded to strike a piñata when there is no piñata. According to Strawson, the use of definite descriptions **presupposes** the existence of their referents. To use them does not normally amount to *saying* that their referents exist, or more broadly to say something which logically *entails* that they exist.

The cash value of the distinction between presupposition and entailment is this:

> If P entails Q, then if Q is false then P is false.
> If P presupposes Q, then if Q is false then P is neither true nor false.

Crucially, Strawson holds that the meaning of a *referring expression* of the form 'The F' does not depend on whether it is used successfully to refer. Meaning, for Strawson, is a feature of expressions; whereas reference is a feature of speech acts, of the *use* of expressions. Referring is something we *do*, not a property of expressions considered in the abstract.

In effect, Strawson argues for a return to Fregean ideas: the meaning of 'The F is G' is such that if there is no such thing as the F, the meaning of the sentence is unaffected, but nevertheless it cannot be used to say anything with a truth-value. So meaning for Strawson looks a lot like Fregean sense. Therefore, at least at first blush, he will fall into the problems discussed in Chapter 2 surrounding true claims of non-existence, such as 'The King of America does not exist'. However, his emphasis on the concrete use of language rather than the rarefied air of functions, propositions and senses brings him down closer to the practice of ordinary language; it's not for nothing that together with Austin he is routinely put forth as a quintessential *ordinary language philosopher*. They've made a plausible case that by sticking closer to the surface phenomena of ordinary language, such problems as the puzzle over negative existentials are not intractable. And the idea of presupposition, so central to the approach, has been enormously influential in both philosophical and linguistic pragmatics.

Another observation of the ordinary use of definite descriptions that seems to upset Russell's picture, but also upsets Strawson's, and which nevertheless does imply that at least sometimes they function as referring expressions, was made by Keith Donnellan. We are in the audience to see Jones being tried for Smith's murder. The real murderer, however, is Brown, who is a very sane man, a cold-blooded killer as we say. But no one knows save Brown that Brown killed Smith, and in fact you and I are both persuaded that Jones killed Smith. And this is partly because of Jones's egregiously bizarre behaviour on the witness stand; in fact, Jones is insane. I whisper to you, 'Smith's murderer is insane!' to which you reply, 'Yes, I think so'.

It seems plain that I did communicate to you a truth *about Jones*, in some way equivalent to 'Jones is insane'. Yet I did this by means of a sentence that, according to Russell, is false because it expresses a proposition that is about Brown, a sane man, not Jones – in the sense that Brown satisfies the description 'Smith's murderer' ('The person who murdered Smith'). Donnellan (1966) therefore distinguishes the **referential use** from the **attributive use** of definite descriptions: one's use of a definite description is *referential* if one uses it to enable the audience to identify the referent;

one's use of a definite description is *attributive* if one says something about whoever or whatever satisfies it, just as Russell's view would have it. The key is that a referential use involves the description only inessentially; it is merely a tool for communication, not part of what one communicates. It doesn't matter how one packages the message, so to speak, so long as one successfully communicates it. The trouble with Russell's view is that there seems to be no way to characterise such cases – such cases of a successful use of a description to refer to a thing when the thing does not satisfy the description.

The theory outlined in Strawson's 1950 paper cannot accommodate the distinction either: Strawson's theory agrees with Russell's in that if the F exists, then a use of a term of the form 'The F' simply refers to the F.

In the above example, I spoke only vaguely of 'what he communicated' rather than the 'proposition expressed by' my utterance of 'Smith's murderer is insane'. Does that sentence, in that context, express a false proposition about Brown or true proposition about Jones? If we say the former, then perhaps there is no objection to Russell here, but the account will be silent about the actual linguistic transaction. But if the latter, then it seems that you, apprised of the facts of the case, would have to agree that 'Smith's murderer is insane' is somehow true, even though you know that Jones is *not* Smith's murderer.

Kripke urged in 1977 that the matter can be cleared up, leaving Russell's theory relatively unscathed, by invoking an important distinction closely related to Gricean distinctions. If, in amid a heist, one burglar says to his partner, 'The cops are around the corner', then it is evident that what is intended is different from the literal meaning of the sentence used in the particular context: he meant something like 'We can't wait around collecting loot; let's go!' Thus *speaker's meaning* can be distinguished sharply from *semantic meaning*: whereas the latter is determined by linguistic rules governing the use of expressions, the former is determined by various special intentions of the speaker, including Grice's cooperative maxims (thus conversational *implicature* is most plausibly reckoned a matter of speaker meaning).

Similarly, Kripke distinguishes between semantic and speaker's *reference*. You and I see Bob in the distance, but both mistake him for Jaroslav. I ask you, 'What is Jaroslav doing?'; 'Raking leaves', you reply. The semantic referent is Jaroslav, but the speaker's referent is Bob. It seems very plausible we can say exactly analogous things about the case of Smith's murderer: the semantic referent is Brown, the speaker's referent is Jones. The difference, then, is a pragmatic difference, not a semantical one – that is, it is not something that would affect the analysis of referring terms or definite descriptions. Donnellan's phenomenon is no more mysterious than the fact that tools can unintentionally but successfully be misused, as when a screwdriver is used as a chisel by someone who thinks that that is what it's for.

• 6 A PRAGMATIC APPROACH TO SEMANTICS

The classical theorist of meaning regards pragmatics – the use of language – as built upon a foundation in semantics, where semantics fundamentally involves reference: singular terms paradigmatically *refer* to objects, predicates *refer* to properties and relations. Once one learns the semantics, one can employ the words in various kinds of speech-act, including the drawing of inferences.

An alternative, championed by Willard Sellars (1912–1989) and articulated recently by Robert Brandom, regards pragmatics, and in particular inference, as fundamental. Consider the logical particle 'and' (where its role is that of connecting whole sentences, not its role in forming collective subjects, as in 'Laurel and Hardy'). A truth-table for the word is as follows, letting 'P' and 'Q' stand for any declarative sentences:

P	Q	P and Q
T	T	T
T	F	F
F	T	F
F	F	F

This tells us that if P and Q are both true, then 'P and Q' is likewise true; otherwise 'P and Q' is false. The standard inference rules – employed in proofs or derivations – are as follows:

$$\frac{P, Q}{P \text{ and } Q} \qquad \frac{P \text{ and } Q}{P} \qquad \frac{P \text{ and } Q}{Q}$$

These tell us that anytime one has P and also has Q, one may infer 'P and Q'; and if one has 'P and Q', one may infer P, and likewise may infer Q.

The classical theorist regards the truth-tables as fundamental; the inference-rules – instructions for how to *use* the word – are *based* on the truth-tables, which specify the *meaning*, the semantics, of 'and'. But for the inferentialist, the inference-rules are fundamental: they set forth what one has to know, if only implicitly, to be credited with mastery of the word 'and'. If one possesses such mastery, nothing else is required for grasping the meaning of 'and'; one understands the word just insofar as one performs with the word as specified by the inference rules. The rules make explicit what was originally a matter of practice, of the use of words – a matter of *knowledge-how* as opposed to *knowledge-that*. Such are *interlinguistic* rules; there are also 'language-entry' and 'language-exit' rules, which come to the fore with non-logical sorts of words. Instead of explaining the word 'red', for example, in terms of its *reference* to a certain property, we specify rules such as: if an object is seen to be red, one may assert 'it is red'; if commanded to 'get the red one', one should get the red one (in this case there are also such interlinguistic rules as: from 'it is red' one may infer 'it is coloured', and 'it is not blue', and so on).

This approach disenshrines the concepts *reference* and *truth* in favour of those fundamental to the statement of such rules as just described; in particular, the general form of such rules tells one what one is *obligated* to do, what one *may* do, with words; such are **normative** concepts, not essentially semantic concepts. Indeed, the words 'refers to' and 'is true' can themselves be subjected to the same treatment. Very roughly, one is entitled to assert *P is true* just in case one is entitled to assert P; and similarly one is entitled to assert *the referent of 'b' = A* just in case one is entitled to assert $b = A$.

Not *all* inferences one is prepared to draw can plausibly be explained as justified by one's mastery of words; for example, if one happens to know that one has a sandwich in one's backpack, one's inferring 'Here is some lunch' from 'Here is my backpack' is not justified merely by one's mastery of words. But many inferences can be seen in that way; for example, the inference from 'A is north of B' and 'B is north of C' to 'A is north of C'. It is plausible that the sum-total of inferences of this sort constitute one's linguistic mastery, one's knowledge of meaning.

• 7 METAPHOR

This book is an introduction to the philosophy of language, but not a comprehensive introduction. And the subject of metaphor is relatively an untamed beast, which is liable to lead us into a dizzying variety of issues in psychology, epistemology, literary criticism, philosophy of science, philosophy of mind and other things. Here, I just say enough to be provocative and perhaps more opinionated than I have striven to be at other points in the book, and to convince you that the tools we have been introduced to shed some light on the phenomenon; beyond that I refer you to the further reading.

Here are some metaphors:

> Richard is a lion.
> Life is a yo-yo.
> What he said casts some light on the matter.
> She was carried away by passion.
> Light consists of waves.
> He burns for her.
> I've some new ideas floating around in my head.
> She was the finest flower of her generation.
> I'm on a highway to hell.
> Money doesn't grow on trees.
> Giovanni followed in his father's footsteps.

What *is* a metaphor? Many plausible but wrong things have been said about this. For example:

- A metaphor states a *comparison*. No, because it doesn't *state* a comparison; 'New York is bigger than Paris' states a comparison. At most, the metaphor implies or suggests a comparison.
- A metaphor states a *similarity*. No: *similes* do that, such as 'My love is like a rose', as opposed to 'My love is a rose'. Similes are often literally true.
- Metaphors simply *are* similes. No: metaphors typically are more powerful than their corresponding similes; 'Richard is a lion' versus 'Richard is like a lion'.
- Metaphors are literally false. No: 'Money doesn't grow on trees' is literally true.
- A metaphor is equivalent to a conjunction of literal sentences. No: what conjunction of sentences is equivalent to 'potatoes piled in pits, blind-eyed'? None; the metaphor causes an event of visual imagination in the reader or hearer.
- In a metaphor, the meanings of words shift from literal meanings to metaphorical meanings. No: 'Richard is a lion' *could not* have the metaphorical significance that it does if 'lion' were not understood as denoting the usual African felines.

Metaphor is easier to think about if we view the property of *being metaphorical* as a matter of *pragmatics*. This means that it is not *sentences* or *propositions* that are metaphorical; rather it is certain *speech acts* – even though the sentences will typically be without a reasonable literal use. The shortcomings of the ideas just mentioned are all due to the mistake of trying to describe metaphor in terms of a special type of *meaning*. Instead, we should try to characterise metaphor as a kind of *use* of language. Metaphor is not a locutionary matter, and we'll see in a moment, there are even doubts about whether it is an illocutionary matter.

Even so, the task is difficult, because we cannot be sure that all things called 'metaphors' have something distinctive in common. But here are some elements that should be incorporated into any theory of metaphor.

1 A correct metaphorical utterance would violate Grice's cooperative principle if taken literally (that is, as expressing a statement whose content is the conventional meaning of the sentence). Thus, for example, 'She burns for him' would hardly make sense; 'Richard is a lion' would obviously be false; 'Money does not grow on trees' would too obviously be true. Thus the listener, expecting the speaker to obey the cooperative principle (that is, expecting the speaker to have a reasonable purpose in speaking), is prompted to take the utterance in some other way.
2 Metaphorical significance depends on literal meaning: as before, 'Richard is a lion' *could not* have the metaphorical significance that it does if 'lion' were not understood as denoting the usual African felines.
3 Metaphors may have a *cognitive* function. For example, it is scientifically useful and informative to think of light as a wave, when literally it cannot be a wave; a wave is a moving region of compression in a physical medium (water, air etc.), and light can propagate through a vacuum.

4 Metaphors may have an *expressive* function. In poetry, or when we use metaphors to describe how we feel, think or perceive, we often do so in order to convey *what it is like* to feel, think or perceive as we do.

There is very little agreement in philosophy, linguistics, literary criticism or psychology on what metaphors are. But the distinction between (3) and (4), in my view, is crucial. Very often, one side or the other of this distinction is emphasised at the expense of the other. We have seen already that literal language has both cognitive (representational) and expressive functions. So it is with metaphor: we make metaphors in order to describe, but also in order to express.

It is plausible that what these functions have in common is the involvement of the *imagination*. For a cognitive example, we imagine tiny objects moving round a larger object at the centre; such proved a useful model for the *atom*, even though the atom is not actually like that. For a non-cognitive, expressive example, we imagine the pain of being stabbed; we thus get the point of someone's saying 'I realised with a stab that she was being unfaithful to me'. For an example that is perhaps both, we imagine a beautiful girl, and also the sun; as I. A. Richards put it, the distinctive 'feel' of Romeo's 'Juliet is the sun' arises from an 'interaction' among those acts of the imagination. It may be impossible to sum up all such activities of the imagination. What we can say, however, is that it is the overarching *purpose* of the metaphorical utterance to stimulate such activities in the imagination of the audience. In the terminology of speech act theory, metaphor is characterised by a type of intended *perlocutionary* act.

• HISTORICAL NOTES

Ludwig Wittgenstein's work – both his famous *Philosophical Investigations* of 1953, and his *The Blue and Brown Books* of the 1930s, which was unpublished during his lifetime but circulated unofficially in mimeographed form around Cambridge in the 1930s – played a decisive role in the rise of so-called 'ordinary language' philosophy, which reached its peak in the 1950s and 1960s. Gilbert Ryle (1900–76), Peter Strawson (1919–2006), John Austin (1911–60), Norman Malcolm (1911–90), O. K. Bouwsma (1898–1978) and many others applied the subtleties of careful observation of ordinary language to philosophical problems with sometimes striking results. The legacy lives on in that philosophers as a whole are usually much more sensitive than previously to how philosophical theories are so seldom reflected unambiguously in ordinary linguistic practice, in 'what we say'. But undoubtedly a much greater effect of ordinary language philosophy was its invigoration of pragmatics – understood as a sub-discipline of linguistic study alongside syntax and semantics, though sometimes contending with them. By 1970, Austin's work in particular had inspired John Searle in writing his *Speech-Acts: An Essay in the Philosophy of Language* (1969), and then his *Expression and Meaning: Studies in the Theory of Speech-Acts* (1979); meanwhile the influence of H. P. Grice (1913–88), especially his essay 'Logic and Conversation' (1975) began to make itself felt. The Austin-Searle and Gricean paradigms have since then been subjected to massive development, revision and also pressure: (1) The literature on implicature has grown enormously in the past 30 years, with various types of implicature being identified, new maxims being formulated, and new ways to cope with cases in which the original maxims are found wanting. (2) According to **relevance theory**, proposed by Dan Sperber and Deirdre Wilson, Grice's maxims should be replaced by a single, general principle of optimal relevance or communicative efficiency: roughly, given at the outset a speaker's understanding of the context, including information about the likely cognitive states of the listeners, the speaker says only enough to affect the audience's cognitive states in the desired way. Grice's theory and relevance theory conflict in certain cases, and not always in favour of relevance theory, but relevance theory is an intuitive, flexible and compact alternative to Gricean maxims.

• CHAPTER SUMMARY

The mood of a sentence is a syntactical feature that is conventionally tied to the type of force that may be attached to an utterance of the sentence. For example, switching the order of subject and verb – e.g. 'you are' versus 'are you' – is a standard difference between the declarative and interrogative moods. Speakers sometimes break the principle, as when asking a question with the declarative mood.

The standard force-types – assertions, questions, commands – give rise to a more fine-grained theory. If what we are considering is a speech act of assertion, Austin famously distinguishes the locutionary act of expressing a proposition from the illocutionary act of assertion of a proposition, and from the perlocutionary act of getting the listener to believe a proposition. Locutionary and illocutionary acts depend mostly on the actions of the speaker, the perlocutionary act depends entirely on the effect on the listener. The precise extent to which illocutionary acts are conventional as opposed to intentional is a matter of dispute. Normally, we intend the perlocutionary act we succeed in performing, but often the actual perlocutionary act is not what we intend. The perlocutionary act, however, is always something that the speaker did in speaking as he did.

A statement in which P *implicates* Q is: P does not logically entail Q, but a well-informed, competent speaker would take the speaker to be intending to convey that Q. This captures the ordinary sense in which we sometimes say: 'I know you didn't actually *say* that he's ugly, but you *implied* it'. There are no strict rules for what is known as 'conversational implicature', but the idea is that the practice of conversation possesses the following constitutive rules, known collectively as the cooperative principle: do not say what you believe to be false. Do not say anything for which you lack adequate evidence. Avoid obscurity, ambiguity, vagueness. Be brief. Be relevant. Make what you say neither more nor less informative than is required for the purposes at hand. Working out conversational implicatures involves the assumption of fidelity on the part of the speaker to the rules of conversation; a speaker may not have said anything that logically entails Q but the assumption that the speaker aims to satisfy the cooperative principle may involve that he did mean to convey Q.

Another key concept put forward by philosophers approaching language in a pragmatic spirit is that of *presupposition*: if P presupposes Q, then if Q is false then P is neither true nor false (whereas if P entails Q, then if Q is false then P is false). This formed the basis of Strawson's attack on the theory of definite descriptions: if there is no unique F, rather than saying as Russell does that 'The F is G' is false, we can say that 'The F is G' presupposes reference on the part of the speaker's use of 'The F', and that since that presupposition is false, the use of the sentence does not express a statement with a truth-value. Donnellan presses harder, pointing out that 'The F is G' can serve to express a true statement, even when it is false taken in Russell's sense; he calls the two readings the referential sense and the attributive sense. Kripke in effect saves Russell, suggesting that *speaker's meaning* can differ from *semantic meaning*; both Strawson's and Donnellan's phenomena be explained purely pragmatically, with no threat to Russell.

There are many theories of metaphor, but it is plausible to regard it as strictly a pragmatic phenomenon – in particular, that it will violate maxims of cooperativeness if taken literally (according to semantic rules), and it always involves the dominant intention to achieve a perlocutionary affect of stimulating the audience's imagination in certain distinctive ways. Thus the semantic or literal meaning may be false and it may be true, but the point is always to engage the audience's imagination. The difficult work is to describe these effects on the imagination.

• STUDY QUESTIONS

1 Eavesdrop on a conservation – unobtrusively! – and try to identify the various illocutionary acts that you hear. How many of them sit comfortably in one of the basic categories of *force* we identified in Section 1?

2 What would be wrong with following claim: 'The purpose of an utterance is always the same: to express one's mental state!'

3 Of the three basic varieties of force of Section 1, is it possible to regard one to be basic, explaining the others in terms of it?

4 To work out by Gricean means conversational implicatures seems rather complicated; what would a defender of Grice say to the charge that complicated and recondite procedures of linguistic analysis he describes cannot possibly take place in ordinary conversation?

5 Consider:

I ate some of the cake.

Suppose it turns out that the speaker ate *all* of the cake; has the speaker lied (has the speaker wilfully uttered a sentence which he knows is false)?

6 'It's not the case that the King of America is rich'; non-technically, is that true?
7 'Money doesn't grow on trees' – literally true, therefore not all metaphors are literally false. But are there literally true metaphors that do *not* contain negation? What of 'Business is business'? Is that a metaphor? How does an utterance of it achieve its intended effect?

• PRIMARY READING

Austin, J. L. (1962) *How To Do Things With Words*, second edition, (eds) J. O. Urmson and M. Sbisá (Cambridge, MA: Harvard University Press).
Donnellan, K. S. (1966) 'Reference and Definite Descriptions', *Philosophical Review*, 77: 281–304.
Grice, H. P. (1989) Logic and Conversation' ([1975]; in Grice).
——(1989) *Studies in the Way of Words* (Cambridge, MA: Harvard University Press). Contains the celebrated essay 'Logic and Conversation'.
Kripke, S. (1977) 'Speaker's Reference and Semantic Reference', in P. French, T. E. Uehling Jr and H. K. Wettstein (eds) *Studies in the Philosophy of Language*, (Bloomington: University of Minnesota Press).
Searle, J. (1969) *Speech Acts: An Essay in the Philosophy of Language* (Cambridge: Cambridge University Press).
——(1979) 'Metaphor,' in *Expression and Meaning: Studies in the Theory of Speech Acts* (Cambridge: Cambridge University Press).
Strawson, P. F. (1950) 'On Referring', *Mind*, 59 (235): 320–44.

• SECONDARY READING

Sperber, D. and Wilson, D. (1995) *Relevance: Communication and Cognition*, second edition (Oxford: Blackwell).

• NOTES

1 Grice distinguishes between *conversational* implicature and **conventional implicature**. In the conventional case, the implicature is not *cancellable*: there are no circumstances in which one could assert the sentence without being responsible for the implicature. An example is 'He hurried home', which always implicates that he had a reason to get home quickly, even though it would not be a logical contradiction to say 'He hurried home, but for no reason'. By contrast, there are circumstances in which one can say 'He hasn't been expelled' without implicating that he is not doing well in school (for example, the parents of an unruly boy ask,

'Has he been expelled?'; the headmaster answers 'He hasn't been expelled'; even in the case discussed in the text, the Headmaster could cancel the implicature by adding, 'just in case you were worried – nearly half his classmates were sent home yesterday due to the unpleasant events that took place in the refectory').

2 According to the truth-functional account (the truth-table account), a conditional is false in just one case: when the antecedent is true, and the consequent false. Otherwise it's true.

3 The case is different for subjunctive or counterfactual conditionals, like 'If dogs could talk, they would be honest' – in those cases we say something that *would* be so if a certain *false* proposition were true. Unlike the material conditional if-then, however, the counterfactual conditional is not truth-functional: its truth-value is not determined by the truth-values of its antecedent and consequent.

4 The disjunction is truth-functionally equivalent to 'If Marie's car is not a Fiat then it's a Volkswagen'; since Marie's car is a Fiat, the conditional is true but pragmatically incorrect to assert. Likewise for 'If Marie's car is not a Volkswagen then it's a Fiat'.

7

˙the propositional attitudes

• 1 EXTENSIONALITY REVISITED

A language is extensional just insofar as the principle of substitutivity (introduced in Chapter 2, Section 6) holds of it; in particular:

(i) For any occurrence of a sentence within a larger sentence, the former can always be replaced by another sentence of the same truth-value, and the truth-value of the larger sentence will be unchanged.

(ii) For any occurrence of a predicate within a sentence, the predicate can always be replaced by another with the same extension, and the truth-value of the sentence will be unchanged.

(iii) For any occurrence of a singular term within a sentence, the singular term can always be replaced by another with the same reference, and the truth-value of the sentence will be unchanged.

Extensionality is highly intuitive. Consider (iii): if a sentence says that a certain object satisfies a predicate, and another sentence says that the *same* object satisfies the very same predicate, then surely if the original sentence is true then so is the new one, and if the first sentence is false then so is the new one. For example:

(1) Paris is north of Vienna.
(2) 'Paris' and 'the capital of France' are co-referential.
(3) The capital of France is north of Vienna.

Whether or not (1) is true, it seems that (2) tells you that (3) will have the same truth-value as (1). Similarly for (ii):

(4) This goldfish has a pancreas.
(5) 'α has a pancreas' and 'α has a spleen' are co-extensive.
(6) This goldfish has a spleen.

Supposing (5) to be true, then again the truth-value of (4) must be the same as that of (6). Sameness of truth-value, remember, is not sameness of *meaning*.

But there are cases of non-extensionality or substitution-failure in English. The simplest and most obvious cases are counterexamples to (i), involving non-extensional **sentence-connectives** such as *because*. For example:

(7)   The cat meowed because the dog barked.
(8)   The cat meowed because Paris is in France.

Assuming that (7) is true, hence that 'The cat meowed' and 'the dog barked' are true, replacing the true 'the dog barked' with the equally true 'Paris is in France' yields (8), which is false.

• 2 REFERENTIAL OPACITY AND FREGE ON THE ATTITUDES

Now consider:

(9)   'Venus' has five letters.

'Venus' and 'the Morning Star' refer to the same object, the planet Venus. But we cannot validly infer:

(10)   'The Morning Star' has five letters.

Unlike (9), (10) is false. A Fregean explanation is that 'Venus', as it occurs in (9), is not a singular term referring to Venus; rather it refers to 'Venus' – it's a name of a name, not of a planet. The position in which it occurs is **referentially opaque** as opposed to **referentially transparent**. Inserted into that position, the name 'Venus' does not do its customary job of referring to Venus. That is why the context

(11)   '___' has five letters.

is not open to substitution of co-extensive expressions; it is non-extensional. 'Venus', as it occurs in (9), is simply not in the business of naming Venus. Instead, what happens when we insert an expression into the blank of (11) is that the quotation marks together with the expression form a name of that expression, and the sentence says something about that.

But this context, subtly different from (11), *is* referentially transparent:

(12)   ___ has five letters.

or:

(13)   α has five letters.

Frege held that something very similar goes for *indirect* quotation, and for the related expressions of propositional attitude such as belief. Let us briefly revisit the view we introduced in Chapter 2. Consider the following example involving indirect quotation:

(14) Adam said that Venus is a planet.
(15) Adam did not say that the Morning Star is a planet.

These can both be true, even though of course:

(16) The Morning Star = Venus.

For if Adam does not know of the truth of (16) – for example, if he had no notion of 'the Morning Star' – then surely both (14) and (15) can be true. Indeed, even if Adam *does* know (16), it seems that the fact that he spoke as (14) says he did, does not establish that he actually *said* that the Morning Star is a planet. For reasons which will become clear below, it is usual to call such non-extensional contexts **hyper-intensional** contexts.

Cases like this are also hyper-intensional:

(17) Adam believes that Venus is a planet.
(18) Adam does not believe that the Morning Star is a planet.

In order to preserve the rationality of Adam, however, we must assume that Adam does *not know* that (16) is true. But with that assumption made, it does appear that (17) and (18) could be jointly true. Frege's explanation is that

(19) that Venus is a planet

is not a sentence, but a complex *singular term* denoting a proposition, the sense of 'Venus is a planet'. The word 'that' converts a sentence into a singular term referring to the sense of the attached sentence. This sense is *different* from the proposition denoted by

(20) that the Morning Star is a planet

This is reflected in the fact that 'Venus is a planet' and 'The Morning Star is a planet' express different propositions, different senses. It thus appears that the context

(21) Adam believes that α is a planet.

is referentially opaque; the truth of a whole sentence formed by inserting a singular term into (21) depends on more than what is referred to by the singular term. More generally, the context

(22) Adam believes that S.

where S represents any sentence, is referentially opaque; it is a hyper-intensional context. Of course, we are not attributing special powers to Adam in particular; the general point is that

(23) α believes that S.

is referentially opaque with respect to the sentences substituted for S. As with quotation, however, the subtly different expression

(24)   α believes β

is simply a two-place predicate, standing for a normal, extensional relation: belief (compare (23) and (24) with (11) and (12)).

Thus for Frege, the opaque context (23) is really very much like (11). A sentence formed by filling the blank of (11) with a referring term does not thereby yield a sentence about the referent of that referring term, but about the term itself. Likewise in the case of (23), except that instead of getting a sentence about the *term* inserted there, we get a sentence about John and a *proposition*, the sense of a sentence (at-a-context-of-utterance).

Moreover, according to Frege, a sentence like (17) does *not* contain an expression referring to the planet Venus, or to the Morning Star. The sentence refers to Adam, and to the proposition expressed by 'Venus is a planet', and it says that the former believes the latter. But, although an element of the *proposition* in fact *determines* Venus, a singular term *of* this proposition – (20) – does not *refer* to Venus.

In fact this is in accord with intuition, because we do assert such things as

(25)   Le Verrier believed that Vulcan is smaller than Mercury.

This is true, despite the non-existence of Vulcan; hence the truth-value of a sentence containing the belief-operator does not require that singular terms within the scope of the belief-operator refer to their customary objects. All that is required is that the that-phrases – the indirect clauses as grammarians know them – pick out a proposition. Which is the case in the above example: although 'Vulcan is smaller than Mercury' lacks a truth-value owing to reference failure on the part of 'Vulcan', it does express a sense, a proposition, and the statement says that Le Verrier believed it.

● 3 FURTHER DISCUSSION: LOSS OF SEMANTICAL INNOCENCE AND MULTIPLE HYPER-INTENSIONAL EMBEDDING

For Frege, in hyper-intensional contexts terms undergo a referential shift. And the shift can happen multiple times, as in

Dudley believes that Adam believes that the Evening Star is a planet.

If we call cases like (17) cases of *type-1 hyper-intensional embedding*, involving what Frege calls the term's indirect sense and its indirect reference, then (26) exemplifies *type-2 hyper-intensional embedding*, involving *doubly* indirect sense and reference. A table may help:

Table 7.1 The sense and reference of a term as used in three contexts

Extensional Context	Type-1 Hyper-extensional Context	Type-2 Hyper-extensional Context
Customary Sense	Indirect Sense	Doubly Indirect Sense
Customary Referent	Indirect Referent	Doubly Indirect Referent

The first column depicts the normal, extensional case: in a case like 'The Evening Star is a planet', the term 'the Evening Star' has its customary sense, which determines its customary referent, Venus. The lines indicate identity: in a type-1 non-extensional context – such as 'Adam believes that the Evening Star is a planet' – the customary sense becomes the referent of 'the Evening Star', i.e. the customary *sense* is the indirect *referent* of 'the Evening Star'. Similarly, the indirect sense of the term is the term's doubly indirect referent. And, in principle, the pattern must continue, since there is no end to the possible embeddings of a term using 'believes that'; we have 'A believes that B believes that C believes that...' and so on.

Some have urged that this loss of 'semantic innocence' is a serious defect of Fregean semantics. Does not a term mean the same thing, wherever it is used? If not – if indeed there are infinitely many possible embeddings and hence references for a term – doesn't this pose difficulties for compositionality, the claim that it must be possible to state the meaning of infinitely many sentences by laying down the significances of finitely many terms and modes of composition? For where do the indirect senses, the doubly indirect senses, and so on, come from? It seems that according to the above chart, they emerge anew, so to speak, from each embedding with a non-extensional operator such as 'believes that'.

• 4 *DE RE* AND *DE DICTO* NECESSITY

An important sort of non-extensional context is generated by modal adverbs such as 'necessarily'. We've touched on the topic before (Chapter 4, Section 2; Chapter 5). As before, let us assume the customary view that the truths of mathematics are necessary truths, truths that could not have been otherwise. Thus consider:

(26) Necessarily, two is less than three.

That's true. Now Mars has two moons, Phobos and Deimos. So the singular term 'the number of Martian moons' has the same reference as 'two'. But we cannot infer from that fact and (27):

(27) Necessarily, the number of Martian moons is less than three.

It's a fact but only a contingent fact that Mars has less than three moons; Mars might easily have had more. 'Necessarily', then, creates a non-extensional context. But this is an intensional context, not a *hyper*-intensional context. The reason for this terminological distinction is that modal adverbs do not cut things as finely as propositional attitude verbs do (for example). For example, it is a necessary truth that any kangaroo is a kangaroo. Therefore, the possible worlds in which Beckett was born in 1906 are exactly the same as those in which Beckett was born in 1906 and any kangaroo is a kangaroo. But a person can wonder whether Beckett was born in 1906, without wondering whether Beckett was born in 1906 and any kangaroo is a kangaroo. The semantical difference is not reflected in the sentences' intensional truth-conditions.

Sentence (27) is false. But now consider:

> (28)   Two is such that necessarily it is less than three.

Quine – about whom you'll hear more about in Chapter 9 – called the step from (26) to (28) a step of *exportation*. (26) and (28) illustrate the distinction between **de dicto** statements of necessity – of things said – like (26), and **de re** statements of necessity – of things – like (28).

In (28), the term 'two' is *outside the scope* of the necessity operator. 'Two' has shifted from an intensional position to an extensional one. Thus since two = the number of Martian moons, we *can* infer:

> (29)   The number of Martian moons is such that necessarily it is less than three.

Like (28), and unlike (27), this sentence is *true*: it says, consider the number of Martian moons – two, i.e. the number of ears on Prince Charles, call it what you will – *that object* is necessarily less than three.

• 5 *DE RE* AND *DE DICTO* BELIEF

The same distinction can be made with respect to hyper-intensional contexts. To explain and illustrate, let us consider Quine's famous example involving statements of propositional attitude. Ralph has seen a certain man in a brown hat behaving suspiciously. Abbreviating 'the man in the brown hat' as 'the MBH', we write:

> (30)   Ralph believes that the MBH is a spy.

One might think that this establishes that

> (31)   The MBH is such that Ralph believes that he is a spy.

It looks just like the inference from (26) to (28): it involves moving 'the MBH' from inside the scope of 'believes' to outside its scope, from a *de dicto* statement of belief to a *de re*. This seemingly innocuous transition from the *de dicto* to the *de re* turns out to have immense epistemological significance. To bring it out, consider an existential quantification of the *de re* case (31):

> (32) There is an x such that (Ralph believes that x is a spy).

(32) represents a much more interesting state for Ralph than simply the *de dicto*:

> (33)   Ralph believes that there is an x such that (x is a spy).

Ralph believes there are spies, but so does everyone; the point of (32) is that unlike most of us, he suspects someone.

Considered in itself, the step from (31) to (32) is plainly valid, since the place quantified into – the occurrence in (31) of 'The MBH' – is a perfectly normal occurrence of a singular term, an occurrence that is referentially transparent; it is *not* bound by or within the scope of 'believes that', but stands *outside* the occurrence of 'believes that' (the second occurrence of the variable 'x' has replaced the word 'he'; in this use of the word 'he', it has the same function as the variable).

But looking through our Fregean microscope, the inference from (30) to (31) seems not to be valid. For at the end of Section 2 we saw that within belief contexts, terms refer not to their customary referents, but to their customary senses. (30) states a relation of Ralph to a proposition, *not* to such objects as the MBH. In fact, (30) does not even entail that there *is* such a man, as we learned from thinking about La Verrier and Vulcan; therefore it cannot entail (31), which *does* entail the existence of the MBH. (32), and hence (31), is made true partly by the existence of a certain man, namely the MBH, when strictly speaking (30) makes no mention of that man, the MBH. A referentially opaque context in a sentence like (30) appears to be sealed off from such devices as quantifiers; one cannot, without further ado, *quantify into* positions *within* that context by means of a quantifier placed outside the context. (30) can usefully be compared to a statement about a painting: Ralph's taking a certain painting to be of real events does not entail that the events exist, or that elements of the painting themselves refer.

It seems that the further premise that we are assuming in moving from (30) to (31) is that 'The MBH' expresses an object determining sense, that is, that it refers. Roughly, the assumption is:

> There is an x such that the sense of 'The MBH' determines x.

• 6 RALPH'S PREDICAMENT

We now add to Ralph's story. A certain Bernard J. Ortcutt is known to Ralph as an upstanding member of society, certainly no spy. Hence

> (34)   Ralph believes that Ortcutt is not a spy.

Just as we inferred (31) from (30) on the grounds that the MBH exists, and hence (32) from (31), we can from (34) infer:

(35)   There is an x such that (Ralph believes that x is not a spy).

– on the grounds that Ortcutt exists. Yet, unknown to Ralph,

(36)   The MBH = Ortcutt.

Now (32) says that Ralph believes, of someone, that he is a spy. This man is the MBH, otherwise known as Ortcutt. Thus, concerning Ortcutt, Ralph believes him to be a spy. But, by exactly parallel reasoning, concerning Ortcutt, Ralph believes him *not* to be a spy. What is Ralph's attitude towards this man? For Ralph, of course, it depends on how he is thinking of that man; thinking of him as MBH, he thinks him to be a spy; thinking of him as Ortcutt, he thinks him not to be a spy. But what about for *us*? Obviously Ralph's attitude towards that man does not depend on how *we* are thinking of that man. Concerning Ortcutt, does Ralph believe him to be a spy, or not?

Having appreciated Frege's lesson of the Morning Star, it is plausible to say: both. We are not charging Ralph with inconsistency or irrationality, as if we were saying of a proposition P that he believes that P and that he believes that not-P. The idea is that in (30), the term we employ inside the scope of 'believes' must reflect Ralph's way of thinking of Ortcutt, i.e. he is thinking of him *as the MBH*. Likewise in (34), except that he is thinking of him *as Ortcutt*. In (30) and (34), the position occupied by 'the MBH' is referentially opaque, not open to substitution by co-referentials. The context 'Ralph believes that __ is a spy' depends for its applicability on something other than simply the object referred to by whatever singular term we insert into the blank. It is not, as we might put it, simply about the object.

In (31), by contrast, 'the MBH' need not perform any such function: the position occupied by 'the MBH' is fully and transparently referential, open to substitution by co-referring singular terms (such as 'Ortcutt'). The operation of exportation on (30) to yield (31) is a transition from a *de dicto* construction to a *de re* one; (32), meanwhile, explicitly purports to tell us that *there is* a certain object that satisfies that predicate.

The epistemological significance of the *de re/de dicto* distinction is manifold but there are two phenomena that stand out.

(i)   **The indispensably of the de re.** Russell once suggested the example 'I thought your yacht was longer than it is'. Let A be the yacht in question. Obviously what Russell is saying about his own beliefs at a certain time in the past cannot represented like this:

(37)   Bertrand believes that A is longer than A.

He does not profess to have believed an explicit contradiction. What we want to say is not that Bertrand thought that the length of A is longer than the length of A, but rather that *there is* a length, such that Bertrand believes that the length of A is greater than *it*. We must export material from inside the scope of 'believes that' to outside its scope:

> (38)   There is an x, and there is a y, such that (x = the length of A & y is greater than x & Bertrand believes that y is the length of A).

That is, in order to describe Bertrand's mistake, we have to quantify from outside into the scope of 'believes'; the *de re* approach is mandatory.

(ii)   ***A further restriction on exportation.*** Suppose Ralph's friend Leo has, unlike Ralph, no reason whatsoever to suspect anyone of being a spy. Still he has reason to believe that the two most vertically challenged spies are not exactly the same height; and suppose he's right on that score. So apparently we must accept:

> (39)   Leo believes that the shortest spy is a spy.

Since the shortest spy exists, we may apply exportation to (39), to yield:

> (40)   The shortest spy is such that Leo believes that he is a spy.

And then we may quantify on 'the shortest spy' in (40):

> (41)   There is an x such that (Leo believes that x is a spy).

But something has gone wrong; for (41) appears to have Leo suspecting someone of being a spy, which we explicitly said is not the case. Again, the inference from (40) to (41) is watertight: it's merely of the form 'B is thus and so' to 'There is something that is thus and so'.

The problem must be with the exportation step from (39) to (40). Merely having a *de dicto* belief appears not to be sufficient for having the corresponding *de re* belief; belief that a proposition containing a denoting, descriptive singular term is true is not sufficient for having a belief *about the thing* denoted by the singular term. It is not sufficient for having a belief with respect to a singular proposition involving that object. So exportation – the transition from the *de dicto* to the *de re* – requires something more than we have so far recognised.

It's natural to say that the problem with Leo and the shortest spy is that Leo doesn't *know who* the shortest spy is; if a premise were added to the effect he does know who the shortest spy is, then surely (40) would be forthcoming. That thought has been famously sharpened, refined and elaborated on by David Kaplan. We'll just say enough to get a taste. Kaplan puts the thought by saying that the inference requires the term subjected to exportation – 'the shortest spy' in (39) – should put the subject of the belief – Leo – into a position of being epistemically *en rapport* with the object of belief (the object to which the *de re* statement purports to relate the believer). The key is Kaplan's notion of a *'vivid designator'* – a singular term that is an element of a person's inner story; it is a 'conglomeration' of mental images, partial descriptions, and ordinary names, which, *if* the object exists, serves to bring the object to a given person's mind; even if the object does not exist, it is from the subject's point of view *as if* it did. Vivacity is what is known in the philosophy of mind as an *internal* phenomenon: a vivid name need not have a referent, and one may be mistaken as to the truth-value of identity statements, even when both sides of the statement are vivid.

The crucial thing is that if a given person thinks in terms of a vivid designator, *and* if there exists an object such that the designator is suitably related to the object for the believer, then, as Kaplan puts it, the designator *represents* the object *to* the believer. In such a case, exportation is allowed. In the non-vivid case – terms such as 'the shortest spy' which are not directly referential – the term expresses a certain conceptual halo which might be sufficient to contribute to certain beliefs, but which do not sustain exportation.

• 7 BELIEF ATTRIBUTIONS AND EXPLICIT INDEXICALS; BELIEF *DE SE*

Suppose at a cocktail party Jones gestures toward Brown, who is across the room, and indulges in the following bit of gossip:

(42) The president of the university believes that he's a charlatan.

How are we to interpret Jones's utterance? On Frege's scheme, strictly speaking, we require the sense that *the president* uses to pick out Brown, *not* the sense Jones uses to pick out Brown. Yet (42) gives us no clue as to what sense that is. Moreover, it seems plain – if uses of indexicals do express senses – that 'he' expresses the sense employed by Jones, rather than the president's employment of a sense to pick out Jones.

The problem is exacerbated if Jones generalises his remark about the infamous Brown:

(43) Everyone in the university believes that he is a charlatan.

Jones surely uses 'he' to refer to Brown, and it seems that a Fregean must agree that the indexical expresses the sense that Jones expresses, not somehow all the various senses employed by members of the university to pick out Brown.

In Chapter 5, Section 6, we pointed out that indexicals are not just referring devices; they also can serve to locate *oneself* in space and time in a peculiar and ineliminable way. Looking at a map, one sometimes wants to know where *here* is; looking a calendar, one sometimes wants to know which day it is *now*, or which day is *today*. Mere descriptions couched in terms of general concepts can never scratch that itch. Such was the lesson of what Perry calls the essential indexical. The matter crystallises around the use of first-person pronouns – 'I', 'me', 'myself'. For example, if I find during a performance of classical music that the F's phone is ringing, it is a minor irritation compared with my panic and embarrassment if I learn that the F is *me*. This issue crops up in such a sentence as the following; imagine as before that Jones is the speaker:

>   (44)   The president of the university believes that I am a charlatan.

Such self-ascribing beliefs are called beliefs *de se*. Jones is now complaining that the president takes a dim view of Jones himself, not of Brown. Again, the indexical pronoun 'I' cannot express the *president's* sense in which *he* thinks of Jones. 'I' expresses Jones' own way of thinking of Jones, of himself. It *seems* therefore that the corresponding proposition – what Jones expresses by 'I am a charlatan' – is available to, is thinkable by, only Jones himself, not the president.

We could try to analyse the speech act involving (42) in terms of Kaplan's scheme, using an existential quantification combined with the indexical:

>   (45)   At the envisaged context, the referent of 'he' = Brown, and there is a
>   vivid name y, which represents Brown to the president, and the pres-
>   ident believes the proposition expressed by 'y is a charlatan'.[1]

Something along those lines; similarly for (43) and (44). But there are other approaches to the problem; we shall investigate one.

• 8 AN IMPLICIT INDEXICAL ELEMENT?

We pointed out in Chaper 5 that the direct referential view of proper names – associated with Kripke – amounts to simply denying the considerations that brought Frege to posit sense in the first place. For if proper names are directly referential, if they have denotation but not connotation, then it remains a puzzle how to explain situations like this:

>   (46)   Alice believes that Marilyn Monroe is a famous actress.
>   (47)   Alice believes that Norma Jean Baker is not a famous actress.
>   (48)   Marilyn Monroe = Norma Jean Baker.

For on the direct reference view, the singular terms 'Marilyn Monroe' and 'Norma Jean Baker' are synonymous; therefore Alice believes a proposition and its negation, which is apparently irrational on the part of Alice; but surely the situation represent by (46)–(48) can happen without irrationality. Whereas on Frege's view, 'Marilyn Monroe' and 'Norma Jean Baker' express different senses, so no such contradiction is imputed to Alice.

But there is a powerful reason for doubting that the Fregean line is satisfactory. Suppose you hear a little about Paderewski – that he was the second prime minister of Poland.[2] Then later, you catch a glimpse of a pianist in the film *Moonlight Sonata*, who is also called Paderewski. It never occurs to you that these are the same man; but they are: one man, one name. Since there is just one name, then on Frege's view it can hardly help having one sense. So it seems that you accept a proposition – that

Paderewski is a politician – and its negation – that Paderewski is not a politician. *It's crucial to note that this problem is independent of the thesis of direct reference*: however the term 'Paderewski' is explained – as Fregean or Kripkean – it appears that you accept that Paderewski is a politician and that you accept that Paderewski is not a politician. It looks like you accept a logical contradiction. Yet the mistake you make is surely a mere factual mistake, not a failure of rationality.

Frege does have a sneaky dodge: perhaps, *in your idiolect*, there is not one name 'Paderewski' but two, corresponding to what you think are two men. But the sort of phenomenon observed in the Paderewski tale is capable of occurring almost anywhere. It is usually at least *conceivable*, if not at all likely, that what you had assumed to be a single self-same object or type of object are in fact two, or even more than two. Maybe what you thought of as your left hand is in fact a sequence of entities, one for each day, created by evil scientists; you could name them 'my left hand$_1$', 'my left hand$_2$', ... Maybe your left hand$_1$ ≠ your left hand$_2$. Since you can't *absolutely* rule out such possibilities, though they are vanishingly unlikely, it seems that they not the sort of things to be decided by semantical decree, by stipulation – in particular, they are not *analytic*, as pointed out by Kripke. And some cases are not so unlikely. Suppose you look out your window and see, from the side, the front of a limo; then you look through another window on the same wall, seeing, from the same side, the back of a limo. You wonder – quite reasonably given the various lengths of stretch limos – 'Is that limo that limo?'

The singular terms in this case are not proper names or natural kind terms but indexicals; in particular, they are different occurrences of the same demonstrative, each with a different accompanying demonstration – an act, perhaps only implicit or intended, of pointing out of each window. But we pointed out in Chapter 4 that Putnam quite plausibly thinks that natural kind terms such as 'water' contain a tacit or hidden *indexical* element. Until to the nineteenth century what people were calling 'jade' was discovered to be two distinct minerals, now called by mineralogists 'jadeite' and 'nephrite'. Each such case can be made sense of by making explicit the hidden indexical or demonstrative: *this* (pointing at a sample ordinarily called jade) versus *that* (pointing at another).

In view of such cases, it looks as if, were we to hang on to Frege's conception of language, we would have to maintain that what we vaguely call 'English' is really a vast assemblage of idiolects, each exquisitely complex and fine-grained. But to give up on this is at least partly to renounce one of the principal aims of Frege's theory: the theory was to lay bare the common, public structure underlying the surface hubbub of speech.

• 9 A PRAGMATIC PICTURE

The foregoing paragraphs suggest that the subject of the propositional attitudes is not intertwined with semantics in the way one might think upon reading Frege ('the

Morning Star' and 'the Evening Star' are very far from being typical proper names!). Cognitive attitudes do not divide up exactly along the lines laid down by language. Of course, cases such as jadeite and nephrite, Padewerski, and the limo in the window, are rare, and no surprise: language, among other things, serves the purposes of communication, and it would merely impede that purpose if you required a separate name for each portion of stuff conventionally called by a natural kind term you've encountered, just on the off chance they are distinct substances. So far as semantics is concerned, it's a sensible policy that if it walks and quacks like a duck, then, until reasons emerge to the contrary, it is a duck.

Nathan Salmon has proposed the following. The semantic or informational value of a proper name, natural kind term or indexical is nothing more than its referent; such is his Millianism, the direct reference view that proper names and indexicals refer without expressing descriptive content. But many sorts of properties tend to get *defeasably* attached to the term, in such a way that for many purposes, the *illusion* is created that they are attached still more intimately to the term – that they are attached to it as a matter of the very meaning, what Frege calls the sense of the term.

Suppose the story is real, in the case of 'Superman' and 'Clark Kent'. According to Salmon's view, the information-value of the two names, the semantic content of the two, is identical. Nevertheless, when Lois Lane hears 'Superman is here!' how she responds is different from how she responds when she hears 'Clark Kent is here!' In particular, Lois *grasps* this proposition in different *guises* – grasped in one guise, she is disposed to assent to 'Superman is here', and grasped in another guise, she's disposed to *dissent* from 'Clark Kent is here', despite that fact that the two statements are statements of the very same proposition.

The key point is that the different guises under which Lois grasps the proposition are not part of the semantics of the names 'Superman' and 'Clark Kent'. The guises are not a part of the meaning of the statements *Superman is here* or *Clark Kent is here*. Instead, they are cognitive or psychological features *in Lois* that need not show up in an arbitrary person's use of the crucial terms 'Superman' and 'Clark Kent' – not even if the person is fully competent in using the terms. A person who knows all about Clark Kent's identity with Superman might understand the terms as interchangeable (or if that strikes you as wrong, use another example, such as 'Mark Twain' and 'Samuel Clemens', 'Sean Combs' and 'P Diddy', or of someone's calling a boy by his middle name on some occasions and other times by his first name).

Let us now apply this way of thinking to sentences that explicitly contain propositional attitude terms. The crucial thing is that in Salmon's theory, guises must appear in an analysis of the attitudes, of belief sentences. If Lois, for example, believes that Superman is here, then there is a guise and a proposition such that Lois stands in certain cognitive relation to the proposition under that guise; we call this relation 'BEL', which is just a more articulate version of the ordinary belief relation. Generalising, and understanding 'p' as indicating a proposition and 'g' as indicating a guise:

> *A believes p* if and only if: There is a *g* such that [A grasps *p* by means of *g* & A stands in the BEL-relation to *p* under *g*]

Suppose as before that 'Superman is here' and 'Clark Kent is here' express the same proposition – call the proposition 'P' – but are associated by Lois with different guises; then we have the following:

> Lois grasps P by means of 'Superman is here' & Lois stands in the BEL-relation to P under the guise she associates with 'Superman is here'.

> Lois grasps not-P by means of 'Clark Kent is not here' and Lois stands in the BEL-relation to not-P under the guise she associates with 'Clark Kent is not here'.[3]

Thus, Lois comes out as believing a proposition P and also its negation not-P: she believes that Superman is here, but also that Superman is not here. She would, of course, deny that she has such a belief as the latter, *expressed in those words*. But just because one dissents from a sentence doesn't prove that one doesn't believe the proposition it expresses. She is not thereby characterised as *irrational*; that charge would stick only if she both believed and disbelieved a proposition under the *same guise*, which is not the case. The same goes in other cases; one might reasonably dissent from the sentence 'Mark Twain is Samuel Clemens' yet believing the proposition all the same: the proposition is just of the form $a = a$, but the guise under which one grasps it in denying it is of the form $a = b$.

We saw in Chapter 6 that Grice offered an explanation as to why certain sentences are semantically correct but pragmatically improper, such as 'If Paris is in Germany then Paris is in Morocco': according to the classical truth-functional account of conditionals, that sentence is true, but the statement made by it, normally, is drastically misleading. Similarly, Lois Lane believes that Superman is Clark Kent, or, in the above situation, that Clark Kent is here, but it would be pragmatically improper to say it in those words. Guises, as it were, take up the cognitive slack left on the ground by the semantic properties of expressions. Salmon, of course, allows that normally we do endeavour, in ascribing propositional attitudes, to convey something of the subject's point of view; we often try to use the same or similar words that the subject would assent to in characterising his or her attitude. But still this is a matter of what Salmon calls 'pragmatically imparted information'; it remains the case that it is possible to characterise anomalies such as Lois' while maintaining that proper names are directly referential, and do not express Fregean senses.

• HISTORICAL NOTES

After the Second World War, interest in the propositional attitudes picked up dramatically, and shows no signs of petering out after 65 years. Frege and Russell set the table long before the war, but it was Rudolf Carnap and Alonzo Church working broadly in a Fregean framework in the late 1940s and the 1950s, that really got the subject up and running. Carnap came out with *Meaning and Necessity* in 1947 (Carnap 1956), then Church with his 'A Formulation of the Logic of Sense and Denotation' of 1951 and 'Intensional Isomorphism and Identity of Belief' of 1954. Then came Quine's 1955 paper 'Quantifiers and Propositional Attitudes' (in Quine 1975), according to which Fregean referential opacity cannot be all there is to the attitudes – the attitude cannot be *merely* a relation between a subject and a Fregean proposition – because quantification into the scope of a propositional attitude verb seems ordinarily to make sense. Quine ultimately decided against ordinary common sense, but many people took up his challenge, including Kaplan, who published his landmark paper 'Quantifying In' in 1968 (see Kaplan 1969). The 1970s saw a move away from Frege and towards Millianism or direct reference theory; Kaplan moved that way in later papers, and Kripke published 'A Puzzle About Belief' in 1979, in which he makes the case that, even aside from issues over quantification, Fregean semantics is not nearly so good as one might have thought in coping with belief-puzzles. Nathan Salmon published his *Frege's Puzzle* in 1986; it was one of several attempts to combine an approach to the propositional attitudes with direct reference; others in recent years have included Mark Richard and Scott Soames. Another stream that we haven't space for is the 'paratactic' approach of Donald Davidson, according to which sentences ascribing attitudes do not indicate relations between a subject and a proposition, but between a subject and a token of a sentence supplied by the ascriber.

• CHAPTER SUMMARY

In Frege's scheme, expressions appearing in hyper-intensional contexts do not refer to their customary referents, but to their customary senses: 'Venus' in 'Venus is a planet' refers to the planet Venus, but in 'Bob believes that Venus is a planet', 'Venus' refers to the sense of the term 'Venus', not to its referent, not to Venus. This explains why 'Le Verrier believed that Vulcan orbits the sun' can be true although 'Vulcan' has no referent. And it explains the apparent consistency of 'Bob believes that Venus is a planet' and 'Bob does not believe that the Morning Star is a planet'. Hyper-intensional contexts are referentially opaque, meaning that substitution of co-referential expressions within such contexts is blocked. These phenomena can be reiterated endlessly: we have hyper-intensional contexts, hyper-intensional contexts within hyper-intensional contexts, hyper-intensional contexts within hyper-intensional contexts within hyper-intensional contexts, and so on, as in 'Jim believes that Bill believes that Fred believes that p'.

Unlike hyper-intensional contexts, intensional contexts *de dicto* do not require sameness of sense for substitution; they require only the preservation of the modal characteristics of the expression being substituted for. '1 + 1' can be substituted for '2' in the *de dicto* 'Necessarily, 2 < 3', but not the co-referential 'The number of Martian moons'. Full referential transparency is characteristic of *de re* necessity – such as 'The number of Martian moons is such that necessarily it < 3'; such statements are implied by but do not imply the corresponding *de dicto* statements of necessity. The step from the *de dicto* to the *de re* is called 'exportation'.

At first blush, exportation in propositional attitude sentences also seems valid, so long as the term subject to exportation succeeds in referring. If *a* is a referring singular term, then 'Bob believes that *Fa*' seems to imply '*a* is such that Bob believes it to be *F*'. This seems to hold, even if there is another singular *b* such that *b* = *a*, and Bob believes that not-*Fb*; for then *b* is such that Bob believes it to be not-*F*, in which case *a* is such that Bob believes it to be not-*F*. A certain object is such that Bob both believes it to be *F* and believes it not to be *F*; no irrationality is ascribed to Bob in the way it would if, for example, we charged Bob with believing *Fa* and believing not-*Fa*.

However, exportation seems to require more. For sentences like 'Ralph believes that the shortest spy is a spy', even where the shortest spy exists, do not seem to sustain exportation. A common suggestion is that what is missing in such a case is that Ralph must know who the shortest spy is in order for exportation to go through. David Kaplan suggests a lucid formalisation of the idea, requiring that the term subjected to exportation be a *vivid designator*; such designators are like rigid designators in that they sustain exportation and the converse, importation, but unlike them in being subjective, i.e. whether or not a designator is vivid potentially varies from person to person.

The broadly Fregean picture explored so far comes under severe strain from considerations involving indexicals and demonstratives. Certain propositional attitude sentences explicitly contain indexicals, as in Jones' statement 'The president of the university believes that I am a charlatan'. We learned from John Perry that such *de se* statements are not epistemically equivalent to any statement free of the first-person pronoun, yet 'I am a charlatan' as used in the statement does not express a proposition available to the president of the university. Furthermore, it appears that a Frege-type puzzle can be generated for any object of reference, e.g. if one speaks somewhat slowly, one could conceivably wonder whether 'that sun = that sun', where the statement is in fact true, and the first occurrence of 'that sun' is accompanied by a different demonstration from the one accompanying the second. It thus appears that the propositional attitudes do not map onto the contours of language as straightforwardly as one may have thought upon reading Frege. The attitudes are potentially much finer, and the cognitive states they involve more various, than what can be expressed in language without indexicals.

Nathan Salmon allows the free substitution of co-referring proper names within the scope of operators of propositional attitudes. Since he regards proper names as directly referential, for example 'Hesperus' and 'Phosphorus' are interchangeable in propositional attitude contexts, the account of propositional attitudes becomes part of the philosophy of mind; one does not merely believe a proposition, but one believes it under some guise, where the make-up of such guises is ultimately a matter for the philosophy of mind. We do communicate information about guises, which in standard cases align with the theory of Fregean senses, with the crucial difference that the information is only pragmatically imparted, implicated in the manner of Grice, and is not part of the semantics of the terms. Since Lois believes that Superman is brave, she therefore believes that Clark Kent is brave, even if she sincerely asserts that Clark Kent is not brave.

• STUDY QUESTIONS

1 Consider:

Hob thinks a witch has blighted Bob's mare, and Nob wonders whether she (the same witch) killed Cob's sow.

The sentence can be true, even though there are no witches. How can this be made sense of? How can the apparent connection between Hob and Nob be reconstructed when the thing that would tie them together doesn't exist? (The example is taken from Geach 1967).

2 Could a brain-in-a-vat have precisely the same beliefs as you on Fregean semantics? Would typical beliefs such as that *the cat is hungry* be false, or neither-true-nor-false, or would a brain-in-a-vat be incapable of such beliefs?

3 A likely condition for expressions being synonymous – for their expressing the same sense – is that they be interchangeable in *all* contexts (save quotation). But now take any two synonymous expressions, say 'to buy' and 'to purchase'. Consider:

    (a) Nobody doubts that whoever believes that x buys a hot dog, believes that x buys a hot dog.

This and the proposed condition of synonymy jointly entail that

    (b) Nobody doubts that whoever believes that x buys a hot dog, believes that x purchases a hot dog.

Is that correct? Does (b) express *exactly the same* proposition as (a)? (The example is taken from Mates 1952)

4 In this book, we have been blithely assuming that, for example,

    (a)   that the cat is white

means

    (b)   the sense of 'the cat is white'.

But maybe this is a mistake. For surely, *translation* is a matter of preserving sense. A French translation of (a) would be:

    (c)   que le chat est blanc

(b) would be

    (d)   le sens du «the cat is white»

For (b) pertains to a particular English sentence; it contains a mode of presentation of that sentence. Therefore, since sense determines reference, a translation must preserve reference to that sentence. So (d) is synonymous with (b), but not with (a). So (b) is not synonymous with (a). But if (b) is not strictly equivalent to (a), what is? Nothing? Or is there some flaw in the argument we've just been through?

5 Are the guises in Salmon's theory just Fregean senses by another name?

• PRIMARY READING

Kripke, S. (1979) 'A Puzzle About Belief', in *Meaning in Use*, (ed.) A. Margalit (Dordrecht: Reidel).
Salmon, N. (1986, 1991) *Frege's Puzzle* (Atascadero, CA: Ridgeview)

More difficult:

Kaplan, D. (1969) 'Quantifying In', in D. Davidson and G. Harman (eds) *Word and Objections: Essays on the Work of W. V. Quine* (Dordrecht: Reidel).
Quine, W. V. (1975) 'Quantifiers and Propositional Attitudes', revised edition, in his *Ways of Paradox* (Cambridge, MA: Harvard University Press).

• NOTES

1 I have quantified into the quotation marks, which is strictly speaking nonsense. But I think a correct presentation of the view, in this context, would be too tedious.
2 The example is adapted from Kripke 1979.
3 I'm pretending that guises are simply sentences.

8
davidson's philosophy of language

The work of Donald Davidson (1917–2003) was largely inspired by Quine, the subject of Chapter 9. Quine propounds a form of naturalism, and is a noted sceptic about the concept of meaning employed by Frege, Russell and others; he proposes an alternative conception of what having language amounts to that does not assume the concept of meaning. Davidson agrees with Quine that linguistic phenomena should be investigated without making the sorts of presuppositions found in Frege and Russell. And he agrees that *if* it possible to theorise fruitfully about meaning, then the concept must be explained as empirically answerable, applicable to language-users from a third-person point of view. But he is more optimistic than Quine; he is, at any rate, much less inclined to say that if the theory of meaning cannot take its place among the hard sciences, then so much the worse for it. He thinks, roughly, that it is undeniable that meaning is something we *know* about, and thus that it must be possible to give a systematic description of what we know. And he is encouraged in this thought by his rather remarkable success in showing how a theory of meaning *can* be made into something empirically answerable, in a way that Frege and Russell hardly stopped to consider. Davidson wrote after Quine did and was influenced by him, but because his positive views do not depart so radically from the mainstream as Quine's, we will consider him first, before we consider Quine.

1 METHODOLOGY

Davidson's key concept is the idea of a *theory of meaning for L*, which is a theory that states all the semantic facts about a given natural language L, such as Portuguese: ideally, for each meaningful expression of L, such as a sentence, the theory states its meaning, in the sense of *entailing a theorem* that states its meaning. The language that the theory of meaning is *about* is called the 'object language', and the language that we *use* to state the theory is called the 'metalanguage'. Such a theory, it is worth stressing, is an *empirical* theory, since it seeks to describe a contingent phenomenon such as Portuguese. Davidson's primary methodological ideas are that if (i) we can say what a theory of meaning for L would be like for *variable L* – any language L you like to take – we thereby know the shape or form of a theory of meaning, and (ii) if we can say how, in general, such theories are to be confirmed 'in the field', then we have said what there is to say philosophically about meaning-in-general. General philosophical knowledge about meaning – an explication of concept of meaning – can thus be summed up by describing (i) the form of a theory of meaning, and (ii) how such a theory is confirmed.

Unlike other sorts of phenomena such as gravity or respiration, meaning is essentially something *known*, in the following sense: the meaning of every meaningful linguistic expression is (or has been) known to someone, or is logically entailed by something that is or has been known to someone. But a theory of meaning, for a particular language such as a linguistic theorist might devise it, will likely be a rather technical beast, using lexical concepts and so on of which the typical speaker of a language has no inkling. So Davidson envisages the relation between theories of meaning and commonsense knowledge of actual speakers in the following way: an ordinary speaker cannot normally *explicitly state* a theory of meaning for the language he speaks, but it is plausible to think of a theory of meaning as making explicit what the ordinary speaker *implicitly* knows. A theory of meaning, that is to say, *describes* what it is that an ordinary speaker implicitly knows.

• 2 THE GENERAL FORM OF A THEORY OF MEANING

(A) Compositionality

What would such a theory look like? First, such a theory must be *compositional*: it must, that is, show how the meaning of a sentence is determined by the meanings of its parts. Consider a speaker who knows the language L, in whatever sense it is that a speaker knows a language. Ignoring sentences that are too long or complicated, such a speaker understands each sentence of L, in the sense that if presented with it, he will know what it means. Beyond a certain point, sentences will be too long for the speaker to understand; so the set of sentences that the speaker would actually understand is finite. Nevertheless, it seems undeniable that the finiteness of this set is due only, so to speak, to limitations in the hardware, and not to limitations in the programme. Where a sentence is simply too long for a given speaker to understand, the problem is not that the speaker does not (implicitly) know the principles that determine the meaning of the sentence, but that he is unable to apply them correctly.

To take a simple example, we all grasp the principle that determines the meaning of 'the father of X' for any singular term put for X. But X may itself be of the form 'the father of...'; so we get the singular terms 'the father of the father of X', and 'the father of the father of the father of X', and so on. This reflexive behaviour – of the device accepting as inputs its own outputs – is what is known as **recursion.** From this device we can get sentences of arbitrary length, for example of the form 'The father of X was fat'. Beyond a certain point, we will be unable to interpret them, because we will become confused, sleepy, or dead. Still, we do grasp principles that would enable us to understand them, if we were not contingently limited in the ways that we are.

The demand for compositionality also emerges in another way. Knowing what a sentence means, in the sense in which a speaker knows the meanings of sentences of his own language, is more than simply knowing *that* s *means that* p, for some s and p. For example, one might know that 'La neige est blanche' means that snow is white without *understanding* the French sentence (imagine being told that a certain sequence of Laotian symbols means that snow is white; do you thereby *understand* the sentence of Lao?) In order to understand it, one has not only to know what its meaning happens to be, but also what its constituent words mean, and how its meaning what it does depends on the meaning of those words and the way it is constructed from them. Understanding, hence knowledge of meaning in the sense we have in mind, is essentially compositional.

Linguists sometimes put the point by saying that an account of meaning must show how the capacity for linguistic competence, at least considered in the abstract, is *generative*, or *productive*. Frege himself stressed that the linguistic capacity is a *creative* capacity.

A theory of meaning, then, must take the following form: first, it assigns meanings to the simple (non-composite) expressions of the language (of which there will be only finitely many). Second, it states principles that determine, for a given grammatically correct way of combining meaningful expressions, the meaning of the composite expression.

(B) A wrong path

Following this lead, we might suppose that for each simple or complex expression *e* of the object language, the theory will entail a theorem which says:

> The meaning of *e* is ….

where the place of '…' is taken by a singular term that names an object, i.e. a meaning. This seems perfectly natural. The theory would take the form of a *recursive assignment of meanings to expressions*.

However, it will not quite work that way, as will emerge if we ask; what are these meanings? What *sorts* of entities get assigned to the simple and complex items? According to Frege, we can distinguish sense from reference. So it might seem that since the sense of an expression is what is understood by it, a Davidsonian theory of meaning should assign *senses* to both simple and complex expressions. If we now ask how exactly this would work, we run into trouble right away. Senses, in Frege's scheme, are special sorts of entities. The sense, for example, of 'Theaetatus' is such an entity. But what *is* this entity? We cannot literally say 'The sense of "Theaetetus" is the man who…', where 'the man who…' is some description such as might be taken to *express* the sense of the name. For such a sentence says that the sense of the name is a certain *man*, which is absurd. All we can really say, by way of *naming* the sense of 'Theaetatus', is that it is the sense of 'Theaetatus'. So we are told: the sense of 'Theaetatus' is the sense of 'Theaetatus'. This is completely uninformative; it is merely an instance of the law of identity, i.e. that x = x.

In addition, an explicitly Fregean approach will leave us with saying something like 'The sense of "Theataetus flies" is composed of the sense of "Theaetatus" and the sense of "flies"'. What is meant here by 'composed'? Clearly, *this does not actually tell us the meaning of the sentence, because it does not enable us to understand it, how to interpret it*: merely being told what entities go to make up the meaning of a sentence is not sufficient for being told the meaning of the sentence. For a theory of meaning requires more than a *list* of entities; we need to know the way the entities go together. Especially striking is the case of relational sentences such as 'Socrates taught Plato'; to be told that the meaning comprises the meanings of the three expressions does not distinguish the meaning of 'Socrates taught Plato' from that of 'Plato taught Socrates'.

It is also worth saying that, for example, a monolingual French speaker ought to be able to gain explicit knowledge of his or her language, by having a theory of meaning *expressed* in French that is *about French itself*. And if such a theory were translated, say into English, it ought to tell the English speaker about the semantics of French – in exactly the same way that knowledge of the theory of general relativity can be translated from French into English. But this is blocked under the present proposal: an English translation of the French theory about French will include such sentences as 'The sense of "boire" is the sense of "boire"', which does not tell an English-only speaker the meaning of the French word.

(C) Davidson's way: T-sentences

Davidson's way forward is to *reject* the idea that the meaning of a sentence should itself be an entity of some kind. That is, we should stop looking for a singular term to fill the blank of

> The meaning of *e* is ___

Instead, as a first step towards Davidson's actual proposal, consider the following:

> *s* means that *p*

Earlier we assumed that 'that p' is a singular term referring to the proposition expressed by 'p'. But we do not have to look at it that way: we could think of 'means that' as an expression that joins a name of a sentence with a sentence to form a new sentence. Thus if s is a sentence of the object language under study, then the place of 'p' will be taken by a sentence of the metalanguage, the language we are using to describe that language. An example might be

'Le neige est blanche' means that snow is white.

– if the object language were French.

Remember the task was to make a theory that would tell us, for an arbitrary sentence of the language, what it means. Would a theory that entailed theorems of the above form do the trick? It looks as if it would, but a very large problem confronts the attempt to devise such a theory. The problem is that the theory would be *using* the expression 'means that'. If we have a true sentence of the form 's means that p', the result of replacing p by another sentence q of the same truth-value need not result in a sentence 's means that q' with the same truth value as 's means that p'. In a word, the place occupied by 'p' in such sentences is *non-extensional* – in fact it is not intensional but *hyper-intensional*, in the language of the last chapter. It is unlike the case, say, of 'p and q', where we can replace the sentence q with any sentence r of the same-truth value as q, and the result will have the same truth-value as 'p and q'. What this means is that it is not clear from what statements a statement of the form 's means that p' follows, and it is not clear what statements follow from a statement of that form (unlike the case of extensional forms such as 'p and q'). Therefore, it is unclear how our knowledge of meaning could be explained in terms of a theory of meaning that uses precisely that form of words. *It seems that we would be explaining the concept of meaning only by presupposing the concept of meaning.*

What we really want, according to Davidson, is a theory of meaning that avoids non-extensional notions such as 'means that'. We want a theory which tells us something *like*

'La neige est blanche' means that snow is white.

– that is, we want it to yield statements which somehow enable us to interpret a *named* sentence of the object-language by means of a sentence of the metalanguage, a sentence that is *used*, as 'snow is white' is used in the above. But we want to do it in a way that is purely *extensional*, so that we clearly understand the logic of what we are doing.

Davidson's proposal is that we can do this by using the predicate 'is true'. Consider the following:

'La neige est blanche' is true iff snow is white.

Such a sentence, following Alfred Tarski, is called a 'T-sentence'. Generalised, the suggestion now is that the theory should entail a T-sentence of the form

> *s* is true iff *p*

for each sentence *s* of the object language. The connective 'iff' – 'if and only if' – is certainly extensional, so its logic and meaning are clear (it has a complete truth-table). Furthermore, the predicate 'is true' is extensional: from '*s* is true' and '*s* = *s**', we can validly infer '*s** is true'.

A T-sentence can plausibly be regarded as stating the *truth-condition* of a sentence. According to Frege, the sense of an expression is the condition under which something is the expression's referent. Since the referent (or extension) of a sentence is a truth-value, the sense of a sentence is the condition under which its referent is truth. So the sense of a sentence is its truth-condition. Therefore a T-sentence can plausibly be regarded as stating the sense of a sentence – its *meaning*, in the ordinary sense of 'meaning'.

Does 'Can plausibly be regarded' state the sense or meaning? Does it really? Does it literally tell us the meaning of a sentence, as '*s* means that *p*' does? No, it does not in itself. In fact, Davidson's claim is *not* that T-sentences directly state the meaning of each sentence of the object language. His claim is that a theory of truth for the language as a *whole* can be regarded as a theory of meaning for the language *as a whole*. This is Davidson's famous doctrine of *holism*. In order to see the basis of this claim, we need to look in more detail at (1) the structure of a theory of truth, and (2) the way in which a theory of truth for a language can be known to be correct.

• 3 THE EXACT FORM OF A THEORY OF MEANING

Since there are infinitely many well-formed sentences of a language, there are infinitely many T-sentences for that language. So if a theory of truth is to serve as a theory of meaning, and a theory of meaning must be something knowable, the theory must admit of being formulated as a finite set of statements. Here is an example of a theory of truth for a simple 'toy' language L, consisting only of atomic sentences and truth-functional combinations of those; the lesson here is actually easier to learn if our object-language is an imaginary language rather than a familiar one such as English or French, with all their forbidding complexity. (The terms 'S_1' and 'S_2' are used below in the metalanguage as *metalinguistic variables*.)

(A) Syntax

L consists of:

(a) Names: a, b.

(b) Predicates: Fα, Gα.

(c) Connectives: ♥, ∇.

(d) Sentences: The result of replacing all the Greek letters in an L-predicate with names is an atomic sentence of L. Every atomic sentence of L is a sentence of L. The result of prefixing a sentence L with '∇' is also a sentence of L. The result joining two sentences of L with '♥' is also a sentence of L. Nothing else is a sentence of L.

(B) Semantics

(a) The referent of 'a' = Socrates.
The referent of 'b' = Plato.

(b) For any x, x satisfies 'Fα' if x is wise.
For any x, x satisfies 'Gα' if x is a philosopher.

(c) Any atomic sentence of L is true if the referent of the name satisfies its predicate.

(d) Suppose that S_1 and S_2 are any sentences whatsoever of L. Then:

∇S_1 is true if S_1 is not true.
S_1 ♥ S_2 is B true if either S_1 is true or S_2 is true.

That's it.[1] Now let us see an example of how the theory entails T-sentences. Consider the L-sentence '∇Gb'. From clause 2d, we have:

(1) '∇Gb' is true if 'Gb' is not true.

By clause 2c, we have:

(2) 'Gb' is true if the referent of 'b' satisfies 'Gα'.

Since clause 2a tells us that referent of 'b' = Plato, we have from (2):

(3) 'Gb' is true if Plato satisfies 'Gα'.

So by clause 2b,

(4) 'Gb' is true if Plato is a philosopher.

Which is logically equivalent to

(5) 'Gb' is not true if Plato is not a philosopher.

So from (1) and (5), we derive:

(6) '∇Gb' is true if Plato is not a philosopher.

(6) is a T-sentence for the L-sentence 'Gb'. Obviously, the '∇' is a sign of negation (and the '♥' is a sign of disjunction). (1)–(6) constitute a *derivation* of a T-sentence *for* the language L, but the derivation is *carried out* in the metalanguage; in particular, we

use English to state and reason about the semantics of L. (1)–(6) *mention* sentences of L but do not *use* them. (6), a T-sentence for L, is of special interest: *It states the truth-condition of an L-sentence.* (6), along with the whole theory of meaning we have just given for L, states something that a speaker of L would be expected (implicitly) to *know*: the L-speaker may not speak English, but he does (implicitly) know what is stated by (6), just as he may know, without speaking English, the fact that is stated by 'The moon orbits the Earth'.

In similar fashion, our little theory of truth entails a T-sentence for every sentence of L, even though L, modest as it is, has infinitely many sentences. For more complicated languages, the truth-theory must be more complicated, but our example gets across the basic idea: a truth-theory assigns semantic properties (reference – we can think of satisfaction as the analogue for predicates of reference for names); and uses 'recursive' (repeatedly applicable clauses like 2c and 2d) to assign truth-conditions to sentences on the basis of those.

• 4 THE EMPIRICAL CONFIRMATION OF A THEORY OF MEANING: RADICAL INTERPRETATION

Our overarching task was to show how the theory of meaning can be empirically applicable in the third-person style. We've explained that such a theory is really an extensional theory of the truth-conditions of a language, and shown essentially how that works via a simple example. But we haven't seen how to devise and confirm such a theory; we've merely looked at a made-up one, true by virtue of stipulation.

So imagine you are a linguist exploring the Indonesian jungle, searching for previously unknown languages. You discover a previously unknown tribe whose language has never previously been identified or even heard by the outside world. Your task, as a **radical interpreter**, is to devise a correct Davidsonian theory of meaning for this language (a theory of truth for it). How do you do it? How do you begin, and how do you know whether or not the theory you come up with is correct (how is it empirically confirmed)?

You begin by hanging out with natives a little. What sorts of things do you watch out for? Suppose you notice that from time to time they make a certain sequence of sounds, 'Gav-a-gai' (the example is due to Quine). Looking out for what they could be talking about, you notice that they say it only when a rabbit appears. Next time a rabbit scuttles by, you try saying to one of the natives, in a questioning tone of voice, 'Gavagai?', without any idea of what sounds correlate to the words of the language. They smile and say 'Jai!' Now you try it when no rabbit is present; 'Nie!', they say.

You conjecture that 'Jai' is a sign of assent (like 'yes'), and 'Nie' a sign of dissent. You now write down, as a provisional hypothesis, that the following is a T-sentence for the language which you dub 'Nove':

'Gavagai' is true-in-Nove if a rabbit is present.

You do the same with other sentences. So far, you are assigning truth-conditions directly to sentences. But as you know, this piecemeal, sentence-by-sentence approach could never suffice for the semantics of the whole language. What you need is to assign meanings to sub-sentential sentences, with an eye towards formulating a *compositional* semantics, a truth-theory for the whole language.

How can you formulate hypotheses concerning sub-sentential expressions? Suppose you come across a sentence whose provisional T-sentence you formulate thus:

'Bavagai' is true-in-Jungle if a monkey is present.

Now you have a clue: surely 'agai' is an expression meaning something like 'a … is present', or 'there is a…', and 'Gav' means *rabbit*, and 'Bav' means *monkey*. Suppose in some similar way you come to interpret 'Bollo' as *snake*, and try saying 'Bollo-agai' when a snake is present; assent from the natives will tend to confirm these hypotheses.

In these and similar ways you work up a semantics for Nove. Now suppose that one day an *ape* enters the scene. A child of the tribe shouts 'Bavagai!' You now have two choices: you could suppose that 'Bav' means not *monkey* but *monkey-or-ape*; this would be plausible, since monkeys and apes are so similar. Or you could suppose that 'Bav' means monkey, but that the child falsely believes that the chimp is a monkey.

How do you decide which course to take? The two options, let us suppose, look *equally plausible*. You decide, let us say, on one of the two options. Proceeding on that basis, you might find that things run pretty smoothly. But eventually other, similar cases will arise, forcing you to choose between either revising an earlier interpretation or attributing a false belief to the native speaker. As interpreter it seems your position is this: given such a case, there will always be more than one way to accommodate the observations you make; accommodating the data one way might require you to revise earlier theoretical choices. According to Davidson, there is not going to be a rule for deciding each case *individually*; what you have to do, rather, is to look at the overall patterns you come up with that would accommodate the data, and decide which one fits it best.

This is Davidson's celebrated doctrine of *holism*, or *meaning* holism or *semantical* holism. The interpreter's task cannot be described as finding empirical confirmation for the interpretation of each *word* individually or each *sentence* individually, but finding the best *overall* fit between theory and evidence. Strictly speaking, it makes no sense to ask, 'is this interpretation of this word correct?'; we can only ask whether an entire theory of meaning is correct, is empirically confirmed. Of course, we do often ask such questions about particular words, but the fact that we can regard an answer to such a question as justified shows that we are always assuming a background interpretation of the language as a whole.

Lurking in the foregoing considerations is a more unsettling idea. It might be that whole patterns of attributions fit the data equally well; they look equally plausible. In that case you'll have multiple finished theories that seem individually to be empirically confirmed: you can use them to understand the natives, and you can use them to say things to them. Yet the two theories will disagree; they will depict the native language and beliefs differently. Indeed, if you recognise this possibility, then if you had just one empirically corroborated theory, you know that you *could have* made different choices along the way, and come up with a different theory that fits the data just as well.

Such is the *indeterminacy* of interpretation, which was preceded in a slightly different context by Quine's argument that translation is indeterminate. It is important to recognise that Davidson does not regard this as a limitation to his approach; he does not accept that his approach *falls short* of meaning, as if facts about meaning somehow elude the attempt of a radical interpreter. *There are no such facts outside the ken of a radical interpreter*. If there is one way to interpret a language-user, then there are bound to be other ways.

5 THE PRINCIPLE OF CHARITY AND THE INTERDEPENDENCE OF BELIEF AND MEANING

So far we have been a little bit vague about what it is to 'confirm' a theory of meaning, about what it is for such a theory to 'fit' the evidence, and what exactly the evidence *is*.

For Davidson, the principal evidence available to the radical interpreter will be manifestations of the native's *holding-true* a certain sentence in a certain circumstance. For example, the native manifests this attitude by *assenting* to the sentence as described above, or by asserting it (just as the interpreter must begin by guessing as to what manifests assent, he must also guess as to what kind of *utterances* of a sentence constitutes *asserting* it).

Roughly, what the interpreter is first looking for are correlations between the attitude of holding-true a sentence and observable circumstances. The interpreter finds, for example a correlation between holding-true a sentence and the circumstance that it is raining; he infers that the sentence is true if and only if it is raining.

What is most useful, then, are sentences whose truth-values *vary* depending on circumstance, such as 'Gavagai', or a sentence that means that it's raining. These are called **occasion sentences**. Their opposite, **standing sentences**, are not as useful; since natives will always hold-true a sentence that means that granite is heavier than wood, and granite always is heavier than wood, we cannot find correlations between varying dispositions to assent to the sentence and varying truth-values of the sentence.

In general, the attitude of holding-true a certain sentence is the product of two factors: the native *belief*, and the *meaning* of the sentence:

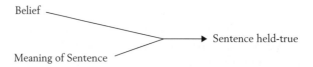

Figure 8.1 The two factors responsible for holding a sentence true

The native holds 'Gavagai' true in a certain circumstance because he believes that a rabbit is there, and 'Gavagai' means that a rabbit is present. But once in a while, the natives might have a false belief, thereby holding-true something that's false. Hence what Davidson calls the *interdependence of belief and meaning*: in fact, the role of the concept of belief is just to take up the inevitable slack between *holding*-true and *is* true. If it is false that P, but we wish to interpret a sentence that is held-true by a certain subject as meaning that P, then we may do so, provided that a *false belief* that P is ascribed to the subject.

And now it might occur to you: how do we know that this doesn't go on all the time? After all, we *could* make the interpretation of 'Gavagai' consistent with the data by assuming that the natives are always wrong about rabbits: perhaps they believe that a rabbit is present if and only if a rabbit is *not* present, and we interpret 'Gavagai' as 'No rabbit is present'. Or we could interpret 'Gavagai' as true if and only if the moon is on fire, and suppose them to believe that the moon is fire just when a rabbit is present. These hypotheses seem bizarre, but what rules them out?

What rules them out is that if such hypotheses are entertained, then *no* theory of meaning can be justified – or rather, *any* theory of meaning, any scheme of interpretation, could be made to accord with any set of evidence. In order to get started with an interpretation, and in order to sustain it, we *must* assume that the natives are usually correct, especially about relatively obvious things such as whether or not it is raining, whether or not that's a rabbit, and so on. Think of what goes on when a child learns a language. If the people around him or her were in the habit of speaking falsely as often as truly, the child could never guess the meanings of words, since there would be no observable correlation between what is said and what the child observes.

This is Davidson's celebrated **principle of charity**. Since no interpretation – hence no understanding – is possible except under the assumption that speakers generally have true beliefs, the discovery that speakers generally have false beliefs is impossible. In order to make such a discovery, we would have to interpret their language, which requires the assumption of true beliefs. Thus it is a methodological imperative that the subject being interpreted be assumed to have mostly true beliefs. In order to understand another creature, we must attribute beliefs to that creature that are mostly true; we must, that is, assume agreement between ourselves and the subject (compare this with Grice's maxims of cooperation, Chapter 6, Section 3).

At one time Davidson drew the more radical metaphysical conclusion that no language-using creature *could* be systematically wrong. For consider the conceivable possibility of an *omniscient* interpreter, 'The OI'. The OI would be able to interpret any creature (otherwise the OI would not be omniscient). But since the OI's beliefs are all true, and interpretation requires the principle of charity, the subject OI must attribute mostly true beliefs to the subject. Since the OI is omniscient, the OI cannot be wrong to do so. Therefore the subject's beliefs are mostly true.

This argument has been challenged. One might think that the OI would not have to use the principle of charity, since the OI, being omniscient, already knows what the subject's beliefs are. On the other hand, suppose we restrict the OI in such a way that it does not already know the subject's beliefs; it knows, say, only all those publicly observable facts that would be relevant to an ordinary interpreter. If interpretation requires charity, hence agreement between interpreter and subject, then perhaps the OI *could not* interpret the subject.

• HISTORICAL NOTES

Donald Davidson stresses in his intellectual biography that he was impressed early on by the idea that whatever meaning is, it has to be something public; it has to be something which, in principle, can be made available to an interpreter, or a child learning language. He thought a great deal before publishing, but once he came out with 'Theories of Meaning and Learnable Language' in 1965 (in Davidson 1984) and 'Truth and Meaning' in 1967 (see Primary reading, below), a series of papers came thick and fast, articulating the ramifications and applications of his view, and revising it as well. Almost immediately he attracted attention; Richard Rorty (1931–2007), Tyler Burge, John McDowell and Ernie Lepore are some well-known commentators. Davidson's theory of language has been extraordinary fertile, setting philosophers and linguists to work on finding ways to interpret within a Davidsonian theory of truth-conditions such recalcitrant beasts as adverbs, predicative adjectives, indexicals and demonstratives, tense, mood, causal statements, the propositional attitudes and more (Davidson himself provided at least the beginnings of the work on most of these subjects). He is equally prominent in the philosophy of mind, developing his view known as 'anomalist monism', according to which mental description is not reducible to physical description, but concerns the same (physical) objects.

• CHAPTER SUMMARY

Davidson approaches the phenomenon of meaning with two key requirements: a theory of meaning for a particular language L must, for each sentence of L, entail a theorem that in some sense states or displays its meaning; and we must explain how such a theory is empirically confirmed. If we succeed in describing such a theory in general – irrespective of the details of any particular L – we will have described meaning in general. Since the range of possible sentences constructible in a language is potentially infinite, such a theory must be compositional.

It is not possible, according to Davidson, for the theory simply to take the form of assigning *entities* to expressions, such as Fregean senses. Such a scheme inevitably is uninformative, as well as incapable of getting round the list problem. Instead, Davidson first considers the idea that a theory of meaning for a language should issue in true statements of the form '*s* means that *p*', for every sentence *s* of the language. The problem however is that such statements are hyper-intensional: they involve the term 'means that', and thus cannot be used in theory whose purpose is to illuminate meaning, without generating a circle. Davidson's proposal is that a theory of *truth* can be regarded as a theory of meaning: the aim should be to generate a true 'T-sentence' of the form '*s* is true if and only if *p*', where *s* is any sentence of the object language, and *p* is a sentence of the metalanguage. Tarski had already shown how to construct such a theory, one that generates an infinitude of T-sentences from a finite base, consisting of reference-assignments for simple singular terms, satisfaction-conditions for simple predicates and so on. Crucially, except for singular terms, no *entities* are assigned to expressions.

The idea is not that a true T-sentence literally states the meaning of a sentence individually; it is that a whole theory that generates all true T-sentences conveys all there is to convey about the meanings of the sentences of the language; a theory of meaning is *holistic*, not atomic.

To explain how such a theory is confirmed, it is sufficient to explain how to devise such a theory for a language that is new to us; such is Davidsonian radical interpretation. This will draw out, will make explicit, anything upon which our understanding of a language depends. Occasion sentences – like 'It's raining' as opposed to standing sentences like 'Wood burns' – afford the interpreter a way to get started. Observing the native linguistic behaviour, for example, '"Gavagai" is true-in-Nove if a rabbit is present' might he tried as a possible T-sentence. Subsequent observations might bear out this hypothesis along with many more. Chopping sentences into parts that are assigned referential and satisfaction conditions will suggest other T-sentences, which can then be tested and so on, until we have a complete theory.

If a native assents to 'Gavagai' in the presence of a rabbit, what is presumed to be going on is that 'Gavagai' is indeed true if and only if a rabbit is present, *and* the native *believes* that a rabbit is present. In other words, 'Gavagai' is *held-true* by the native in a certain circumstance, and 'Gavagai' *is* true in that circumstance. The assumption is Davidson's principle of charity: without this assumption, interpretation is impossible. Sometimes, however, the pattern is broken; we mistakenly hold a certain sentence true. Since we are human beings, interpretation must allow for this. If, once in a while, the native is found to hold-true, for example, 'Gavagai', when it is not the case that a rabbit is present, we can stick to our interpretation as 'A rabbit is present'. But this can happen only within limits; if it happens too frequently, we can no longer pay for an interpretation in the currency of ascription of false belief; we must revise the interpretation. Such is the interpenetration of belief and meaning.

• STUDY QUESTIONS

1 At least some natives believe all sorts of wild things, but still they speak and are understood. Is that not in tension with the principle of charity, which requires that the beliefs ascribed be mostly true? Can a more detailed principle of charity cope better? Perhaps something like: assume that the native speakers have generally true beliefs about what is evident in the immediate environment?

2 If we always had true beliefs, and never had false beliefs, then evidently Davidson would not have to introduce the concept of belief into his theory at all: 'is true' would take the place of 'is *held* true'. It would appear then that there are only *beliefs* if there are *false beliefs*. Is that plausible?

3 Holism entails that the meanings of all the expressions of a language are interdependent. Is it therefore impossible to have a language consisting of just one sentence with a particular meaning? Is the answer damaging to the idea of holism?

4 Holism entails that the meanings of all the expressions of a language are interdependent. Therefore, it is not possible to learn the meaning of a single expression without learning the meanings of all. But in that case, it is impossible to learn such a language; one doesn't learn a language at one fell swoop! So holism is false. What can a defender of holism say in response?

5 What can Davidson say to someone who advances the following objection?

> Consider: '"Gavagai" is true if and only if a rabbit is present and all kangaroos are kangaroos.' This statement assigns exactly the same truth-conditions to 'Gavagai' as '"Gavagai" is true if and only if a rabbit is present'. By your lights, Mr Davidson, they mean the same. But obviously they don't!

• PRIMARY READING

'Truth and Meaning' and 'Radical Interpretation' are essential; they are both in Davidson's *Inquiries into Truth and Interpretation* (Oxford: Oxford University Press, 1984) and *The Essential Davidson*, edited by K. Ludwig and E. Lepore (Oxford: Oxford University Press, 2006). The former includes much more on the philosophy of language, including 'Belief and the Basis of Meaning', 'Reply to Foster', 'Reality Without Reference' and 'The Inscrutability of Reference'. The latter includes 'A Nice Derangement of Epitaphs'. Both volumes have 'On Saying That' and 'What Metaphors Mean'.

• SECONDARY READING

Evnine, S. (1991) *Donald Davidson* (Cambridge: Polity Press).

J. Malpas, 'Donald Davidson', in the *Stanford Encyclopaedia of Philosophy* http://
plato.stanford.edu/entries/davidson/

• NOTES

1 The use of brackets to indicate grouping has been suppressed. It would be easy to
add more names and predicates to the language (though adding relational predicates makes it slightly more complicated to give the semantical clauses). All truth-
functional connectives can be defined using the two given, so nothing essential
would be added by adding more of those. Significant new complexity comes when
we add quantifiers to such a language, but the platitudinous character of our
simple example remains.

9

quine's philosophy of language

W. V. Quine (1908–2000) has one of the biggest names in the philosophy of language, but so far we have said comparatively little about him. The reason is that despite his enormous influence on the philosophy of language since the Second World War – and we have seen something of his role in framing the debate over propositional attitudes – his actual theory is something of an outlier. On the one hand, a great deal of what he is most famous for is seen by many as unjustifiably critical or negative, and is felt as an irritant that needn't stand in the way of the positive or constructive proposals being advanced. On the other hand, his own positive proposals have not been taken up widely. We'll try to gain some appreciation of both the destructive and constructive sides of Quine, especially of how the two sides support one another.

• 1 QUINE'S NATURALISM

Such philosophies of language as Frege's or Russell's can seem rather high-falutin'. They make substantive *a priori* assumptions about language, its relationship to the world and its relationship to the mind. These include assumptions about what sorts of concepts – such as *sense, understanding* – could be assumed as sufficiently clear, and determinately applicable to actual phenomena, to utterances in the real world. Quine's main project in the philosophy of language was to avoid making those sorts of assumptions. Instead, we should examine what happens if we try to approach language, and especially the theory of meaning, from the point of view of natural science; what would a rigorous *science* of language be like? Can the concept of meaning be made scientifically respectable? Frege and Russell spoke rather airily of meaning and of meanings, of grasping propositions, of reference and truth-conditions, as if the existence of those things, and the explanatory value of those concepts, could be either presupposed, or established *a priori* by philosophical reflection. But they did not say very much about how such concepts can be known to apply to objects and events in the real world; they just assumed that they have determinate application, or stipulated their application in laying out their formal or symbolic languages. Yet language and its meaningfulness, surely, are phenomena to be met with in the real world of noise-making animals; shouldn't a theory of meaning describe what makes it the case that a certain noise or mark has the significance that it does? Shouldn't a theory of natural language be an empirical theory that describes what certain animals *do*, and which can be confirmed by comparing it with observable evidence? Do we really have to assume that immaterial meanings or propositions explain human cognition, the stuff of axons and synapses?

Quine asked that sort of question, and his answer, to cut a long story short, is that there cannot really be a science of meaning: *practically* speaking, the notion of meaning is probably indispensable – that is, we need it to get by in our dealings with each other – but from a scientific point of view there is really no such thing. Ascriptions of meaning are inescapably *pragmatic* and *interest-relative*, and none are uniquely justified by any conceivable objective evidence. How we describe the meaning of a statement is, to significant degree, a matter of convenience, of our always shifting interests, and there is no theoretically useful way to make more of it than that.

Quine promotes his general philosophical point of view he terms *naturalism*: it is the sum of natural science, and not philosophy conceived as an *a priori* discipline above or behind science, that sets the standard for knowledge and reality. Philosophy from this point of view is rather a hodgepodge without a defining essence; but in general it has its legitimate place by virtue of its generality, its abstractness, and especially its penchant for those problems, paradoxes and confusions thrown up by the human endeavour to know, which for some reason or other continue to resist clarification. There is, Quine famously proclaims, no 'first philosophy; it is only within science itself, and not in some prior philosophy, that reality is to be identified and described' (1981: 21). Quine often uses an image from the Austrian philosopher of science Otto Neurath (1882–1945): as scientists or philosophers we all are aboard a ship at sea, having to make running repairs, but it is only a philosopher's illusion to think we can deconstruct the whole ship without sinking, in the manner of Descartes. There is no knowledge that is somehow unscientific; if some discipline resists being subject to the norms and standards prevailing elsewhere in natural science – caricature examples include astrology and homeopathy – then that is a reason to doubt whether it's really knowledge.

But as we said, Quine's outlook is not merely negative. He is also very much concerned to propose a positive conception of language, one that can account for communication, especially those aspects of language that house our beliefs and knowledge, in ways that are immune to the sorts of objections just mentioned.

• 2 THE JUNGLE LINGUIST

Suppose you had a sort of register that described *all* of the linguistic dispositions of a given human being, at a certain moment; call the person Jo and the moment *t*. The register needn't predict what sentences if any Jo would actually say at moments directly after *t* – that depends on what goes on around Jo – but it would tell you, for each sentence of Jo's language and set of circumstances, whether Jo *would* assent to if asked under those circumstances, and similarly for cases of dissent, and for cases where Jo is undecided. Such a manual contains all the data relevant to the meanings of Jo's sentences. In Quine's view, indeed, it would be enormously problematic to ask for more. If you thought there must be more, you're saying that even if you knew all of Jo's linguistic dispositions, nevertheless you would not understand her language; there is something you might not know about what Jo means by her sentences. But what you would know about Jo is the most anyone knows about anyone, so far as language is concerned; we learn language by observation of others, observing what people say when.

So it should be possible to construct a 'theory of meaning' – an account describing all of Jo's language – strictly based on such a register. In order to sharpen the scenario, we can imagine venturing into an hypothetical region of the globe where the language spoken is a previously untranslated language, which we'll call 'Jungle'. We conceive the task, as Quine does, as that of devising a systematic *translation* from Jungle-to-English; if we assume, as we do, that we understand English, then this is to give a manual which pairs each Jungle sentence with an English sentence we deem appropriate in an equivalent circumstance. Such is the task of **radical translation**. It is close to Davidson's radical interpretation described in Chapter 8 – in fact Quine proposed the thought-experiment before Davidson did – but as there are some important differences, I'll tell the story again.

Our focus, as usual, is on declarative sentences. To begin, we might watch the Jungle-speaking natives going about their business, watching out for speech, and especially for hints as to what they are talking about. Suppose it so happens that a rabbit appears, and a native cries 'Ga-va-gai!' This could be a sentence equivalent to 'Rabbit!' – in the use where it is equivalent to 'There's a rabbit!' – it could be a name of that particular rabbit, or it could be something else entirely, whose connection with the appearance of a rabbit on this occasion is purely contingent – maybe the appearance of a well-fattened rabbit prompted the native to remark on how good dinner is likely to be – or it was thoroughly accidental, i.e. he was talking about his grandfather, and the rabbit just happened to appear at that precise moment. So you try it, while the rabbit is still visible; 'Gavagai?', you ask; 'Ja', says the native. A little later, when the rabbit is gone, you try again: 'Gavagai?', you ask; 'Nie', says the native. Here then is an hypothesis: 'Gavagai' is translatable as, perhaps, 'There is a rabbit' or something like it, and 'Ja' and 'Nie' are signs of assent and dissent, the equivalent of 'Yes' and 'No'. Suppose you then test this hypothesis, trying it on various members of the tribe, in the presence or absence of rabbits; and that the test is borne out.

There are two differences from Davidson's radical interpretation. Crucial for our purpose is that Quine strives to describe the natives only in *causal* terminology – being caused to utter certain sounds in certain circumstances and so on. Whereas Davidson describes the natives from the beginning in terms of assertion, as saying things that have truth-conditions, as referring to objects. Less crucial for us is that a *translation* of a native sentence as 'That's it' – a sentence involving indexicals – is sufficient for Quine, whereas Davidson, in seeking to apply the notion of truth to utterances, also requires a scheme that tells the interpreter how to find the referents of indexicals.

'Gavagai' is what Quine calls an **observation sentence**. Observation sentences go from true to false depending on what is apparent in the immediate observable environment; such is what Quine once called the *intersubjective stimulus-meaning* of an observation sentence. They are not *subjective* as in 'My stomach hurts', which pertains to things not observable publicly. And they are not what Quine calls **standing sentences**; these normally are intersubjective or public, but once established as true or as false, do not change their truth-values. Examples in English include 'Neil Armstrong walked on the Moon is 1969', or 'A helium atom has two neutrons in its nucleus'. It is obvious that what you are looking for at the beginning of radical translation are observation sentences like 'Gavagai', not subjective sentences, and not standing sentences; as Quine says, observation sentences constitute the 'entering wedge' of translation. A native's disposition to assent to 'Gavagai' will come and go depending on the comings and goings of rabbits. But since, for example, a helium atom always has two neutrons in its nucleus, a native sentence translatable as helium atoms have two neutrons in their nuclei, cannot be discovered by watching for correlations between dispositions to assent and changes in the observable environment. Like every other standing sentence, correlations of that kind are irrelevant to their meaning. They all have equivalent stimulus-meanings, because they all tend to retain their truth-values whatever is happening in the environment.

In fact, we speak of things happening in the environment only as shorthand. Strictly, the stimulus meaning of an observation sentence will involve only the actual nerves being stimulated in characteristic ways; for a native sentence whose role is that of 'It's hot!' it will be relatively simple, but for 'Gavagai' it will be extraordinarily complex, taking in all the various possible sightings, glimpses and other sensory manifestations of rabbithood, as well as events at the sensory surfaces that are typically not caused by rabbits but by events which fool the subject into assenting to rabbit when there is no rabbit. But this introduces further complexity, which for our purposes is best avoided.

In order to progress beyond the observation sentences of Jungle, you have to begin to disassemble the sentences, assigning translations not to sentences but to smaller words or expressions. You know anyway that merely translating sentences one by one would never suffice for the translation of the whole language; the idea is to provide a means for translating *all* the sentences of the native language, of which there are in principle infinitely many. This is where the idea of compositionality, or rather what Quine calls a system of 'analytical hypotheses', sets in. A simple example is that if we translate, say 'Gavagai blei' as 'There is a white rabbit' and 'Bollogai pirg' as 'There is a black snake', an obvious guess at translation is that 'blei' goes with 'white' and 'pirg' goes with 'black'. If a black rabbit should be available, you can try out 'Gavagai pirg' on the natives. Quine terms this procedure 'analogical substitution'.

Those are still observation sentences, but the translation of individual terms is the key towards the translation of standing sentences. Essential to translating those will be the translation of Jungle-terms for logical relations, the equivalent terms in Jungle for 'if-then', 'all' and the like. You can get a rough idea of how this would work by considering the following. Suppose we think that 'og' is a sentence-connective of Jungle. If, for any translated observation sentences # and %, a representative native assents to '# og %' if they assent to both # and % individually, and otherwise dissent from '# og %', then one can be fairly sure that 'and' translates 'og'. Similar strategies are employed for other logical connectives; we can thus extract the logical skeletons underlying Jungle, and thus cope with such standing sentences and indeed theoretical sentences as that whose English translation is 'If it's snowing, then it's cold'.

But we shall not pursue this further, as we are in a position now to understand the main Quinean lesson.

• 3 INDETERMINACY

Even if 'Gavagai' can be translated in this way as 'Rabbit!', it by no means follows that there are not other translations which, intuitively, are semantically inequivalent, that is, which do not mean the same. The observation sentences 'Rabbit' and 'Rabbit-stage!' – the latter reports a momentary temporal stage of a rabbit – or 'There's a rabbit!' and 'There a rabbit-stage!', are associated with the same observable circumstances; one is assertable just when the other is. Further 'stimulus-synonymous' sentences are 'There's an undetached rabbit-part!', 'Rabbithood is manifested!', and other more artificial things. Thus the fact that 'Rabbit!' (or 'There is a rabbit!') and 'Gavagai!' are equivalent *sentences* in this respect does not imply that 'rabbit' and 'gavagai' are synonymous or co-extensive *terms*. In particular, we have to find out whether the term 'gavagai' has the same *reference* as 'rabbit' or 'rabbit-stage'; and to find that out, we need to translate some native expression as 'is the same as' or equivalent.

Suppose we have identified the native construction 'ipso' as a candidate for 'is the same as', and 'yo' as a demonstrative pronoun, like 'that' in English. The native, we find, affirms:

(1)   Yo gavagai ipso yo gavagai.

He affirms this, we find, when and only when we point at the same rabbit both times. This would seem to confirm the hypothesis that 'gavagai' means rabbit rather than rabbit-stage. But it doesn't. Here are two translations of the sentence (1):

(2)   That rabbit is the same as that rabbit.
(3)   That rabbit-stage is part of the same animal-history as that rabbit-stage.

(2) and (3) are correlated with exactly the same observable circumstances; indeed we have the same rabbit if and only if we have rabbit-stages that are part of the same

animal-history. So the native's speech-dispositions will not fix the reference of the term 'gavagai'.

Of course, the expressions involved in (1) – 'gavagai', 'ipso' – have uses in the rest of Jungle, so the translations of these will have ramifications for other translations. But just as the data left us with choices in assigning references to the parts of (1), so these choices can be compensated for where other choices emerge in connection with other parts of the translation manual. This is not to say we or the natives do not know the difference between rabbits and rabbit-stages – as long as we are speaking a language such as English, 'rabbits = rabbit-stages' remains false; but all the same, we can translate the word of Jungle in either way, so long as corresponding adjustments are made elsewhere.

It's a little like an answer of 'seven' to the question of how far a certain address is – is it seven blocks?; miles?; kilometres?; leagues? Except in this case, at least Quine thinks, there is no way in principle to settle the question. This does not mean that translation is impossible; it means that translation is too *easy*, with too many right answers. Beyond the parameters set by linguistic behaviour, there is nothing to be wrong or right about. In practice, one will simply select the option that is most familiar – one can just stipulate that the term 'gavagai' is equivalent to the term 'rabbit', but one ought to be aware that doing so is only a convenience, that in so far as the facts are concerned one might as well have chosen another from amongst the alternatives. And who knows, maybe to the native way of thinking, another choice *would* have seemed more natural.

Such is the simplest argument for what Quine calls the *inscrutability of reference*, part of his broader thesis called the *indeterminacy of translation*. There are several further arguments and implications we could consider, but this is enough to bring out the crucial point: The notion of proposition, of sameness of meaning, has no determinate application to the plain facts of the use of language, but is *not needed for an account of such facts*. Pre-theoretically, perhaps, we think one expression correctly translates another just in case it has the same *meaning* as the other; a sentence correctly translates another just in case it expresses the same proposition as the other. We think that two translation manuals, insofar as they are successful, converge; we should expect them to deliver the same translations (allowing, of course, for discrepancies on points of emphasis, style and other grammatical and lexical alternatives that, as we say, amount to the same thing). Quine denies this. Even if you and I were to go about our respective tasks with unimpeachable correctness, there is no reason to assume that we must devise manuals that converge in this way. The two manuals could correctly translate one sentence of Jungle into different sentences of English that 'stand in no plausible relation of equivalence, however loose', as Quine puts it (1960: 27). Meaning is not something objective; the assignment of particular meanings to expressions is irreducibly intuitive and interest-relative, not something that could be validated by the impersonal procedures of science. Indeed, if we find that two inequivalent verdicts are respectively each part of a complete analysis of a given person's language – an analysis that painstakingly catalogues all the person's linguistic dispositions – then the only way to maintain that the two verdicts herald different ascriptions of meaning is to suppose that the differences of meaning are real but do not show up in the person's linguistic dispositions. But to deny that, as noted at the outset of this chapter, is basic to Quine's naturalism; he holds not only that it assumes an unfeasibly high standard, but that it's unclear what could possibly meet it.

● 4 MEANING AND ANALYTIC TRUTH

So according to Quine, there are no facts that would justify a science of meaning. However, Quine is well aware that the word 'meaning' is a well established word of ordinary language; we do ordinarily speak of the meanings of words, and indeed we have such things as phrase books and dictionaries, such people as lexicographers and translators. Quine does not think all this is a scam. He thinks that at least much of what we say when we speak of the meanings of words can be explained in terms of linguistic dispositions: one mentions a word or phrase that one would be willing, in the cited circumstance, to use in place of the word or phrase in question. One could just as well say 'I would be disposed to say…' rather than 'It means…'. As part of this general attitude, he explains how in fact the word 'meaning' is employed by ordinary people as well as in a more informed and systematic manner by professional lexicographers, and finds a miscellany of different uses that do not add up to anything like a systematic theory. In order to 'give a meaning', sometimes one cites an equivalent word or phrase, or one that is equivalent for certain purposes, but another that's equivalent for different purposes; other times one directs one's listener or reader, not to another form of words, but to the thing itself, as in '"tiger" is a word used for those large Asiatic cats that normally are orange with black stripes'; other times we get the point across by means of analogies, hints or a list of examples of correct usage. It is a profoundly useful but ultimately imprecise service, not so much a science as an art.

Since at least the days of Hume, philosophers have spoken of an important division of statements into those that express 'matters of fact' and those that express 'relations of ideas'. Kant introduced the terminology that persists today, distinguishing 'synthetic' statements from 'analytic' ones. A modern definition – one that explicitly takes the things said to be analytic or synthetic to be *statements* – strictly, sentences-at-context-of-utterance – rather than propositions, judgements or thoughts-in-the-mind, would be: a statement is *analytic* if and only if it is a logical truth, or can be transformed into a logical truth by exchanging synonyms. Consider then 'No bachelor is married'. As it stands, this is not a truth of logic; it is of the logical form 'No A is B', which has plenty of instances, such as 'No human is on Venus', which are true but not logically true, and also such instances as 'No human is in California', which are not logically true because they are false. But 'bachelor' is synonymous with 'unmarried man'. So 'No bachelor is married', by substituting synonyms, can be transformed into 'No unmarried man is married'. And that is a logical truth, an instance of the logical form 'No not-B, C, is B'.

We can characterise synonymy as two expressions having the same sense, which for present purposes is the same as characterising it as two expressions having the same meaning. So the standing of the notion of analyticity assumes that of the notion of meaning. And as we've seen, Quine, although he agrees that the notion of meaning is useful for ordinary purposes, denies that the notion of meaning has a more exacting use, that for precise scientific and philosophical purposes the notion is best left aside in favour of the notion of linguistic dispositions. Quine is thus very much against the idea that analyticity should play a serious and indispensable role in philosophy.

• 5 THE ARGUMENT OF 'TWO DOGMAS'; THE EPISTEMOLOGICAL SIGNIFICANCE OF THE CONCEPT OF MEANING

In fact, Quine attacked the notion of analyticity *before* directly attacking the notion of meaning; the original attack on analyticity was only an indirect attack on meaning (his famous or infamous article 'Two Dogmas of Empiricism' appeared in 1951 [it appears slightly revised in Quine 1961], and the book *Word and Object* appeared in 1960). It was Rudolph Carnap's view that was Quine's primary and explicit target, but also in the picture were Ayer's view, the views of Strawson and Grice, and many others who depended on the distinction that Quine sought to undermine (in 1956 Grice and Strawson co-wrote a famous reply to Quine, 'In Defense of a Dogma').

In Quine's article, he argues that no definition or characterisation of analyticity is possible that does not presuppose the legitimacy of the notion of meaning, or notions very close if not identical to meaning such as *conceptual content, verification conditions, propositional content* or Fregean *sense*. But this might leave one puzzled if one thinks that some such concept is all right, even if rough round the edges. The key is that the overarching question for Quine is one about the nature, structure and dynamics of knowledge. We can sketch a caricature of the view that Quine attacked, one that is not however misleading on the fundamental points. There are statements about what is immediately given in sensation or experience; then there are statements that are not themselves experiential statements, but which are conceptually related to those that are. The nature of the linkage is analytical. It is because of various complex analytic relations to experiential statements that a non-analytic statement S – an ordinary one like 'There is beer in the refrigerator' or 'She's single', or a theoretical statement like 'Squirrels do not live as long as 25 years' or 'Ethanol freezes at –114 degrees Celsius' – comes to have the particular meaning that it has, and will logically entail certain experiential statements E1, E2 and so on. Those statements count collectively as an experiential test for the veracity of statement S; if E1, E2 ... are all true, then S must be accepted as true; if at least one of E1, E2 ... is false, then S must be rejected as false. Inevitably, then, some statements will be confirmed *irrespective* of experience; an obvious case will be 'Either there is beer in the refrigerator or there is no beer in the refrigerator'. These are the analytic truths, including 'No unmarried men are married' and 'No bachelor is married'. Such is known as *epistemological reductionism*: the justification of statements always proceeds from a foundation in experience upwards, to theoretical statements that cannot in practice be compared directly with experience, but each of which is nevertheless equivalent to some perhaps complicated combination of statements which can be. For our purposes we can count Ayer's verification theory of meaning as an instance of this, according to which every cognitively meaningful statement is either analytic, or is equivalent to a verification condition. In addition, the distinction between the *a priori* and the *a posteriori*, and that between the necessary and contingent, Ayer among others believed, can be explained as analytic.

Quine's idea is to replace this picture whereby justification is *linear* with what is known as epistemic **holism**. Suppose a statement S is up for testing, and a correspondingly expected experiential statement E5 is *falsified*. Typically, statement S will entail the truth of E5 not by itself, but only in concert with many other statements: statements pertaining to the nature and reliability of the testing equipment, the chemical composition and behaviour of various substances, logic and arithmetic, and so on. In principle, then, what we test is a whole raft of statements, not just S in particular; it's just that normally the other members of the raft will be more firmly established than S itself, for in an actual case we are testing S precisely because it seems more vulnerable than the others, its credentials comparatively suspect. But that is a matter of degree, not a matter of kind; in principle, one could, in the case where E5 proves false, withdraw not S but some other member of the raft of statements which together with S entailed E5. And those statements will in turn be connected with others, and the others with others, and so on. It's very much an 'in-principle' point, but in principle we are testing the whole of science with each particular test, experiment or observation – including the so-called analytic statements, which in turn include the statements of mathematics. Yes, even the statements of arithmetic or mathematics generally are *revisable*: in certain, dimly glimpsed and exceedingly improbable circumstances, we could adjust them.

In a famous passage, Quine writes:

> The totality of our so-called knowledge or beliefs, from the most casual matters of geography and history to the profoundest laws of atomic physics or even of pure mathematics and logic, is a man-made fabric which impinges on experience only along the edges. Or, to change the figure, total science is like a field of force whose boundary conditions are experience. A conflict with experience at the periphery occasions readjustments in the interior of the field. Truth values have to redistributed over some of our statements … [T]he total field is so underdetermined by its boundary conditions, experience, that there is much latitude of choice as to what statements to reevaluate in the light of any single contrary experience. No particular experiences are linked with any particular statements in the interior of the field, except indirectly through considerations of equilibrium affecting the field as a whole.
>
> (Quine 1961: 42–3)

According to holism, the sum of human knowledge, speaking a bit figuratively, is a loose-jointed web of belief; it is not a rigid, vertical structure built upon a foundation of experiential statements, with analytic statements providing the cement. So knowledge can be characterised without making use of the concept of analyticity or the concept of meaning. The problem Quine was attempting to solve is an epistemological problem, not a problem about linguistics – but Quine's solution to the epistemological problem had a direct effect on linguistics, and indeed during the period of writing 'Two Dogmas' saw Quine branching out from logic and the philosophy of mathematics to the philosophy of language.

• 6 QUINE PROPOSES REPLACEMENT, NOT ANALYSIS

Quine surfaced in Chapter 7 as the instigator of a problem for the propositional attitudes. The problem with respect to belief that eventually emerged is that it is difficult to formulate a genuinely informative criterion for when a *de dicto* belief – belief in a proposition – entails a *de re* belief – a belief about ordinary objects. We mentioned briefly a couple of solutions, a broadly Fregean one advanced by Kaplan, and a broadly Millian or Kripkean one advanced by Salmon. And what was Quine's solution? Ultimately, none! The problem was one that he saw fit to walk away from. The distinction rests ultimately upon the subject's *knowing what* the object is – but that, for Quine, is a thoroughly context-bound business; sometimes we know the face but not the name, other times we know the name but not the face. There cannot be a serious, general theory of that notion, no general notion of 'intentionality'. It is a useful practical device in certain situations, nothing more: sometimes we find it convenient, rather than displaying the full content of a person's belief – a *de dicto* belief-report – to specify what the belief is about without characterising the subject's own way of characterising it, reporting the person to have a *de re* belief. Rather than the *de dicto* 'A believes that b is F', we use the *de re* style, 'You know b? – A believes it to be F'.

The ins and outs of that issue are not as important as understanding Quine's motivation. Quine rejects the idea of the meaning of an individual sentence, and thus naturally does not believe there is a well defined task called 'conceptual analysis'. His aim is never to discover, isolate and investigate the concepts or meanings expressed by terms of ordinary language; strictly speaking he denies that there are any such things. Such things are irredeemably vague, and from a scientific point of view, there aren't such things. Instead, Quine's remarks on these sorts of issues are driven by his aim to fashion *replacements* of certain imprecise or otherwise problematic ordinary locutions with theoretical language that is free of those defects – the aim not being linguistic reform for its own sake, but to provide a rigorous mode of expression for the statement of one's official theory of a given subject-matter, especially when one is aware of danger in the ordinary mode of expression. The *de re/de dicto* distinction is ordinarily useful, but pressed harder it falls apart, and encourages one to make distinction where in reality there isn't one; the distinction can be maintained only in a manner that is arbitrary or misleading, resting upon ideas that are thoroughly unscientific. The notion of the meaning of a sentence suffers a similar fate, and is replaced for theoretical purposes by that of a linguistic disposition.

Further examples include the idea of proper names. They are rife in ordinary speech, but they are notoriously difficult to account for satisfactorily, as we have seen. Quine's solution is that they can be replaced – not analysed – in a language free of them. The important aspect of their ordinary use can be duplicated by a language without them: if, for example, we have a particular interest in having a 'name' that would serve as the ordinary name 'Socrates' does, we can simply invent a predicate – 'α Socratises' – stipulating that it is to be true of just that particular man. Then whenever we used to use the name 'Socrates', we form the definite description 'the Socratiser', defining it in Russell's way; clearly 'Socrates is Greek' will be true so long as 'There is an x such that x uniquely Socratises and x is Greek' is true. Crucially, if for whatever reason the description in fact fails to denote anything, the latter such statements will simply be false, not lacking truth-value.

• 7 THE PLACE OF NATURALISM

The conclusion of indeterminacy does not mean translation is impossible, that the alien mind is unknowable; it's that translation is too easy to sustain the idea that there is any one right way to portray the alien mind. This goes for the minds of our fellows, and indeed for our mind. The idea is that certain mentalistic notions – the mind's grasping propositions, of the mind's having a kind of non-causal contact with things outside it, and so on – are from Quine's scientistic point of view ill-equipped to serve as materials for genuine explanations. I say 'scientistic' point of view, but for Quine that covers any domain of knowledge, and any domain of knowledge must submit to the strictures of naturalism. Of course, ordinary knowledge, because it doesn't measure up the most stringent demands, is not without epistemic value or not in any sense knowledge; it just fails to be rigorous and maximally objective.

There is hope for one who likes naturalism but is loathe to accept Quine's negative conclusions for the idea of meaning. Suppose, as many have argued, that translation in Quine's sense is not indeterminate as he says. Staying within the naturalistic constraints on Quinean radical translation, suppose Quine has missed certain facts that determine translation. In that case, a notion of the meaning of a sentence would readily be available: take all sentences in which a given sentence can be correctly translated, i.e. are synonymous. These make up a set of sentences of intuitively equivalent translations (an equivalence class under the relation *x correctly translates y*). This set can perform the function of what previously we were calling the meaning, proposition or sense expressed by the sentence: as a vehicle of truth, as what (by definition) all sentences that are synonymous with the original sentence have in common, and as the object of propositional attitudes. Call the set a meaning*. Thus, Quine's picture could conceivably be brought in a closer harmony with common sense, as well as with the idea of a theory of meaning. Nevertheless, the explanation of *why* the classes are as they are would be independent of, and prior to, the application of the concept of meaning*. The concept of meaning* would still be without causal robustness, and would be incapable of serving in genuine explanations: fundamentally, it's not *because* a sentence has a certain meaning* that it plays its part in linguistic behaviour; for saying that it has that meaning* does not add anything to saying that it plays the behavioural role. Indeed, within naturalism it is completely unclear what role a causally robust notion of meaning could play; to think that it can play such a role would be to commit the sin of private language as discussed by Wittgenstein, our next and final topic.

• HISTORICAL NOTES

W. V. Quine came upon the scene in the first instance as a mathematical logician; most of his published papers and books until the 1950s were on logic and set-theory. But his meeting of Rudolf Carnap (1891–1970) in Prague in 1933, who was working on epistemology and the philosophy of language as well as logic, made a lasting impression. He was impressed but had doubts, some of which were expressed in 'Truth by Convention' of 1935, when Quine was all of 26. After the war – during which Quine put his logical skills to work on finding algorithms for designing more efficient electrical switching circuits – his criticisms of uncritical use among philosophers of analyticity were famously expressed in his 'Two Dogmas of Empiricism' of 1951, together with his sketch of the dynamics of knowledge, which dispensed with the notion. Then came *Word and Object* of 1960, which among other things set out the case for the indeterminacy of translation, and provided more in the way of detail for an explanation of human knowledge and language without relying on the concept of meaning. He went on developing and fine-tuning the view through the 1990s, especially with the *Roots of Reference* (1974) and *Pursuit of Truth* (revised edition 1992). More generally, Quine has influenced the course of analytical philosophy deeply in various ways, but most conspicuously by setting some of its leading problems, and for articulating solutions to them for philosophers to celebrate or criticise. There aren't many out-and-out followers of Quine; but recent figures who have been broadly supportive include Gilbert Harman, Daniel Dennett and Peter Hylton. In the 1960s Donald Davidson, partly inspired by Quine, developed a view which has in many ways gained a more visible following, even if it ultimately departs from Quine on the central question of whether a rigorous theory of meaning is possible.

• CHAPTER SUMMARY

Quine's criticisms of the work going on in the philosophy of language were motivated by his scientific naturalism, by the position that a serious understanding of linguistic phenomena should not uncritically help itself to the idea of meaning and related concepts. Closely connected is that linguistic significance must be accessible from a third-person point of view; in particular, it must be reconstructable in terms of linguistic behaviour.

The thought experiment of radical translation involves translation into English of a previously unknown (to the translators) language; this clarifies what naturalism requires and prohibits, and affords a way of finding out the objective standing of the idea of cognitive meaning, of propositional content. The meaning-free concepts with which translation begins include the concept of an *observation sentence*, which goes from true to false depending on what is apparent in the immediate observable environment; the concept of a *standing sentence* which does not change its truth-value once established as true or as false. Quine's conclusion is that radical translation is indeterminate; for example, there is no objective difference between a translation of a native observation sentence as 'There is a rabbit' and 'There is a rabbit-stage' – for one can make adjustments to the translations of individual expressions to even out the bumps. The conclusion of indeterminacy does not mean translation is impossible, that the alien mind is unknowable; it's that translation is too easy to sustain the idea that there is any one right way to portray the alien mind.

Analytic truth is truth due solely to meanings of words. Quine dismisses meaning from the arsenal of naturalistic concepts, and thus dismisses analyticity. Analyticity played a central role in theories of knowledge from Hume and Kant to Ayer and Carnap. In holism, Quine sketches an alternative theory of knowledge that dispenses with the concept: rather than a false prediction enjoining a specific alteration of theory according to analytic rules, the effect of a false prediction is a more flexible response, with various alterations possible. Human knowledge is like a loose-jointed web of belief, not like a vertical structure built upon a foundation of experiential statements.

It is easy to read some of Quine's work as attempting to *analyse* ordinary expressions, but in fact he proposes *replacement* of ordinary or scientific language. Ordinary expressions are often vague, imprecise and even contradictory in their implications; Quine's solution is not to find out better what they mean – that path is ruled out by the indeterminacy arguments – but, if the need is felt for some theoretical purpose, to propose replacements which serve the necessary functions without those problems.

• STUDY QUESTIONS

1 If the notion of meaning is *indispensable*, from a practical point of view, how can science take the view that it is ultimately not real?

2 Suppose Mary speaks only English, and Bob speaks only a variant of English, called Quinglish. Strangely enough, Bob's language and Mary's have never been in contact, not even indirectly. But then Bob and Mary meet, and set about at once to undertake radical translation of each other, as one does. Bob translates an English sentence S, 'A rabbit is present', as the Quinglish sentence S*, 'A rabbit-stage is

present'. Mary, sensible girl that she is, translates the Quinglish sentence S* as the English sentence S** 'A rabbit-stage is present'. Therefore since S** translates S*, and S* translates S, S** translates S. But then the English sentence 'A rabbit is present' is equivalent to the English sentence 'A rabbit stage is present'! How should Mary respond to this?

3 Does Quine's theory imply that we don't know our own minds, our own thoughts?

4 An alternative way of defining analyticity is this: a given statement is analytic if and only if *accepting* it is a criterion for *understanding* it (that is, in order to understand the concepts involved, one must accept a given statement). Would such a definition fare better against Quine's criticisms?

5 Suppose that B and C are native Jungle-speakers. But B and C have very different sensory organs, so that 'Gavagai!' has for B a different stimulus-meaning from what it has for C. In that case, in virtue of what are they speakers of the same language? How can they communicate using the observation sentence 'Gavagai!'? Compare that with Russell's conception of how communication takes place.

• PRIMARY READING

The first Quine is inevitably the hardest; I recommend 'Speaking of Objects' in his *Ontological Relativity and Other Essays* (New York and London: Columbia University Press, 1969) and 'Two Dogmas of Empiricism', in his collection *From a Logical Point of View* (Cambridge, MA: Harvard University Press, second edition, 1961), then the essay 'Things and Their Place in Theories', in his collection *Theories and Things* (Cambridge, MA: Harvard University Press, 1981). Not for the faint of heart is *Word and Object* (Cambridge, MA: MIT Press, 1960).

• SECONDARY READING

Hylton, P., 'Willard van Orman Quine', in the *Stanford Encyclopaedia of Philosophy*, http://plato.stanford.edu/entries/quine

10

wittgenstein's alternative

Ludwig Wittgenstein (1889–1951) wrote two books: the *Tractatus Logico-Philosophicus* (1921) and the *Philosophical Investigations* (published posthumously in 1953). Superficially the two are similar; each contains a philosophy of language, and neither is organised into continuous prose which carries the reader along an argument to a conclusion. Each is an assemblage of remarks, seemingly arranged by cutting and pasting, as if the rich variety of connections between remarks resisted the conventions of linear ordering.

But the difference between the two could not be greater. For our purposes, we can think of the younger Wittgenstein, the author of the *Tractatus*, as accepting the essentials of the Frege-Russell view of the functioning of language – even though in the *Tractatus* Wittgenstein disagrees with both Frege's view and Russell's in seemingly profound ways. From the point of view of the later Wittgenstein, the author of the *Investigations*, those disagreements can seem inconsequential. He now thinks there is no systematic and definitive way of mapping the multiplicity of language, in all its unfathomable diversity. To look for systematic generalities would be like imposing a grid onto a medieval Italian city, with all its twisting lanes, dead-ends, irregular *piazzi*, tunnels, bridges, even streets atop streets. You could do it, but it would be arbitrary and distorting, and you would not thereby get to know the city in the way you would by exploring it on foot. And it is this later, much more radical view that our final chapter is about.

• 1 LANGUAGE GAMES

According to Frege, Russell and indeed most philosophers of language, including the younger Wittgenstein, reference or naming is fundamental. In the words of the *Tractatus*, that is the point at which language reaches out to reality, where it touches the world. Other words that play fundamental roles in the classical conception are 'understanding' and 'meaning'. According to the later Wittgenstein, these words foster illusions of clarity, as when we say, as if we were reciting a religious slogan, that to *understand* a sentence is to *grasp* its *meaning*. On the contrary, understanding is a multiple-dimensional business (what counts as understanding one word may be quite different from understanding another), and there is no way to cut out the specifically linguistic capacity for dissection and investigation. There is no one thing that constitutes understanding; it depends on details of the case. Furthermore, understanding something is not all-or-nothing, but a matter of degree.

This emerges quite clearly when we consider one of the **language games** that Wittgenstein describes at the beginning of the *Investigations*.

> I send someone shopping. I give him a slip marked "five red apples". He takes the slip to the shopkeeper, who opens the drawer marked "apples"; then he looks up the word "red" in a table and finds a colour sample opposite it; then he says the series of cardinal numbers – I assume that he knows them by heart – up to the word "five" and for each number he takes an apple of the same colour as the sample out of the drawer. – It is in this and similar ways that one operates with words.
>
> (Wittgenstein 1953, Section 1)

Although of humdrum sort, the skills that the shopkeeper and the shopper have to master in order to play such a game are diverse. There is no one kind of thing that one has to master, and it seems somewhat arbitrary to call some of the skills *linguistic* skills and others not. Taking the list to a certain place and handing it over, finding the drawer marked 'apples', attending to a colour sample and responding appropriately, taking the correct apples out of the drawer, and so on – these constitute what Wittgenstein calls '**forms of life**'. They are partly linguistic, partly not, and have the full significance they have through their being embedded in a larger framework of overall life or culture. To isolate and pull out linguistic phenomena for examination is precisely to look at parts out of context, as if we were examining a disembodied gallbladder on a lab bench, trying to describe it while remaining completely ignorant of the role it plays in the body.

Part of the point of calling such activities 'language games' is to stress the affinity between the words employed and pieces in a game. The significance of identifying a certain piece as a *rook* depends upon a certain framework, namely the overall rules of the game of chess – which collectively describe the moves that one may do with a rook. Furthermore, in playing chess one doesn't just follow the rules; within the rules there are unendingly many opportunities for creativity and drama. Likewise in the case of language games, except the overall framework is *much* wider and less definitely bounded than criteria for reference or meaning; and insofar as the rules lay down necessary conditions of saying something intelligible, they are often treated in practice as themes for variation, as means that can be altered for some end.

This is not to criticise normal linguistic description. One could correctly *say* 'five' refers to five, 'red' to red, and 'apples' to apples. But one would not be adding anything to the above description of the language game; one would not thereby be explaining what is really going on. On the contrary, to suppose that one would thereby be identifying what is really going on is to submit to the *craving for generality* embodied in such words as 'refers' and 'means'. Such words do serve the purpose of summing up various linguistic activities, but the insight so afforded is only of a superficial sort, precisely because it is so general. The job of such a word is to conceal differences, not to bring them to light in a way as to afford insight.

The proper role of such expressions as 'refers', or 'means that', is to indicate, *once a background is understood,* or once a place has been conceptually carved out, what particular word one is to use for a certain purpose. A somewhat artificial example, but one that makes the point clearly, is the case of a starter's saying 'Set!' to a field of sprinters about to commence a race: it's clear that it is only a complicated background of rules, expectations and traditions, that that syllable, uttered in that exact context, has the significance that it has. Likewise, if we say of the language game described above that 'red' refers to redness, it is only because so much has been presupposed. Normally, we share so many forms of life that we never notice them, they go without saying. Compare walking down a busy street: it is in fact a very complicated business, but we cope effortlessly because we are so utterly used to it. Again, the semantical vocabulary has its point only when forms of life, comprising various habits and dispositions, are understood as being in the background.

Another important thing to notice about the language game is that, as described, it is *complete* – the point is not that more detail could not be added to the description, but that one could perfectly well imagine such a skill-set being the only one mastered, or rather the only one mastered that one is tempted to call linguistic. There is no reason to maintain that the language game is incomplete or partial. The shopkeeper fully understands the words he is using; he is fully competent in the activities carried out by means of them, and that is that.

• 2 FAMILY RESEMBLANCE, TOOLS AND CITIES

Suppose a child has mastered the shopper's role in the above language game. If we now imagine the child as mastering more and more language games – each perhaps borrowing some elements from others, but also requiring the acquisition of new forms of lingo – we have a picture of his overall skill-set as consisting of various cells, each interwoven or related to others but having its distinctive territory, its distinctive cluster of purposes. The language of storytelling and make-believe, of being a pupil at school, of joking, of professing wants, of asking favours, and so on; there is no one place at which we declare him a master of language; it's a matter of degree. And learning language involves many capacities, many kinds of mastery, as just intimated. What then is language? No one thing; Wittgenstein is anti-essentialist about language. No neat definition is possible. Instead, the concept of *language* is a **family resemblance** concept.

There are other examples of family resemblance concepts. Consider the concept of a *game*. What are the necessary and sufficient conditions for something being a game? According to Wittgenstein, there aren't any; but the concept, or rather the word, is none the worse for it. Some games involve a board and pieces (backgammon, Parcheesi) others don't; some involve competition – others don't (solitaire, charades); some have an element of luck, others don't (chess, noughts and crosses or tic-tac-toe); some are for the diversion of the participants, others not (professional sports). Instead, there are various features that are sufficient for being an instance of the concept: things having attributes A and B, or B and C, or C and D – but there are no features distinctive of or common to all games. Nor is it right to say that the concept is *disjunctive* in character, as if we could define it thus: something is a game if and only if it has attributes A and B, or B and C, or C and D, or … for some finite number of terms, covering all actual games present and past. Besides being a case of merely 'playing with words' as Wittgenstein says – and note that no one is likely actually to come up with such a disjunction – this misses a fundamental feature of family resemblance concepts, namely that the concept of a game is *open-textured*. Even if we had such a definition involving an exhaustive disjunction as above, such a definition fails to reckon with past possibilities that went unrealised, and with *future* possibilities. If the linguistic community is faced with a new thing, with a novel set of attributes which does not qualify it for inclusion under the concept as it has been applied in the past – the concept may nonetheless be stretched to the new thing, if the community sees fit. Thus with time the concept may expand its field of correct application; the model thus provides for conceptual change over time.

Once one has the idea of a family resemblance concept, one can seem to spot them all over the place, often in philosophically sensitive areas.

Returning to the concept of language, 'language' itself expresses a family resemblance concept; no one thing is common to the sundry activities we characterise by means of the word. Instead of thinking of language as something of which the essentials can in principle be characterised at one fell swoop, Wittgenstein suggests an analogy with cities – not planned ones like Milton Keynes or Brasilia, but organic and historical ones such as London or Mumbai. The former are planned out in advance of being used and constructed, sometimes by a single person; a good analogy would be the notation of chemistry, or logical calculi. The latter, just like a natural language, evolved bit by bit, over time (and it is not necessary for any single person to understand all of it). There need not be an overall logic to its development. London developed over 2000 years, higgledy-piggledy, sometimes expanding rapidly, sometimes undergoing periods of statis, other times shrinking. Likewise the English language, except it took longer. Both are organic, natural products of our evolution. There is no overall grid to be abstracted out. Still, you can get from one place to another: the streets are not all dead ends (English grammar is not hopeless). And certain parts – normally the suburbs but sometimes the centre as when Hausmann redesigned central Paris – are self-consciously designed; in our language, the scientific bits are most conspicuously like that.

Thus we can see various language games as woven together in diverse ways, and a child acquiring language as finding his feet with each of them, some earlier than others, some presupposing others, some having to be learned simultaneously with others; it is a piecemeal business. Thus, as you might expect, Wittgenstein does not regard what we have been calling 'cognitive language' – fact-stating language, the stuff of assertion, truth-conditions and logical implication – as taking peculiar precedence in the order of what in Chapter 6 we called speech-acts. In language, in addition to assertion or statement, we have greetings, insults, commands, betting, haggling, moral praise and censure, aesthetic praise and criticism, poetry, banter, warnings, jokes, slang, simile, metaphor, threats, exclamations, dirty words, words we cry out under duress, in fear, in disgust, during sexual excitement, in pain, when victorious, in encouragement … and many other things. Expressions exist for all these purposes, and some are not *referring* terms at all – 'Goodbye', for instance, or 'Come on!', or 'It's raining'. Again, it would be very hard to say what they all have in common; certainly we cannot assume *a priori* that they do have something in common that is of theoretical importance.

The variety of language games Wittgenstein points to makes it unsurprising that he comes out with the famous saying that: 'For a *large* class of cases – though not for all – in which we employ the word "meaning" it can be defined thus: the meaning a word is its use in the language' (1953: Section 43). Rather than impose a specious uniformity on language by saying such things as that every word expresses a *meaning*, it is more instructive and less misleading to ask after the diverse *uses* of words.

Wittgenstein famously compared language to a toolbox, and words for tools. If we tried to say what all tools have in common, we should end up with something totally uninformative and probably false, like 'all tools are used to alter something' (or even: 'A tool is a thing that is *used*'). Think of the hammer, saw, measuring tape, vice, screwdriver, glue-pot, paintbrush, pliers, plumb bob, soldering iron, sandpaper … and so on. Philosophers often talk as if the stating of facts or the conveying of factual information – and related acts such as questions, understood simply as requests for information – were the sole purpose of language. That would be like someone who looked into a tool box and saw only the hammer. There are certainly limits to this analogy; or at least, it can be question-begging to push it too far. Most conspicuously, we should not assume that all the purposes served by language could be conceived or explained independently of language. We can always explain the intended result of using a tool in a way that makes no reference to tools (except when using tools to make or repair tools!) But it might well be, for example, that our ability to think some kinds of thoughts depends on our mastery of language; so when we use language to record or convey certain sorts of thoughts, the intended result – perhaps that a certain person should acquire a certain belief – cannot be explained except in terms of that person's mastery of language. Perhaps many linguistic activities are themselves inextricable from Wittgenstein's forms of life: those are convention-bound activities that make up certain departments of living, and without which certain kinds of purpose and value could not exist.

• 3 TO FOLLOW A RULE I

We now come to a Wittgensteinian topic that has received a mountain of commentary, especially since Kripke's *Wittgenstein on Rules and Private Language* of 1982. The topic has become frighteningly complex, but the essentials are quite simple.

We'll take an elementary example, but it will serve to make a point that is of completely general significance. Suppose one is walking through a corridor at an airport, and one comes to a 'Y' junction. There appears the sign:

Of course, without any hesitation, you go right. The sign, as we say, *means that* one should go right. But how do you know? What fact do you know? What does your understanding consist of? What feature counts as your understanding?

One might point to a mental occurrence; perhaps a mental image occurs when you understand. But such a mental object or state is not necessary or sufficient for being competent with the sign, for understanding the sign. It is not necessary because one can perfectly well imagine one's being competent with the sign without an accompanying mental image occurring; one sees the arrow and one goes right, but there is no need to suppose that alongside these events is another mental process that explains the event.

But more importantly, it is not sufficient for competence; the existence of such a mental occurrence cannot explain understanding. For if something, so to speak, were to flash on one's inner mental screen at an appropriate moment, that something would be in exactly the same situation as the original sign on the wall. It would have to be read, interpreted; the question of *its* meaning would arise. Suppose, for simplicity, that an internal, mental duplicate of the external, physical sign was thought sufficient for understanding the latter. Then the question of the interpretation of the inner sign arises. It could mean that one is to go *left* – a society in which arrows point the opposite way from the way we take them to point is perfectly imaginable; as is a society in which that particular mark meant 'do not enter' or 'do not use mobile phones'. It's a convention. So merely having another sign appear on one's mental screen is powerless to bring it about that one understands the outer sign. But so it is with anything that might happen in one's mind, no matter how complex in comparison with an inner replica; such inner phenomena cannot constitute understanding. 'No [mental] process', writes Wittgenstein, 'could have the consequences of meaning' (1953, II: 218).

Wittgenstein's reaction is not scepticism; he doesn't suggest that maybe no one understands anything, or that the whole idea of understanding and meaning is a fraud. Instead, he says that we must grasp signs in a way that is not an interpretation at all. He does not mean that understanding is magic: if 'interpretation' is understood as seeing one sign in terms of another, then this follows straightforwardly from the discussion of last paragraph. Rather, learning to follow or obey a sign is a matter of *training*, of acquiring dispositions such as to go right in such circumstances as the sign in the airport. 'Explanations have to stop somewhere', hc points out early in the *Investigations*; digging down, one reaches bedrock, one's 'spade is turned'. Responding as we do is just what one is 'inclined to *do*'; it is just how we roll. And the capacity to learn in this way is a feature of our natural history. Other sorts of creatures, with very different natural dispositions, would simply be unable to respond to the training as we do. The possibility of communication depends on agreement in judgements, as Wittgenstein puts it: if we were not already disposed to respond in similar ways to events, communication could not get started. The comparison is often made with the slave-boy in Plato's *Meno*: by teaching the slave-boy a proof by merely asking him a sequence of questions, Socrates purports to demonstrate that knowledge of geometry is innate.

• 4 TO FOLLOW A RULE II

Does having a disposition to respond to a sign constitute understanding the sign? No; at the minimum, one has to be disposed to respond to it *in the right way*. At the very least, one has to be disposed to respond to it in ways that other members of the linguistic community do. This raises an issue that forms the heart of Kripke's book *Wittgenstein on Rules and Private Language*, of which everyone studying Wittgenstein should have some inkling. We can separate it into two parts.

First, a person has necessarily been exposed to a given rule on only so many occasions, in comparison with the *infinite* range of uses of the rule, actual and potential. One can never know with certainty that one has the right disposition; perhaps the disposition one has and the disposition actually indicated by the rule have matched in the occasions that one has so far encountered, but branch apart in other cases that one has not so far encountered. So there is a sceptical problem, an epistemic gap; how can one ever know that one has got the rule right?

Second, there is a **normative** gap between having a disposition to *respond* to a sign as others do, and *understanding* the sign. Even if I am disposed to go on in what is in fact the right or correct way, it does not follow that my doing so is itself right or correct. For dispositions, in themselves, have no normative force. That a creature behaves with a certain disposition doesn't mean that they are right to do what they do; likewise having dispositions cannot tell me what I *ought* to do, any more than a dog is doing the right thing when he moves his leg up and down when you scratch his back. But that is the whole point of speaking of *rules*, of meaning. On the one hand I might make, systematically, mistakes; that is a case where my performance is systematically incorrect according to the rule, which should not be possible if having a disposition were sufficient for being subject to a rule. There is a difference between a person who grasps a rule but makes mistakes, and a person whose behaviour is exactly the same but isn't following any rule. On the other hand, even my behaviour accords exactly with the rule; it might be a case of *merely* acting so as to match the rule, rather than being *guided* by it (a waffle iron, even if it performs perfectly, is not following rules).

How Wittgenstein responds or would respond to these points has been the subject of much controversy. Kripke's own solution, presented on behalf of Wittgenstein, has won a fair following, but many others have been proposed. I will just sketch what I personally believe was more or less Wittgenstein's own response to the second difficulty. The key is the social context in which such linguistic behaviour takes place. Among the various language games is the habit of correcting people when their linguistic dispositions run off the rails. It is this element of our practice that accounts for normativity, and nothing more; we admonish and criticise such people (in the old days we punished them). Without such a community it would not make sense to speak of speech as being right or wrong – even if it seemed to the language user as if it did. Yes, this does mean that just as the individual cannot have dealt with all questions, actual and potential, of interpretation of a given sign, neither can the whole community – they can have dealt with a great deal more such cases, but not all. But the challenge was only to allow for normativity in the community's practice, which the present suggestion does. As for the first difficulty, I do not think that Wittgenstein would be disturbed by it. He is no more bothered by such things than he is about the principle of induction, the problem of justifying normal inferences from observed cases to unobserved cases. He recommends not a solution to 'the problem' but quietism, that this is a place where we must simply acquiesce in forms of life. But that is long story.

• 5 PRIVATE LANGUAGE

At Section 243 of the *Investigations* Wittgenstein introduces the idea of a language in which words stand for inner experiences, things that can *only* be known to the person speaking (or the person writing down the words). He then proceeds to argue that this – a **private language**, a language that is necessarily understood only by the speaker – is impossible. He does not mean to disturb the evident fact that we use words to refer to inner experiences so long as the words can, in principle, be understood by others (more on that in a moment). He means to argue against the idea of a language that is *necessarily* private.

Thus suppose you try to construct such a language. You have a sensation which you call 'S'. You note it down, intending that 'S' labels S. Later, a sensation intrudes. Is it S? One's natural response is to say that one can simply compare it inwardly with the previous case. The problem, however, is that such an inner comparison makes no sense; for there is no **criterion** available to answer the question. For there is no gap between the *existence* of an inner sensation and its *seeming* to exist. One cannot say: if it *seems* to be S, it's S, if not, not. For a word to be meaningful, it has to be conceivable that one could *mistakenly* misapply the word. If there is no such thing, then one's attempt to mean something by 'S' has failed. As Wittgenstein writes, 'in the present case I have no criterion of correctness. One would like to say: whatever is going to seem right to me is right. And that only means that here we can't talk about "right"' (1953, Section 258). And:

'obeying a rule' is a practice. And to *think* one is obeying a rule is not to obey a rule. Hence it is not possible to obey a rule 'privately'; otherwise thinking one was obeying a rule would be the same thing as obeying it.

(1953, Section 202)

We can ask: what is the criterion for the sameness of a sensation? What is the criterion for re-identifying S? Or: *what is the criterion for being S?* Without one, no standard for 'being S' is determined, so no meaning. Thus the argument, laid out succinctly is:

1 Meaning something by a word requires a distinction between applying the word correctly and only seeming to apply it correctly.
2 A private word necessarily lacks that distinction.

So: no private word is meaningful.

When *Investigations* first came out, many readers supposed that the impossibility of private language implied that sensations are necessarily *public* – or that Wittgenstein was arguing for behaviourism. But the matter is more subtle than that. Learning, for example, a pain-word, is learning a bit of behaviour, which is acquired in connection with pain and its accompaniments:

words are connected with the primitive, the natural, expressions of the sensation and used in their place. A child has hurt himself he cries; and then adults talk to him and teach him exclamations and, later, sentences. They teach the child new pain-behaviour.

(1953, Section 244) ·

Again, words have their meaning in context. They are interwoven in the rich matrix of life, and have their roles only within the whole. We said earlier that it is the fact that we have pre-existing dispositions that makes a language possible. Included in these are 'natural expressions' as Wittgenstein describes; words for inner sensations, such as pain, ride atop them.

We can connect this with a doctrine previously encountered. Russell's theory of language, in the form we studied in Chapter 2, rested on his notion of sense-data and his principle of acquaintance. 'Every proposition we can understand is composed entirely of elements with which we can be acquainted', runs the principle of acquaintance; and sense-data are the ultimate means we have of referring to physical objects. But sense-data are private entities *par excellence*. Clearly Wittgenstein raises severe doubts about such doctrines – including perhaps the more modern notion of *qualia*, in the philosophy of mind.

• HISTORICAL NOTES

Ludwig Wittgenstein came from an extraordinarily wealthy Austrian family. As a young man he went to England in 1908 to study engineering, before switching to the foundation of mathematics and logic, and meeting Russell. It was not long before Russell recognised Wittgenstein's philosophical genius – to the point where his own philosophy not only felt his influence, but momentary came to halt as Russell was so shaken. In 1913 Wittgenstein went to Norway, then home to Vienna; he served his country bravely during the Great War, and published his *Tractatus Logico-Philosophicus* in 1921. In the 1920s Wittgenstein left philosophy, but his work profoundly influenced the philosophers meeting in Vienna called the 'Vienna Circle', known popularly as the logical positivists. Wittgenstein came back to philosophy in 1929, making appearances at the Circle. The meetings did not make a favourable impression on him, and his views in any case were changing rapidly; he soon returned to Cambridge where he lectured, and wrote, or rather dictated, the 'Blue Book' and the 'Brown Book' in the years 1933–5. These proved to be sketches for a bigger book, the *Philosophical Investigations* – which was published in 1953, two years after Wittgenstein's death. The number of books on Wittgenstein's philosophy is enormous. Many of the most penetrating are written from the point of view of disciples, who treat Wittgenstein's writings almost as if they were sacred texts; that is by no means to belittle his disciples, it is just testimony to the quality of and fascination held by the writings. Even among philosophers who have not been quite so keen to follow explicitly in his footsteps, there is a wide range of figures – from Crispin Wright to John McDowell to Stanley Cavell – whose work has been profoundly shaped by Wittgenstein.

• CHAPTER SUMMARY

Wittgenstein proposes a quite different way of thinking about language from Frege's, or Russell's, or his own former self's. Language, according to the later Wittgenstein, may be thought of as a fabric made up of language games, without presupposing that it contains a single unifying thread. *Language* is a family resemblance concept, not a concept such as 'bachelor', which admits of definition in terms of necessary and sufficient conditions; languages are organic entities, protean and diverse, with parts crisscrossing and overlapping. The concepts of reference, meaning and the like distort our understanding of these games, if we try to use them to theorise about all such activities in abstraction. If we 'look and see', for example at the simple example of the shopper and shopkeeper, we find that such language-games can be described without those concepts being privileged in the description. Their applicability presupposes a great deal of stage-setting, but once the stage is set, they do not contribute nearly so much as one might suppose.

A great illusion is that the meaning of a word is queer and mysterious, like a ghost attached to the word, telling us how to respond to it. Careful attention to cases reveals that such a thing would be powerless: if, for example, the meaning were a mental entity that was grasped whenever one used or heard the word, the entity would stand in need of interpretation, just as the word itself does. There is no choice but to accept that understanding is a matter of grasping *without* interpretation; at the bottom-level case, one is *trained* to respond as one does. Such training results not in mere behaviour like a trained parrot, but in *understanding*, because one learns to respond against the background of a linguistic community, whose ways constitute the norms, the standards of correctness, that one strives to match.

Russell along with many others said that the ability to talk about material objects depends upon our acquaintance with sense-data. Wittgenstein argues that such a language is impossible. For meaning something by a word requires a distinction between applying the word correctly and only seeming to apply it correctly; a private word – e.g. one for a sense-datum – lacks that distinction.

• STUDY QUESTIONS

1 Looking back at Sections 1–2 of this chapter, a good question to ask is how or whether Wittgenstein could cope with the demand represented by the principle of compositionality. For in dis-enshrining meaning he appears to remove the one semantical concept in terms of which the compositionality challenge was to be met. How can one respond?

2 Think of language as used on a factory floor, as used among lovers or intimate friends, as used on the street, as used in the court of law, and various other occasions; surely there are norms at work – perhaps Gricean rules – but do they change, depending on context? How? In what manner are they understood by the participants?

3 Does Wittgenstein's picture overplay the differences, and underplay the similarities, among different types of language?

4 John Stuart Mill, and later, A. J. Ayer, proposed the following solution to the problem of other minds (how does one know that they exist): When I'm in pain I cry out. Other human beings are very similar to me. Therefore when others cry out, I can infer by analogy that they are in pain. Having read a bit about the private language argument, what do you think of Mill's solution?

• PRIMARY READING

Wittgenstein, L. (2009) *Philosophical Investigations*, fourth edition, (eds and trans.) P. M. S. Hacker and J. Schulte (Oxford: Wiley-Blackwell).

• SECONDARY READING

Ahmed, A. (2010) *Wittgenstein's Philosophical Investigations* (London: Continuum).

glossary

anaphoric
Of pronouns and indexicals; an anaphoric use of a term 'borrows' its referent from some other referring device in the sentence (or beyond; it may borrow from other sentences in the context). For example, the indefinite pronoun 'it' in 'Bob loved the symphony, but Billy hated it'; one could replace 'it' with another use of 'the symphony' without altering the meaning of the sentence (such have been called 'lazy' pronouns). By contrast, in 'Whatever she wants, you'll buy it for her unless your mother doesn't like it', the role of 'it' is essential to the meaning of the sentence (it is the role of a quantificational **variable**); and in 'I'm ready!', the pronoun refers indexically, not anaphorically.

assertoric
Of sentences, the mood one uses to *say* something, make a statement, to advance a proposition as true; it is primarily the indicative **mood**, as opposed to the non-assertoric moods such as the interrogative (questioning), optative (wishing), or imperative (commanding) mood. Of **speech acts**, it is the act of making a statement, of verbally committing oneself to the truth of a proposition.

atomic proposition
The **proposition** expressed by an **atomic sentence**. See **singular proposition**.

atomic sentence
A sentence containing only one *n*-place **pure predicate** plus *n* singular terms.

attributive use see **referential use**.

biconditionality
A conditional is a statement of the form 'If P then Q'; a *bi*conditional is of the form 'P if and only if Q', which is the same as 'If P then Q, and if Q then P'. It means that P and Q have the same truth-value: either both are true, or both are false.

character
Together with the **context of utterance**, the character is a rule which yields the **content** of a given expression, which in the case of a sentence is the proposition expressed. The character of 'You are beautiful' yields different propositions at different contexts of utterance; in particular the different people referred to by 'You' will yield different propositions. The term was introduced by David Kaplan.

circumstance of evaluation
Given the proposition expressed by a sentence at a given context, we can ask for an evaluation of it as true or false in the actual world, or in non-actual but possible worlds. Similarly, we can ask for the evaluation of definite descriptions; at different circumstances of evaluation different objects may be denoted by a given definite description. Once the **context of utterance** is determined, the reference of an indexical remains unchanged in different circumstances of evaluation. The term was introduced by David Kaplan.

cognitive content, cognitive meaning
As opposed to the expressive content or expressive meaning of a sentence, **singular term**, or **predicate**. It is that element of content that is relevant to truth-conditions and reference.

cognitive value
Also called 'information value'. One can learn something from 'The author of *Middlemarch* is George Eliot' that one cannot learn from 'George Eliot is George Eliot'; Frege calls it a difference in cognitive value, which he explains as a difference in **sense** between 'The author of *Middlemarch*' and 'George Eliot'.

compositionality
According to the principle of compositionality, there is no upper limit to the number of grammatically correct sentences of a natural language such as English, but a finite vocabulary together with finitely many rules of composition engender every possible grammatically correct sentence.

compound see **indexicals**.

concept
In psychology, by a 'concept' one typically means a type of cognitive capacity such as the ability to recognise *flowers* or *the colour red*, or to think such thoughts as *the square of precisely one positive number is equal to adding it to itself*, and so on. It is not normally thought to be tied to any particular language. Frege used the word somewhat eccentrically as the *referent* of a predicate, where predicates are interchangeable so long as their extensions are the same. So 'is a ten-foot tall human' and 'was manufacturing transistors at the time of Julius Caesar' would designate the same concept, since their extensions are the empty set. Much closer though not the same as the psychological use is to let concepts be the *senses* of predicates, as according to Alonzo Church.

conditionality
In this book, the relation signified by '→' between any two sentences P and Q, such that if P is true but Q false, then 'P→Q' is false, and otherwise 'P→Q' is true. This is a precise replacement of the 'if—then' expression of English, whose interpretation is contentious. See **counterfactual conditional**.

conjunction
The conjunction of two sentences is true if both of those sentences are true; otherwise false. Typically formed in English by means of the word 'and'.

connote
The descriptive content of a term; normally contrasted with **denotation**, which are the entities constituting the extension of the term. General terms – 'dog', 'sticky' – are generally considered to have connotation. But whereas Frege held that all singular terms as well as general terms have connotation – they all express **senses** – many people following Kripke maintain the Millian doctrine that proper names only denote objects, and do not have connotation.

content
Normally short for the cognitive content of an expression at a context.

context of utterance
The circumstance in which an expression is uttered or might be uttered; includes time, place, identity of speaker, listeners, items demonstrated. See **circumstance of evaluation**.

context relativity
Many words shift their reference depending on the circumstances of their use; this is obvious in the case of **indexicals** such as 'here', less obvious in the case of words such as 'tall'. Some philosophers hold that context-relativity is rampant, infecting even philosophically important words such as 'knowledge', 'permissible' and 'necessarily'.

context-sensitivity see **context relativity**.

contextual definition
Unlike explicit definition, a contextual definition of a subsentential expression does not provide an equivalent expression, but provides a rule for converting whole sentences containing the defined expression to equivalent sentences that do not contain the defined expression. The classic example in the philosophy of language is Russell's contextual definition of definite descriptions: The F is G $=_{df}$ there is an F, there is not more than one F, and all F are G. No expression equivalent to 'the F' appears on the right-hand side of the definition.

contingent
A proposition that is true but not necessarily true is a contingent truth; a proposition that is false but might have been true is contingently false.

conventional implicature
A 'non-cancellable' variety of implicature – meaning that one is always responsible for it – but still it is not a matter of formal logic. For example, 'The dog is very old but eats well' has the same truth-condition as 'The dog is very old and eats well', but unlike it in that it conventionally implies some proposition as that the dog's being so old makes him unlikely to eat well. Contrast with **conversational implicature**, which is cancellable.

conversational implicature
A statement that is not logically entailed by a statement but which is such that a reasonable and well-informed person would take the statement to have been intended to be conveyed by that statement, but for which no semantic norms would be violated if the statement were not so intended.

cooperative principle
A general constitutive norm governing conversation which comprises several sub-norms, including: maxim of quality (do not say what you believe to be false; and do not say anything for which you lack adequate evidence), maxim of manner (be brief; and avoid obscurity, ambiguity, vagueness), maxim of relation (be relevant), maxim of quantity (make what you say neither more nor less informative than is required for the purposes at hand).

co-referential
Of two terms which refer to or stand for the same thing; 'Norma Jean Baker' and 'Marilyn Monroe', 'The first man to walk on the moon' and 'Neil Armstrong'; co-referential terms may have different meanings or senses.

counterfactual conditionals
A conditional whose antecedent is understood as false. Normally expressed in the subjunctive mood, e.g. 'If you *had scored* the goal, you *would have* won', said to someone who missed the goal. Normally, a non-counterfactual conditional – an indicative conditional, a material conditional – is uttered when one does not know the truth-value of the antecedent or the consequent. A popular analysis of 'If P had been, then Q would have been', is that in the possible world most similar to the actual world at which P is the case, Q is the case.

criterion
This word is used in various ways. The most famous user of the word was Wittgenstein, and his use of it has been the subject of considerable dispute. Roughly, to say the predicate B is a criterion of the predicate A is to say that one's understanding of the predicate A depends upon one's facility with B, where B is in some sense more basic than A or closer than A to being an observational predicate, and where it is at least a *prima facie* rule that either (a) nothing can satisfy A without satisfying B (being B is a *necessary* condition of being A); or (b) everything satisfying B satisfies A (being B is a *sufficient* condition for being A). However the relation between A and B expressed by one's being a criterion for the other was not held by Wittgenstein to be analytic or *necessary* in the metaphysical sense employed by Kripke, and indeed was held to be defeasible, in the sense that it is in some sense thinkable to have the one without the other. But the relationship is stronger than that the one is mere evidence for the other.

declarative or **indicative mood**
The mood of a sentence normally used to express a commitment to something as true, as opposed to the imperative or interrogative moods (in this book, we do not

include the interrogative mood as a type of declarative mood, but we do include the subjunctive and optative as varieties of the declarative). See **assertoric** and **force**.

de dicto
'Of the thing said', in statements of modality (necessity, possibility etc.) and propositional attitude. It is contrasted with ***de re***. They are normally thought to resist **substitutivity** (the substitution of co-referentials). For example, 'John believes that the Uffizi is in Rome' can be true where 'John believes that Florence's most famous art gallery is in Rome' is false, despite that fact that the Uffizi = Florence's most famous art gallery. In a *de dicto* statement of belief, the clause which gives the content of the belief – for example 'that the Uffizi is in Rome' above – is entirely inside the **scope** of the belief operator or predicate.

definite description
Using a noun or noun phrase such as 'book on the table', it is possible to form an expression by attaching the word 'the' to the front, i.e. 'the book on the table', which can in turn be used in a sentence such as 'The book on the table is yours', which is true just when the predicate 'is yours' is true of a single book on the table. It is debateable whether the definite description 'the book on the table' is a singular term, along with proper names as Frege thought, or whether, with Russell, we should think of 'every book on the table' really as a quantifier phrase. See **denote**, **contextual definition**.

demonstration
A gesture such as pointing used to secure the referent of the use of a **demonstrative** (a type of **indexical**).

demonstratives
Indexical expressions such as 'this' or 'that bird', which require a **demonstration** to secure a referent. The demonstration may be implicit, if the intended referent is salient in the context.

denote
Normally a synonym for 'refers to'; sometimes used for 'mean'. Russell used it technically for the semantics of **definite descriptions**, for the relation between 'the F' and the F, when the unique F exists. This is *not* reference, in Russell's view, because reference is a pre-condition of the meaning of expressions; 'The F is G' is meaningful – indeed false – even when there is no such thing as the F.

de re
'Of the thing', in statements of modality (necessity, possibility etc.) and propositional attitude. It is contrasted with ***de dicto*** in their behaviour with respect to **substitutivity**, the substitution of identicals. For example, 'Of the Uffizi, John believes that it is in Rome' (more colloquially might be: 'You know the Uffizi? John thinks it's in Rome'). Together with the premise that the Uffizi is Florence's most famous art gallery, such a statement logically implies 'Of Florence's most famous art gallery, John believes that it is in Rome'. Crucially, the term outside the belief operator or

predicate – 'the Uffizi' or 'Florence's most famous art gallery' – need not reflect the subject of the ascription's own way of thinking of its referent, and indeed may be wholly unknown to the subject. Before the 1960s most philosophers of language thought that in a *de re* statement of belief, some of what specifies the object or objects involved in the belief – 'the Uffizi' or 'Florence's most famous art gallery' – *must be outside* the **scope** of the belief operator or predicate; being *de re* was thus thought to be a syntactical or structural matter. However, the recognition of the direct reference of singular terms seems incompatible with this; for if a term such as 'the Uffizi' is directly referential, it contributes nothing to any statement beside its referent, in which case there cannot be a difference in truth-conditions between 'John believes that the Uffizi is in Rome' and 'Of the Uffizi, John believes that it is in Rome'; thus one is led to the *semantical de re*, as opposed to the *syntactical de re*.

determines

In a Fregean framework, the relation between **sense** and **reference** of an expression. For example, the sense of the term 'The first man to walk on the moon' determines the referent of that phrase, Neil Armstrong. More generally, the components of a typical sentence refer to various entities; the corresponding senses of the parts of the sentence determine those entities as referents. The sense of the entire sentence, the proposition expressed by it, determines a truth-value.

directly referring expressions

An expression that refers to an entity without importing a Fregean sense, a definite description, descriptive condition, or a conceptual representation into the propositions expressed by sentences containing the expression. They are often said to **denote** objects without **connoting** anything. To say that normal **proper** names directly refer is not to say that, for example, one cannot give a causal account of how they refer, but it is to say that proper names contribute only their referents to the semantics of sentences containing them.

disjunction

The *inclusive* disjunction of two sentences is false if both of those sentences are false; otherwise true. The *exclusive* disjunction of two sentences is true if exactly one of those sentences is true; otherwise false. In this book we generally use the inclusive variety, as is typically formed in English by means of the word 'or'. The exclusive sense is often signalled with 'either … or …'.

empty singular terms

A singular term that fails to denote or refer to an object, such as the proper name 'Pegasus' or 'Vulcan', or the definite description 'The man who walked on the planet Mercury'. Empty singular terms are not precluded from having cognitive meaning; Pegasus does not exist – there is no actual horse with wings – but still we can talk meaningfully using the name.

epistemological

An epistemological statement describes knowledge, normally *our* knowledge. Epistemology or the Theory of Knowledge comprises, among other things, theories of perception and of the justification of belief, and of knowledge itself. See **metaphysical**.

existential quantifier

'There exists a __' is an existential quantifier. 'Some', 'something', 'someone', 'a' and others are not always used as existential quantifiers – they also have uses as **universal quantifiers**. It is complicated to explain in any detail the rules for when the expression is an existential as opposed to universal quantifier. But the distinction itself is straightforward; the existential – 'There exists an F' or 'Something is F' – that is true if and only if at least one F exists. A universal quantification epitomised by 'Everything is F', is true if and only if everything is F. Other quantifiers include 'At least three things are F', and 'Most things are F'.

explicit or **direct definition**

The simplest kind of definition; an expression of a given semantical type is given a definition in terms of another expression of the same semantical type. For example: 'x is a <u>mare</u> = df x is a female horse'. The classical line is that such definitions are cognitively eliminative; they are very useful in practice, but in principle, they do not add anything to cognition since, e.g. one could always dispense with the word 'mare', using the expression 'female horse' instead. Contrasted with **contextual definition**.

expressive meaning

A dimension of meaning, contrasted with **cognitive meaning**, which does not play a role in determining the sense, reference or truth-conditions of expressions. If 'bunny' and 'rabbit' have the same sense, then any difference in meaning they have is a difference in expressive meaning. What they express is typically some attitude of the speaker. For example, it's plausible to say that 'Damn!' does not have a truth-condition, and does not refer to anything; but it serves to express a state of the speaker. Includes but perhaps is not exhausted by Frege's terms *tone* or *colouring*.

extension

Of predicates, is the set of things that **satisfy** the predicate (the set of things which the predicate is true of); of a singular term, it is the term's referent, an object; or sentences, it is the truth-value of the sentence, or the set of worlds at which the sentence is true (all of this has also to be relative to contexts of utterance).

extensional

Of a language, it means that in any sentence, a singular term, predicate or contained sentence may be replaced with another of the same **extension**, and the result will have the same truth-value as the original. Individual positions (or contexts) within sentences may also be called extensional. Natural languages such as English are not normally thought of as extensional; **non-extensional** positions include those within sentences ascribing **propositional attitudes**, and those containing modal operators, *viz.*, 'possibly' and 'necessarily'.

external negation
'It is not the case that b is F' is an *external* negation, as opposed to 'b is not-F', which is an *internal* **negation**. On some accounts of singular terms, if b does not exist, then the external negation is true but not the internal negation.

family resemblance
According to Wittgenstein, many terms – including the term 'language' – pertain to things not in virtue of their essence or necessary and sufficient conditions for the term's application, but through various overlapping resemblances. There is no property necessary to a thing's being a *game*, for instance. It is often added that such terms express 'open concepts', that is, the family of resemblances indicated by the term is constantly subject to revision.

fix the reference
According to Kripke, a definite description or indexical may be used to introduce a referring term by specifying its reference – 'fixing it' – without thereby being understood as synonymous with it, as having the same sense or cognitive content as it does.

force
The type of speech act that one performs in uttering an expression (in Austin/Searle terminology, the *illocutionary* act). The most basic varieties are assertoric, interrogative and imperative. Closely but not invariably connected is the corresponding **mood** of the sentence used, which is a matter of grammar, of words and their order. For example, normally one asks a question by using the interrogative-mood sentence, 'Are you shining my shoes?', but one can also do it by using the indicative-mood sentence – a sentence that normally is used for assertion but in this case is used with a special intonation, 'You're shining my shoes?'.

forms of life
Wittgenstein's term for the various kinds of human activity in which the use of language is often embedded. Greeting, performing music, sport, sitting in the seminar room, haggling, ordering food, banter … there are many forms of life, each requiring distinctive skills and know-how.

general term
Terms like 'dog', 'red', 'smokes' and 'kissed', which either (1) combine with the 'is' of predication and a term such as 'a' to form a **predicate** such as '__ is a dog'; (2) combine with the 'is' of predication to form a predicate such as '__ is red', or (3) form a predicate without the benefit of additional words, such as '__ smokes' or '__ kissed __'. The addition of 'a' is the addition of a **quantifier**, replaceable with 'every' and 'the' in such a way as to preserve the grammatically of the sentence. See **singular term, definite description**.

historical chain
Kripke's term for a sequence of reference-preserving links of a term, that connect one's present use to the origin of the chain, normally an act of dubbing. What

preserves the link is in some sense the individual implicit intentions of each user, or perhaps a norm held by the linguistic community.

holism
Suppose we consider a set of objects, and some property that each object in the set is a candidate for bearing. To say that the property is *atomistic* is to say that each case can be decided definitively without reference to the verdicts given for the other cases; to say that the property is *holistic* is to say that none can be decided definitively unless all cases are decided. Quine is an epistemological holist, a holist about knowledge and empirical confirmation; Davidson, in addition to joining Quine's epistemological holism, is also a semantical holist, a holist about meaning. Quine is not strictly speaking a semantical holist because he does not think an objective account of meaning is possible. Midway between semantical holism and semantical atomism is molecularism, according to which clusters of terms can be mastered independently of the rest of language, but still it is not possible to master any term in isolation from the rest of the terms in the appropriate cluster.

hyper-intensional
A non-**extensional** context in a sentence, which does not guarantee substitution by **co-referentials** without changing the sentence's truth-value, unless they have the same **cognitive meaning**. Only synonyms may be substituted. A less demanding type of non-extsensional context is the **intensional context**.

illocutionary act
In the Austin/Searle scheme, an aspect of a speech-act that is typically intentional and under the control of the speaker, and determines the illocutionary **force** of the utterance. For example, a particular kind of illocutionary act is that of asking a question. It contrasts with the **locutionary act** of expressing a certain content or proposition, and the **perlocutionary act** of getting the audience to answer.

implicature
Divides into *conversational* implicature and *conventional* implicature. Not to be confused with *implies*, or with *implication*, which is a matter not of pragmatics but of logic; to say that one statement implies another is to say that the one logically entails the other, that the truth-conditions of the former include that of the latter.

indexicals
Expressions whose reference varies systematically with the context of utterance – shifts in time, place and even possible world. The standard line is that 'here', 'then', 'now' and so on are *pure* indexicals (or have a standard use as pure indexicals). Indexicals that are not pure indexicals – called 'demonstratives' – require objects to be demonstrated;' examples include 'it', 'that', 'this', 'those', 'them', 'there'. However, for example, 'here' typically requires further sharpening by context or the intention of the speaker; the region indicated may be very large or very small. Many terms actually occurring in natural language are mixed or compound indexical expressions, as in 'those trees down there'. See **context relativity**.

indicative mood see **declarative mood.**

intension/intensional context
That associated with an expression that determines the referent (or extension) of the expression at each possible world is called the *intension* of the expression (by the extension of an expression we mean the objects referred to in the case of singular terms, sets in the case of predicates, and truth-values in the case of sentences). 'Jane Austen wrote *Sense and Sensibility*' and 'Jane Austen wrote *Sense and Sensibility* and *Pride and Prejudice*' are both true in the actual world, have the same actual extension, but in some worlds have different truth-values; hence they have different intensions. An intensional position or context is one such that the substitution of a co-extensive expression may affect the extension of the containing expression. Only if the substituted expression has the same intension as the original does the substitution preserve truth-value across all worlds. Intensionality is not as fine-grained as meaning itself; for example 'Any kangaroo is a kangaroo' and '2 + 2 = 4' have the same truth-value in every possible world – they are always true – but don't mean the same. See **extensional, hyper-intensional.**

iterative see **recursive.**

knowledge by acquaintance/knowledge by description
A distinction due to Russell; the former is the direct, conceptually unmediated knowledge of objects and universals; the latter is indirect, conceptually mediated knowledge. Normally, our knowledge of universals (properties and relations) is by acquaintance. Knowledge by description is represented linguistically by means of a definite description involving the concepts via which we think of the object.

language games
Restriction of **forms of life** to those that essentially involve language, and with an emphasis placed on the 'grammar' of the linguistic activity – on the norms or rules implicit in the activity. Due to Wittgenstein.

locutionary act
In the Austin/Searle scheme, an aspect of a speech-act that is the expression of a meaning; usually it is the expression of a proposition. See **illocutionary act.**

meaning
Classically, once the syntax (the grammar) of a language is settled, meaning is what must be mastered in order to speak the language correctly or appropriately, and to understand the language. See **sense.**

mention see **use.**

metaphysical
A metaphysical statement pertains to the nature or essence of reality and of the things that constitute it, irrespective of point of view. See **epistemological.**

mood

Of sentence, a matter of the grammar or the order of the words that compose the sentence. The main varieties are the declarative/indicative, the interrogative and the imperative. They are conventionally associated with certain **speech acts**; normally, one makes a statement by using a sentence in the declarative mood, one asks a question with the interrogative, and one commands using the imperative. But the association is not sufficient or necessary; one can utter a sentence in the imperative mood without commanding (or anything like it), and one can ask a question using the declarative using a rising intonation. See **assertoric force**.

naïve semantics

A simple theory of meaning according to which the meaning of every expression is what it stands for, its referent. At the level of atomic sentences, singular terms mean objects, predicates mean universals (properties and relations), and sentences mean propositions.

necessary

A necessarily true proposition is one that is true in every possible world; 'necessarily' is equivalent to 'not possibly not'.

negation

Classically, the negation of a sentence is true if the proposition is false, false if it is true. Less classically, the wide-scope negation of a sentence is true if and only if the sentence is not true – leaving open whether the sentence is false or neither-true-nor-false.

negative existentials

The negation of a statement that affirms existence. The negative *singular* existential is a problem: assume for example 'Zeus does not exist' is true; on the face of it, this requires that the predicate '__ does not exist' be true of the referent of 'Zeus'. Therefore there must be such a thing as the referent of 'Zeus', namely Zeus. So Zeus *does* exist. Russell's theory purports to solve this problem; Frege's solves it only artificially.

non-extensional

'Not extensional'; see **extensional**, **intensional** and **hyper-intensional**.

normative

Principles or propositions that are *prescriptive* – that tell one what one ought to do, what one must do, what one is allowed to do or may do.

observation sentence

An important type of **occasion sentence** where one's disposition to assent to it depends on the stimulation of one's senses, *and* where witnesses to the scene tend to agree with the verdict. Examples are 'It's cold', or 'That's a goat'. Relevant primarily to Quine.

occasion sentences
In Davidson and Quine, these are sentences that potentially can change in truth-value, as opposed to *standing sentences*, which cannot. Examples include 'I'm hungry', or 'It's autumn', as opposed to examples such as 'Julius Caesar was assassinated on March 15, 44 BC', or 'Lions are carnivores'.

one-place predicates or **monadic predicates**
A **predicate** that has a single empty place (or multiple places that must be filled by the same **singular term**) to construct a sentence. Examples are '__drinks wine', 'The first boxer to beat ___ is dead'. If they are explained semantically as having referents, then, depending on the exact theory of meaning we have in view, their referents are properties, concepts, sets (extensions) or functions (from objects to truth-values).

perlocutionary act
The effect on the audience, desired or not, achieved in a speech-act. For example, one performs the **illocutionary act** of asking a question; the perlocutionary act might be to get the audience to answer, or it might just be to irritate the audience or prompt them to walk out.

possible
A proposition that is true in some possible world (the actual world is one of the possible worlds); is definable as 'not necessarily not'.

pragmatically improper
Used to describe utterances that are semantically correct – which, for example, constitute true statements – but are nonetheless incorrect, because they violate practical norms, or communicative norms. See **cooperative principle**.

pragmatics
A theory of meaning or semantics, in giving the meaning or truth-conditions of sentences, typically leaves many questions concerning the use of language unanswered; many of these are about the information that can be communicated by the use of sentences but which is not contained in the meaning of sentences. This is standard pragmatics. But some think that pragmatics, as concerning the use of language, takes precedence over semantics or the theory of meaning, or even that semantics can in some sense be reduced to pragmatics. Paul Grice had that view, and today Robert Brandom has it.

predicates
An expression with one or more empty places, which becomes a sentence when the empty places are filled with **singular terms**. Examples: '__ is a fine boy'; '__, Groucho Marx, and __ came to stay', 'Everyone here including __ and Joseph is having a good time'. See **one-place predicates**, **two-place predicates**.

presupposes
Whereas P *logically entails* Q if and only if it is impossible for P to be true but Q false, P *presupposes* Q if and only if it is impossible for Q to fail to be true and for P to be

either true or false. In other words, the truth of Q is a necessary condition of P's having any truth-value at all. Strawson believed that definite descriptions presuppose the existence of a referent; if the F does not exist, then 'The F is G' is not false as Russell believed, but lacks a truth-value.

principle of charity
Many people including Davidson believe that it is a necessary condition of interpretation or radical interpretation that the subject's beliefs be mostly true, or at least that their beliefs about obvious things be generally true. Otherwise there is no basis for treating the subject as rational agent, with beliefs and desires, and no interpretation is possible. Often teamed with a principle of rational accommodation, that a person's propositional attitudes must in the main be coherent.

private language
A language (or set of expressions) whose referents are necessarily known only to a single person. Wittgenstein famously thought that no such a language is possible. The immediate implication is that words for such things as tickles or pains are not to be explained, in the first instance, on the simple model of word-referring-to-object.

proposition
Yielded by sentence-meaning and a context of utterance. For declarative sentences not involving **indexicals**, they may be identified with sentence-meaning. Classically, they are the objects of **propositional attitudes** and fundamental bearers of truth and falsity; their existence and identity are independent of particular languages.

propositional attitudes
Belief, wondering whether, desire, hope and so on may be construed as attitudes towards propositions. Belief, for example, may be construed simply in terms of an ordinary binary (two-place) predicate '__ believes __', where into the first blank goes a singular term referring to the believer, and then into the second blank goes a **singular term** referring to a proposition (at the context of utterance), such as 'that tomorrow will be overcast'.

pure indexicals see indexicals.

pure predicate
A **predicate** which contains no **quantifiers**, no **sentence-connectives** and no **singular terms**.

quantifiers
Expressions that indicate how many or how much of a kind of thing there is or are. Example are 'each', 'every', 'some', 'a', 'many', 'most', 'much', 'seven' and so on; attached to a noun or noun phrase – a description in Russell's vocabulary – we get expressions such as 'Every man', which can be inserted into the blank of a predicate to form such sentences as 'Every man is brave'. This commonality with singular terms once led people on the fruitless search for the referents of such expressions as 'Every man' and 'No man'. It was for Frege to recognise quantifiers as a separate

category of expression, working together with **variables** (pronouns in ordinary language) and **predicates**. The following sketch is Tarski's, but it is simpler. Thus the conditional formed of 'it is a man' and 'it is brave' is 'if it is a man then it is brave', which, with the quantifier-phrase 'Everything is such that', yields 'Everything is such that if it is a man then it is brave'. The open sentence 'if it is a man then it is brave' is unfortunately not true of everything (it is not true of cowards); thus the sentence as a whole – 'Everything is such that if it is a man then it is brave' – is false. Thus the semantic explanation of this does not treat the quantifier as singular term.

radical interpretion/radical translation
A procedure where, beginning with no relevant knowledge of a language – a language that has never previously been translated or interpreted in terms of the home language – one arrives at a translation or interpretation of the language. Radical interpretation for Davidson is more demanding than radical translation is for Quine: the translator may translate indexicals just as words, whereas an interpreter must specify rules for determining the referents of each use of an indexical.

recursive
The idea at its most general is that of a process or rule that applies to any example of a certain kind of thing, produces something else of the same kind, and thus can always be applied to its own results. For example, 'sewing on a bead to a string of beads' would be a recursive process. For another, '+2' is known as a recursive function on the set of natural numbers because it takes any natural number as input and yields another natural number as output, which can in turn be taken as an input for the function, and so on. Linguistic examples include the behaviour of 'It is not the case that __', or 'the mother of __'.

reference
The relation of an expression standing for, or denoting, some item (paradigmatically, an object in the case of singular terms; the relation of 'Fido' to Fido).

referentially opaque/referentially transparent
In the sentence 'John believes that the president of the club is dishonest', the position occupied by 'John' is referentially *transparent* – it is open to substitution by **co-referential** terms; whereas the positions that come after 'believes that' are referentially *opaque* – they are not open to substitution by **co-referentials**. See **propositional attitude**, **extensional**.

referential use
Of a definite description, as used by Keith Donnellan: one uses a description *referentially* to refer to an object, if, were the object to fail to satisfy the description, one nevertheless says something about that object. Otherwise, the use is *attributive*, in which case Russell's account applies. See **definite description**.

satisfy
A relation between an object and a predicate, the converse of true-of: an object satisfies the predicate if and only if the predicate is true of the object. More technically, it is a relation between an infinite sequence of objects and a sentence, open or closed (Tarski).

scope; wide or narrow
A relation between expressions generally, but especially between logical operators and the parts of sentences which they govern; in 'If Harold was late then Susan is not happy', 'not' takes *narrow* scope (the scope is 'Susan is happy') with respect to 'if-then', whereas 'if-then' takes *wide* scope (its scope is the two sentences – 'Harold is late' and 'Susan is not happy' out of which the final sentence is composed) with respect to 'not'. In natural language scope is sometimes ambiguous; for example, 'Everyone did not qualify': one reading is that 'Everyone is such that they did not qualify' (the scope of negation inside that of the quantifier); another reading is 'It is not the case that everyone qualified' (the scope of the quantifier inside that of negation).

semantics
The meaning of words or expressions. See **pragmatics**, **syntax**.

sense
In a Fregean environment, every expression has a sense. The sense of a **singular term** such as 'Mars' is a condition that an object must satisfy to be the referent of the term. Alternatively, the sense is a mode of presentation of the referent; it **determines** the referent. The sense of a (one-place) **predicate** determines whether or not an object falls under the predicate (the referent of the predicate is thus itself a rule, in particular a function from objects to truth-values). The sense of a (context-free) sentence is a proposition, what Frege called a thought. Some expressions such as 'Pegasus' or 'The man who walked on the moon in 1894' express senses that fail to determine referents. We sometime *talk about* senses; that is, senses can be referred to by higher-order senses, such as those expressed by 'The sense of "Pegasus"', or 'the thought just expressed by Lauren'.

sense-data
The immediate sensory content of a perceptual state; Russell tended to think of these as indubitable, the state of having them as incorrigible – in the sense that when you have them, there is no room for doubt that you are having them and that you know which one you're having (although one can doubt that they correspond to anything, e.g. that one has apple-shaped sense-data does not itself prove that an apple exists). Russell thought (in 1912) that sense-data (and possibly the self) are strictly speaking the only objects with which we can be acquainted, and for which we can have genuine names, logically proper names. Ordinary proper names function not as genuine names, but as disguised or abbreviated **definite descriptions**.

sentence-connectives
An expression which joins sentences together to make a single sentence, or which attaches to a single sentence to form a longer sentence. Examples of the first type include 'or', 'and', 'if-then' and 'because'; examples of the first type include 'not', 'necessarily' and 'It is true that' (some of these have other uses, as in forming collective subjects using 'and' such as 'John and Susan'; at least some such uses can be explained as elliptical for the sentential use). Some can be plausibly explained as **truth-functional**, but others cannot be; for example the truth-value of P does not settle the truth-value of 'Necessarily, P'.

singular proposition
A singular proposition is the meaning of a sentence containing a **singular term** that (i) fails to have a truth-value if the singular term fails to refer, and (ii) if the singular term does refer to an object O, then the sentence is true if O satisfies the predicate obtained by deleting the singular term from the sentence, and is false if O does not satisfy that predicate. A more positive picture of what exactly are the entities so characterised is the subject of debate, but one can think of '*Fa*', where '*Fa*' is a singular proposition, as an abstract object that actually contains the object *a* and the property *F*. Russell famously imposed an *acquaintance* requirement on singular propositions, for he held that one has to be acquainted with all its constituents in order to grasp a proposition. For Russell, this showed that the only objects that can figure in the singular propositions that one can grasp are sense data and perhaps the self (thus the vital importance of **definite descriptions** in Russell's scheme). Since Russell, people such as Gareth Evans have proposed looser accounts of what acquaintance requires, or jettisoned the acquaintance requirement entirely. See **knowledge by acquaintance**.

singular term
An expression whose function is to refer to a single object; in the extensional case, filling a one-place **predicate** with a singular term results in a sentence which is true if and only if the predicate is true of the referent of the singular term. Singular terms include proper names such as 'Moscow' and 'Barack Obama'; definite descriptions such as 'the present Queen of England'; indexicals such as 'you' and 'here'.

speech-act
An act of speaking; there are many kinds of speech-act – telling, promising, questioning, berating, suggesting, joking, requesting and so on, each with a distinctive set of norms and expectations – but the most basic are acts of assertion, command, and questioning. See **mood**, **assertoric**, **language games**.

standing sentences see **occasion sentences**.

statement
There are different ways of understanding the word 'statement', but according to one way: relative to a particular context – minimally a particular time and place – a declarative sentence expresses a **proposition** whether or not the sentence is actually uttered in that context; a statement requires the context plus an *actual* utterance of a declarative sentence. See **context of utterance**.

substitutivity
A property of subsentential positions or contexts such that any two expressions with the same referent can be exchanged, the one for the other, and the truth-value of the containing sentence will not change. For example, if the **singular terms** *a* and *b* each have the same referent, then the principle of subsitutivity holds for the predicate *F_* if and only if *Fa* and *Fb* have the same truth-value. See **extensional**.

syntax
A precise description that includes much of what has traditionally been known as grammar. The syntax of a sentence is its particular arrangement or structure of words, described purely formally or morphologically, without reference to semantics or meaning; likewise we can speak of the syntax of the entirety of a language. The syntactical part of descriptive linguistics is partly the attempt to find principles that govern the correct composition of sentences in a particular natural language or family of languages, or more ambitiously for any natural language. Related is the understanding of syntax as the formation of rules for artificial or formal languages such as those for formal logic and computing. In the philosophy of language, the traditional practice is to consider partially idealised forms of language, with a simplified syntax.

tense
An indexical feature of most ordinary sentences, with the basic forms being *past*, *present* and *future*: 'The dog barked', 'The dog is barking', and 'The dog will bark'. The language of mathematics, and some scientific languages or notations such as that of chemistry, lack distinctions of tense.

truth-condition
A set of all those circumstances under which a sentence is true. Frege characterised the sense of a sentence as its truth-condition; Davidson later thought of an entire theory that described the truth-conditions for all the sentences of a language as a theory of meaning for that language.

truth-functional
A sentential connective that results, when attached to one or more sentences, in a sentence whose truth-value is entirely determined by those of the attached sentences. (Depending on the precise technical details of the theory we have in view, the truth-functional expressions may take the form of functional expressions; in Frege's scheme for example negation is a functional expression, denoting a function from truth-values as input to the opposite truth-values as output). See **extensional**.

T-sentences
Made famous in logic by Tarski, and in the philosophy of language by Davidson. A T-sentence is '"Le neige est blanche" is true if and only if snow is white'. More generally, they are of the form 's is true if and only if p', where 's' refers to a sentence that means the same as 'p'. Tarski was able to define truth for a particular language by assuming meaning – in particular the translation of object language to metalanguage;

Davidson inverts the idea, arguing that we can explain meaning if we presuppose the general concept of truth.

two-place or **binary predicate**
A **predicate** that has two empty places where **singular terms** go to construct a sentence. Examples are '__kissed__', 'Sally is between __ and __'. If they are explained as referring, then, depending on the theory of meaning we assume, they refer to (binary) relations, concepts, sets of ordered pairs, or functions (from pairs of objects to truth-values).

types or **tokens**
'My cat hates your cat' contains five word-tokens but only four words counted as types. Examples involving homonyms such as 'She left on the left' shows that we have to make the type/token distinction among words considered as syntactical types as well as words considered as semantical types.

universal quantifier
'All', 'every' etc.; see **quantifier** and **existential quantifier**.

use
To use language is to employ its words for some purpose. Some philosophers think that in some sense the meaning of words emerges from, is implicit in, or supervenient on their use; others think that meaning reduces to use, or that for theoretical purposes it is better to speak plainly of use, letting meaning fall where it may. But according to the classical picture, the use of language is sharply distinct from the meaning of its expressions. In other words **pragmatics** should be kept apart from **semantics**. See also **speech acts**.

variables –
In logic and mathematics, one uses 'x' and 'y' and so on for an object that is left unspecified. A *free* variable, in the standard treatment, has a particular *value* – a **referent** – only relative to an assignment of objects from some domain to the variables of the (formal) language (the free variable under an assignment is a kind of temporary name). A sentence that contains at least one free variable is an *open* sentence. A *closed* sentence is one with no free variables; if it has variables, then those variables are *bound*, normally by quantifiers. For example, if a sentence contains just one free variable, and comes out true under every assignment of values to that variable, then the result of prefixing a universal quantifier governing that variable to it is true (under any assignment); if it comes out false for some assignment then the universal quantification is false. Closely analogous are certain aspects of the behaviour of pronouns in natural language. 'If it is a mammal then it has warm blood' makes a true statement whatever is assigned to 'it'; thus we have the true generalisation 'Everything is such that if it is a mammal then it has warm blood', or more colloquially 'All mammals have warm blood' or more loosely 'Mammals are warm-blooded'.

˙bibliography

Ahmed, A. (2010) *Wittgenstein's Philosophical Investigations*. London: Continuum.

Austin, J. (1961) 'Performative Utterances', in *Philosophical Papers*. Oxford: Clarendon Press.

Austin, J. L. (1962) *How To Do Things With Words*, Second Edition, (eds) J. O. Urmson and M. Sbisá. Cambridge, MA: Harvard University Press.

Ayer, A. J. (1946) *Language, Truth and Logic*, Revised Edition. London: Victor Gollancz.

Barcan Marcus, R. (1947) 'The Identity of Individuals in a Strict Functional Calculus of Second Order', *Journal of Symbolic Logic*, 12(1): 12–15.

Barcan Marcus, R. (1961) 'Modalities and Intensional Languages,' *Synthese*, 13(4): 303–22.

Barwise J. and Etchemendy, J. (1987) *The Liar*. Oxford: Oxford University Press.

Carnap, R. (1942) *Introduction to Semantics*. Cambridge, MA: Harvard University Press.

Carnap, R. (1956) *Meaning and Necessity: A Study in Semantics and Modal Logic*, Second Edition. Chicago and London: Chicago University Press.

Carnap, R. (1967) *The Logical Structure of the World* [1928] and *Pseudoproblems in Philosophy*, (tr.) R. George. Berkeley: University of California Press.

Church, A. (1951) 'A Formulation of the Logic of Sense and Denotation,' in P. Henle (ed.), *Structure, Method and Meaning*. New York: The Liberal Arts Press, pp. 3–24.

Church, A. (1954) 'Intensional Isomorphism and Identity of Belief', *Philosophical Studies: An International Journal for Philosophy in the Analytic Tradition*, 5(5): 65–73.

Chomsky, N. (1965) *Aspects of the Theory of Syntax*. Cambridge, MA: MIT Press.

Davidson, D. (1984) *Inquiries into Truth and Interpretation*. Oxford: Oxford University Press.

Davidson, D. (2006) in K. Ludwig and E. Lepore (eds), *The Essential Davidson*. Oxford: Oxford University Press.

Davidson, D. and Harman, G. (1972) *Semantics of Natural Language*. Dordrecht: Reidel.

Donnellan, K. (1966) 'Reference and Definite Descriptions,' *Philosophical Review*, 77: 281–304.

Dummett, M. (1978) *Truth and Other Enigmas*. Cambridge, MA: Harvard University Press.

Dummett, M. (1993) *Frege: Philosophy of Language*, Second Edition. Cambridge, MA: Harvard University Press.

Evans, G. (1985) *Collected Papers*. Oxford: Oxford University Press.

Everett, D. L. (2008) *Don't Sleep, There are Snakes*. New York: Pantheon Books.

Evnine, S. (1991) *Donald Davidson*. Cambridge: Polity Press.

Frege, G. (1974) *Foundations of Arithmetic* [1884], (tr.) J. L. Austin. Oxford: Basil Blackwell.

Frege, G. (1997) in M. Beaney (ed.), *The Frege Reader*. Oxford: Wiley-Blackwell.

Geach, P. (1967) 'Intentional Identity', *Journal of Philosophy*, 64(20): 627–32.

Grice, H. (1989) *Studies in the Way of Words*. Cambridge, MA: Harvard University Press.

Grice, H. P. and Strawson, P. F. (1956) 'In Defense of a Dogma', *The Philosophical Review*, 65(2): 141–58.

Hylton, P., 'Willard van Orman Quine', *Stanford Encyclopedia of Philosophy (Fall 2010 Edition)*, (ed.) Edward N. Zalta. URL: http://plato.stanford.edu/entries/quine/

Hylton, P. (2005) *Propositions, Functions, and Analysis: Selected Essays on Russell's Philosophy*. Oxford: Oxford University Press.

Kaplan, D. (1969) 'Quantifying In', in D. Davidson and G. Harman (eds), *Word and Objections: Essays on the Work of W. V. Quine*. Dordrecht: Reidel.

Kaplan, D. (1989) 'Demonstratives: An Essay on the Semantics, Logic, Metaphysics, and Epistemology of Demonstratives and Other Indexicals', in J. Almog, J. Perry and H. Wettstein (eds), *Themes from Kaplan*. Oxford: Oxford University Press.

Kripke, S. (1971) 'Identity and Necessity', in M. Munitz (ed.), *Identity and Individuation*. New York: New York University Press, pp. 135–64.

Kripke, S. (1977) 'Speaker's Reference and Semantic Reference', in P. French, T. E. Uehling Jr and H. K. Wettstein (eds), *Studies in the Philosophy of Language*. Bloomington: University of Minnesota Press, pp. 255–76.

Kripke, S. (1979) 'A Puzzle About Belief', in A. Margalit (ed.), *Meaning in Use*. Dordrecht: Reidel, pp. 239–83.

Kripke, S. (1980) *Naming and Necessity*. Cambridge, MA: Harvard University Press.

Kripke, S. (1982) *Wittgenstein on Rules and Private Language*. Cambridge, MA: Harvard University Press.

Lewis, D. (1983) *Philosophical Papers, Volume I*. Oxford: Oxford University Press.

Lewis, D. (1998) *Papers in Philosophical Logic*. Cambridge: Cambridge University Press.

Locke, J. (1961) *An Essay Concerning Human Understanding*. London: Everyman's.

Malpas, J., 'Donald Davidson', *Stanford Encyclopedia of Philosophy (Fall 2010 Edition)*, (ed.) Edward N. Zalta. URL: http://plato.stanford.edu/entries/davidson/

Mates, B. (1952) 'Synonymity', in L. Linsky (ed.), *Semantics and the Philosophy of Language*. Urbana, IL: University of Illinois Press, pp. 111–36.

Meinong, A. (1981) 'The Theory of Objects' in R. Chisholm (ed.), *Realism and the Background of Phenomenology*. Atascadero, CA: Ridgeview, pp. 76–117.

Mill, J. S. (1963) *System of Logic, Ratiocinative and Inductive* [1843], in J. M. Robson (ed.), *Collected Works of John Stuart Mill*, vols 7–8. Toronto: University of Toronto Press.

Montague, R. (1974) in R. Thomason (ed.), *Formal Philosophy. Selected Papers by Richard Montague*. New Haven: Yale University Press.

Neale, S. (1993) *Descriptions*. Cambridge, MA: MIT Press.

Noonan, H. (2001) *Frege: A Critical Introduction*. Cambridge: Polity Press.

Perry, J. (1977) 'Frege on Demonstratives', *Philosophical Review*, 86: 474–97.

Perry, J. (1979) 'The Problem of the Essential Indexical' *Noûs*, 13: 3–21.

Putnam, H. (1975) 'The Meaning of "Meaning"', *Minnesota Studies in the Philosophy of Science*, 7: 131–93.

Quine, W. V. (1960) *Word and Object*. Cambridge, MA: MIT Press.

Quine, W. V. (1961) 'Two Dogmas of Empiricism', in *From a Logical Point of View*, Second Edition. Cambridge, MA: Harvard University Press, pp. 20–46.

Quine, W. V. (1969) 'Speaking of Objects', in *Ontological Relativity and Other Essays*. New York and London: Columbia University Press, pp. 1–25.

Quine, W. V. (1974) *The Roots of Reference*. La Salle, IL: Open Court.

Quine, W. V. (1975 [1935]) 'Truth by Convention', in *The Ways of Paradox*, Revised Edition. Cambridge, MA: Harvard University Press, pp. 77–106.

Quine, W. V. (1975) 'Quantifiers and Propositional Attitudes', in *Ways of Paradox*, Revised Edition. Cambridge, MA: Harvard University Press, pp. 185–96.

Quine, W. V. (1981) 'Things and Their Place in Theories', in *Theories and Things*. Cambridge, MA: Harvard University Press, pp. 1–23.

Quine, W. V. (1992) *Pursuit of Truth*, Revised Edition. Cambridge, MA: Harvard University Press.

Russell, B. (1903) *Principles of Mathematics*. Cambridge: Cambridge University Press.

Russell, B. (1905) 'On Denoting', *Mind*, 14: 479–93.

Russell, B. (1911) 'Knowledge by Acquaintance and Knowledge by Description', *Proceedings of the Aristotelian Society*, New Series, vol. 11, pp. 108–28.

Russell, B. (1918) *Mysticism and Logic and Other Essays*. London: George Allen and Unwin.

Russell, B. (1940) *Inquiry into Meaning and Truth*. New York: Norton.

Russell, B. (1956) *Logic and Knowledge*. London: George Allen and Unwin.

Russell, B. (1973) *Essays in Analysis*. London: George Allen and Unwin.

Russell, B. (1985) *The Philosophy of Logical Atomism* [1918, 1924], (ed.) D. Pears. La Salle, IL: Open Court.

Sainsbury, M. (1979) *Russell*. London: Routledge.

Salmon, N. (1986, 1991) *Frege's Puzzle*. Atascadero, CA: Ridgeview.

Searle, J. (1969) *Speech Acts: An Essay in the Philosophy of Language*. Cambridge: Cambridge University Press.

Searle, J. (1979) 'Metaphor,' in *Expression and Meaning: Studies in the Theory of Speech Acts*. Cambridge: Cambridge University Press.

Sperber, D. and Wilson, D. (1995) *Relevance: Communication and Cognition*, Second Edition. Cambridge, MA: Harvard University Press.

Strawson, P. (1950) 'On Referring', *Mind*, 59(235): 320–44.

Tarski. A. (1993) 'Truth and Proof' [1969], in R. Hughes (ed.), *A Philosophical Companion to First-Order Logic*. Indianapolis: Hackett.

Wittgenstein, L. (1958) *The Blue and Brown Books*. Oxford: Blackwell Publishers.

Wittgenstein, L. (1961) *Tractatus Logico-Philosophicus* [1921], (tr.) D. F. Pears and B. F. McGuinness. New York: Humanities Press.

Wittgenstein, L. (2009) *Philosophical Investigations* [1953], Fourth Edition, (eds and trs) P. M. S. Hacker and J. Schulte. Oxford: Wiley-Blackwell.

Whitehead, A. W. and Russell, B. (1962) *Principia Mathematica to *56*. Cambridge: Cambridge University Press.

index